von Mila
Hanns Metsch.
Hanns Pflügk der Elter.
Georig von Harstal.
Georig Spedt
Wolff Goldacker

Milestones of History

5 Reform and Revolt

1517 1519 1521

Newsweek Books New York

Editor Neville Williams

1522

1532

1533

Milestones of History

5 Reform and Revolt

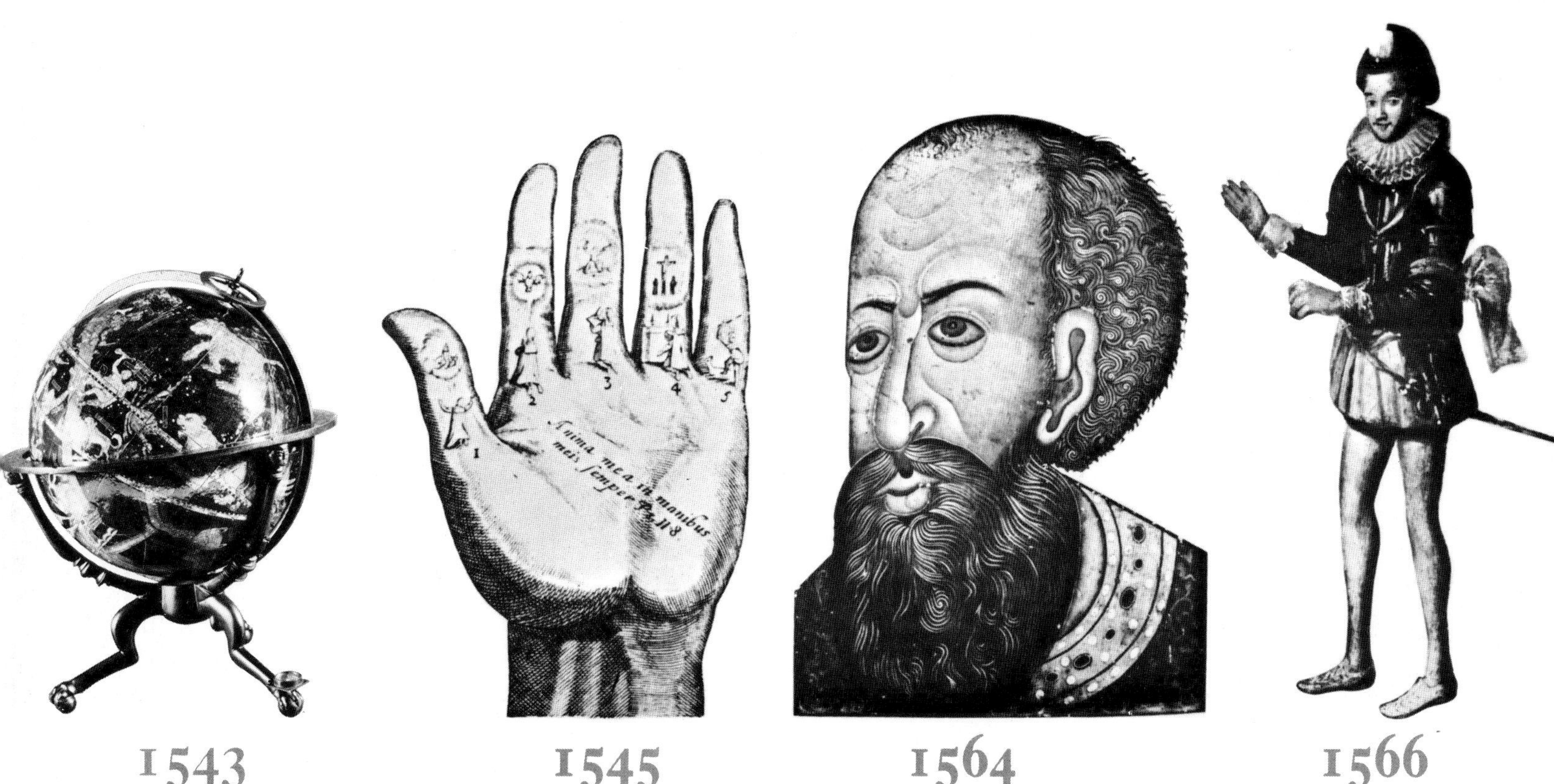

1543 1545 1564 1566

ISBN: Clothbound edition 0-88225-066-3
ISBN: Deluxe edition 0-88225-067-1
Library of Congress Catalog Card No. 73-81687

First published 1970. Revised and expanded edition 1974.

Printed and bound in Italy by
Arnoldo Mondadori Editore–Verona

1571

1572

1573

1588
1593
1600

Contents

Introduction

The themes of Reform and Revolt, the title of this volume, are closely entwined throughout the momentous years spanned in these pages. The relations of Church and State, the grandest of all historical subjects, were fundamental and far-reaching in their consequences. This volume opens with Martin Luther's challenge to papal supremacy at Wittenberg which was to rend Christendom asunder, for the cry for a reform of the Church from within had gone unheeded and thus a revolutionary movement founded Protestantism. Before the breach became irreconcilable, the religious reformers Calvin and Zwingli had devised their own distinctive systems of faith, while extreme sects, such as the Anabaptists, proclaimed a Christian Communism in which revolt was the means and reform the end. The very existence of separate Churches meant that there was now "a state within a state." In turn the Council of Trent formalized the various movements, some originating in the late-fifteenth century, that aimed at reforming Catholicism in spirit and in organization; yet the Counter-Reformation, as it became embodied in the program agreed at Trent, led the Roman Church from the defensive to the attack, notably in Poland and the Hapsburg lands.

Luther's teaching had plunged Germany into civil war, but at last, by 1555, the states agreed to differ in religious affairs. Henry VIII's Erastian Reformation in England, bringing in its train the extinction of monastic life, gave small comfort to those who had fallen under the spell of the continental reformers and thus, on the accession of the boy King Edward VI, revolutionary changes took place in the doctrine and worship of the English Church. Queen Mary attempted to put back the clock, but Elizabeth I sought to tread a golden mean by forming a broad, national Church, though Anglicanism was to satisfy neither the extreme Protestants, who developed a radical, Puritan ethos, nor the professed Catholics who continued to look to Rome and by 1570 were forced to choose between compromising with heresy or being branded traitors to the Elizabethan regime. In Scotland John Knox steeled the Lords of the Congregation to revolt against French, Catholic rule and erect a Presbyterian system of Church government, while in the Scandinavian states, on the periphery of Western Christendom, revolution was swift and the ensuing reforms went largely unchallenged.

By contrast in France and the Netherlands the struggle between Catholic and Protestant was bitter, bloody and long drawn out. The spasmodic warfare for the recognition of Calvinism, beginning in 1562, crippled French development; ten years later the massacre of St. Bartholomew's Eve sent tremors throughout Europe. The wars of religion finally became transformed into a war for the succession to the French throne and the victor, Henry of Navarre, deciding Paris was worth a Mass, finally embraced Catholicism. He subsequently issued his Edict of Nantes in 1598, which gave the Huguenots political safeguards for the limited exercise of their religion.

The Netherlands provide the most striking example of all. Here the lands of the old Burgundian inheritance chafed at Spanish rule. Philip II sought not only to whittle away the traditional independence which the Estates had enjoyed during the reign of Charles V—a ruler revered in the Netherlands by his earliest title "Charles of Ghent"—but, as the Most Catholic King, Philip struck at heresy. Persecution served only to harden the Calvinists from the provinces of Holland and Zeeland in their determination to defy Spanish rule, so that followers of the Reformed faith were essentially rebels in the eyes of King Philip, whose new governor, the Duke of Alva, soon found that he had a large-scale revolt on his hands. In this cockpit of Europe, comprising the land and water within a circle of 150 miles' radius from the international port of Antwerp, the struggle between the Reformation and the Counter-Reformation was fought out. Unity proved impossible; for cultural and linguistic, as well as religious reasons, two nations were born. The Dutch Republic, tracing its origins to the Union of Utrecht signed between the seven northern provinces in 1579, found itself opposed by the southern Catholic provinces, which would one day become Belgium; by the Treaty of Arras, signed the same year, these latter provinces undertook to preserve the Catholic faith and effect a reconciliation with Spain. German troops under John Casimir of the Palatinate and English volunteers came to the aid of William the Silent, while contingents from France, Spain and Italy aligned themselves with the Flemings. The revolt of the Dutch Republic was effectively to last until 1648.

Although most of the articles in this volume are concerned with Western Europe, these are balanced by specialist contributions dealing with Central and South America, India, Russia and Japan. Here, as in the narrative linking passages, the aim has been to see sixteenth-century civilization steadily and to see it whole, taking the entire globe, which the explorers and circumnavigators were opening up, as the historian's parish. No more than five of the decisive events of this period were military or naval battles—Cortes' victory in Mexico, Pizarro's defeat of the Incas of Peru, Don Juan of Austria's annihilation of the Turkish fleet at the Battle of Lepanto, the failure of Philip II's Armada against England and the victory of Tokugawa Ieyasu over his rivals in the Battle of Sekigahara in Japan in the last year of the century. Three articles are exclusively concerned with religion—Luther's stand at Wittenberg, the publication of his German Bible and the papacy's answer to Protestant theology in the summoning of the General Council to Trent to reform the Catholic Church. Four other articles are devoted to particular political repercussions of the Reformation—Henry VIII's breach with Rome, the revolt of the Netherlands, the massacre of St. Bartholomew's Eve in France and, twenty-one years later, Henry of Navarre's acceptance of Catholicism. Three essays deal with particular events in the reigns of other remarkable monarchs—the Holy Roman Emperor Charles V, Ivan the Terrible of Russia and Akbar, the Mogul Emperor of India. The remaining article discusses the one major contribution of the century to science—the work of Copernicus.

If the rhythm of historical development were regular, with major events taking place at neatly-spaced intervals, one might have achieved a volume in which there was a "milestone" every five or six years in this 85-year span. Historical change, however, is fickle and chronology permits no such liberties. Topics for specialist articles have been chosen solely on the grounds of their overriding importance, not because they fit into a preordained plan; as a result there has been some unevenness in the time span between the various contributions. The Battle of Lepanto, the massacre of St. Bartholomew's Eve and Akbar's triumph in India occurred in three successive years, while the publication of Luther's Bible closely followed the conquest of Mexico by Cortes. By contrast as many as twenty-one years separate the first assembly of the Council of Trent and the Boyars' rising against Ivan the Terrible, and there are fifteen years between Akbar and the defeat of the Spanish Armada. There has, accordingly, been a good deal of flexibility in the compilation of the linking passages, although the lay-out of this volume and the easy reference index will enable the reader to find his whereabouts without difficulty.

As in the other volumes of this series, though each of the sixteen essays presented here is complete in itself, these separate contributions by different authorities are not presented in isolation, for the unique events with which they deal are placed in historical context through the means of narrative passages, by a single author, that link each essay to its successor. These linking passages provide the volume with a greater cohesion than would otherwise be the case so, without attempting to cover the whole field of world history with the comprehensiveness of a textbook, they do offer a general survey of the epoch—the movements that underlay it, the economic changes that gave it shape, changes in warfare and the developments in the arts that gave the era its unique style.

Principally these links discuss events and personalities that were of great moment in the history of a particular country, but are of insufficient importance to rank as "milestones" in world history, where selection is all-important. Examples are the significance of the Swiss Protestant leader Zwingli, the contribution to political thought of Jean Bodin, the work Paracelsus achieved in astronomy, Albrecht Dürer in art and Orlando Lassus in music, Pope Gregory XIII's reform of the calendar and Francis Drake's voyage round the world. These, and many more, are facets of sixteenth-century life that need to be placed in perspective, yet cannot attract the same detailed attention as that accorded to our sixteen principal topics. It is in the linking passages, also, that some account is given of the history of minor states, such as the Baltic kingdoms and the Balkans, Poland and Portugal.

These years of Reform and Revolt saw the emergence of the modern nation state in the Western world, which was fostered during the turmoil of the Reformation. They also witnessed the foundation of the great colonial empires of Spain and Portugal in the wake of geographical discovery. England attempted the experiment of Raleigh's Roanoke Colony in Virginia, and it failed. Not until almost twenty years after the defeat of the Armada, which set the seal on England's naval supremacy, were efforts to be made to bring about a permanent settlement in Virginia, the oldest of the North American colonies. Meanwhile the last year of the century saw the foundation of the East India Company, which would lead to British imperial power in India.

In human achievement our period produced three circumnavigations of the globe, the first accurate maps of countries on Mercator's projection, the first microscope and the earliest scientific society (at Naples in 1560).

This was the century of More, Bodin and Bruno, the epoch of Palestrina and Byrd, the age of Ronsard, Montaigne and Spenser. Michelangelo redesigned St. Peter's at Rome and Shakespeare showed the extraordinary range of his dramatic genius. In the face of revolutionary political change and the successful efforts at reform on a scale which civilization had not experienced for seven centuries, there was no dearth of creativity, but instead a remarkable quickening of the pulse in every area of endeavor.

NEVILLE WILLIAMS

heilige
sie/Ich heilige
vnd Opffere
mich für sie
Mit meinen
wunden etc.
Es ist nur ein Mitler.
So wir sundigen, haben
wir einen vorsprecher
beim Vater. Darumb
last uns getrost zu dem
gnadenstuel tretten.
Ich bin der weg/Niemand etc
Sihe dz ist dz lamb Gottes etc.
IN·RI
Trincket alle daraus.
Matthei. 26.
Alle Prophe-
ten zeugen von
diesem/dz kein
ander name vn-
ter dem himel
sey. Act. 4.10.

The Ninety-Five Theses 1517

A papal hireling, in the immediate service of the Archbishop of Mainz, came to Saxony to sell indulgences—remission from sins by cash payments to the proper authorities. His brazen argument that all sins could be forgiven—even in advance—for the right amount of money outraged the Augustinian Father Martin Luther. Luther's argument against indulgences, embodied in his Ninety-Five Theses, were originally intended to form the basis for a theological debate among churchmen. Instead, they touched off the movement that has come to be known as the Protestant Reformation.

When Father Martin Luther, a thirty-four-year-old priest in the Augustinian Priory at Wittenberg, Saxony, sent his printed Latin theses to his archbishop in October, 1517, he could have had no idea of the effect his action would have. The theses were intended to form the basis of a discussion to be held at the University of Wittenberg concerning indulgences—the remission of punishment otherwise due to sin, to be gained by a cash payment.

Soon afterward, the theses were sent to a printer, who numbered them for convenience, and they became known as the *Ninety-Five Theses*. Many years later, Philip Melanchthon, a colleague of Luther, said that Luther had nailed the theses to the church door at Wittenberg. As Melanchthon was not in Wittenberg at the time he is not a reliable witness. It would have been more in character if, as is quite likely, the circumspect young Father Luther had limited himself to sending the theses to his archbishop and bishop. History, however, sees the Reformation as starting with the "nailing" of the *Ninety-Five Theses* to that famous door, and it is possible that the incident is a good example of the manufacture of a myth to provide a more stirring opening to a major event.

Luther's action was hardly more than routine; and the theses themselves were essentially academic and certainly never intended to be widely read. Indeed, only after he had no reply from his superiors, and it appeared that he might have difficulty in arranging a discussion, did Luther send copies to one or two friends. They showed them to others who had copies printed, and soon the propositions put forward by the obscure German priest were being discussed all over Europe.

The reason such interest was shown was that Luther had managed to express the thoughts of many educated men of his time regarding the essential problems that beset the Church at the beginning of the sixteenth century. He had fused theology, protest and common sense into a formula that found a ready response from a wide selection of the population.

Luther belonged to a civilization that was basically religious. Religious belief pervaded everything; educational and charitable institutions were mostly controlled by religious orders, and people accepted religion as a matter of course. Allegiance to the Church was unquestioned. This belief ultimately expressed itself in a variety of symbolic religious actions that were subject to a wide measure of control by the ecclesiastical authorities who had confined virtually the whole life of the Church under the carapace of canon law. Yet the methods of canonical control and the standard of behavior of many ecclesiastics often fell short of the ideals set forth in the New Testament. As a result, anticlericalism and an almost endemic cynicism had long been part of everyday life. Chaucer's *Pardoner's Tale* from *The Canterbury Tales* is typical: this traveling mendicant offered "saints'" relics for veneration, in return for which he expected at least a free drink and dinner. These relics were not human bones but those of pigs. Indulgences had long been a source of scandal and had provoked one other famous outburst. In Prague, in 1412, John Huss had denounced the sale of indulgences to collect money for a war the Pope was fighting against the King of Naples, an action which helped to bring Huss to the flames.

The popes had largely ceased to be spiritual leaders, having become little more than Italian princelings, determined to increase their power and prestige. The Church was wealthy. The current Pope, Leo x, had raised its income considerably by creating and selling new Church offices and increasing the revenue from indulgences, jubilees and regular taxation. The kings of France, Spain and other countries had been able to set limits to the power of the Church in their kingdoms, but there

Bulla contra errores Martini Lutheri ⁊ sequacium.

The title-page of the papal bull condemning Luther's views.

Opposite Luther preaching. The power of Luther's sermons lay in their combination of personal spirituality, definite reform proposals and intense awareness of the hopes and aspirations of his audience.

was no strong central government to bring this about in Germany. The papacy was able to impose heavy taxes on clergy and laity alike. German bishoprics also provided salaries for Italians who remained in the papal court at Rome. Pious people had begun to feel that Christianity was no more the religion of the common people but the preserve of the higher clergy.

Luther's shock at the contrast between ecclesiastical life and Christ's teaching was representative of much that others had experienced. That his initiative suddenly transformed the situation into a violent demand for change lies in the political and economic, as well as religious, context of sixteenth-century Europe. In previous centuries when civil governments were weak the Church had been the chief unifying force in Europe. However, with the emergence of national states it became necessary for national sovereigns, in consolidating their position, to curb the power of the Church. It was, therefore, in the interests of many national states to embrace any reforming proposal that would weaken the Church politically. The wealth of the higher clergy was also coveted by rising capitalist laymen—merchants, manufacturers and landowners. The reformist ideas of Luther were therefore welcomed by the people of northern Germany, and would soon be accepted in Scandinavia, the northern Low Countries, most of Switzerland, Scotland, England and parts of France and Hungary. Reformation would go hand in hand with rebellion.

With the spread of literacy, Christians in greater numbers were reading and interpreting the Gospels. As a response, to protect the Gospels from dangerous interpretations on the part of the laity, the Church tightened its canonical control and exercised greater censorship over the reading of Scripture. The Church developed its organizational control of people as though their religion, like their social and economic life, required a rigid structure.

Coupled with the steady growth in literacy went a similar increase in the circulation of vernacular versions of the Scriptures, following the invention of printing. In England interest in Scripture was fostered—albeit illegally—by the Lollards. On the Continent of Europe it was not always necessary to work underground. The communities of lay people known as Beghards and Beguines were centers of scriptural study in the Rhineland, as were the Brethren of the Common Life, whose spirituality was often referred to as the *devotio moderna*. All were influenced by the Rhineland mystics of the late thirteenth and early fourteenth centuries, associated with the Dominican movement. In particular, Meister Eckhart, Johannes Tauler and Heinrich Suso, sought to establish a direct union between the soul of the individual believer and God through prayer and contemplation rather than through the Church. This development of an emphasis on the inner life, although it called for a more profound reponse on the part of the official Church, did not elicit it.

As momentum grew for a total reform of Church life, the weakness of the structure became evident. In particular, the houses of the religious orders, which had been founded with such idealism and enthusiasm some centuries before, now let their inmates leave without question. The original impulse had been one of extraordinary generosity, an outflowing of the human spirit. Men and women had freely given themselves, and this flowering of the spirit was reflected in the arts and education. The structure remained but the fervor had dimmed, leaving the way open to the zealots and would-be reformists to fill the vacuum with their ideals of a renewed Church.

Luther was ultimately provoked by the arrival in Saxony in 1517 of a papal hireling, the Dominican Johann Tetzel, come to raise funds for the rebuilding of St. Peter's in Rome by selling indulgences. Tetzel was employed by Archbishop Albrecht of Mainz, whom the Pope had authorized to keep half the proceeds. Albrecht needed the money, being in debt to the Fugger banking house of Augsburg for money he borrowed to pay for papal dispensations enabling him to hold three bishoprics at once. Tetzel went about his business with unprecedented effrontery, proclaiming that it was through the grace of the indulgence that man was reconciled with God. He insisted that there was no need for repentance, provided a man paid what he could afford, and he assured his listeners that they could even buy the right to sin in the future. The idea that "everything might be done for money" was anathema to Luther, and he responded with the *Ninety-Five Theses*. That his document was simply the basis for an academic discussion tended to be overlooked as its contents were discussed and spread abroad, and complaints of Luther's outspokenness reached Pope Leo x. The ecclesiastical controversy that the Wittenberg monk stirred up soon expanded to include many more issues than merely the sale of indulgences. Luther had done more than criticize their sale. He had called into question the theory of "justification by good works," of which indulgences were only a small part.

Within a year the *Ninety-Five Theses* had spread over most of Europe, from England to Bohemia, to

The devil playing a tune on Luther, his bagpipes. The papacy claimed that Luther, like all heretics, was being used as a mouthpiece by Satan.

Opposite above An allegorical painting of Luther nailing his theses to the church door in Wittenberg; an example of the way in which major events create their own myths.

Opposite below A woodcut of the sale of indulgences which was permitted by the Church. Luther's criticism of this type of abuse ultimately called into question the theory of "justification by good works."

The Roman Church's worldliness contrasted with the devotion of Luther and his followers.

reach Spain and Italy a few years later. Luther's name became a byword. He was the "new Huss," a religious revolutionary, and hence a heretic. Soon the monk in the little town of Wittenberg realized that he was being thrust up on a gigantic wave of multiple protest. At first he did not relish the experience, but eventually had to accept himself as a living symbol. In 1518 and the following years, he often spoke of his desire to remain hidden in his *angulum*, his own private corner, his little world at the University of Wittenberg surrounded by his friends and colleagues and the people of his local church. In practice he remained loyal to this program all his life. But his fame was carried throughout Europe and students came from every nation to study at Wittenberg and listen to Luther in the lecture hall and round his table in the converted Priory buildings.

Luther soon found himself out of his corner, facing the forum of public opinion. He was a fine orator, always intensely conscious of his audience, whether the young monks at the Priory, the people in the parish church, his university colleagues, the authorities such as the Elector of Saxony, the bishop, the pope or his nuncio. The special power of his sermons lay in their combination of personal spirituality and definite reform proposals. His sensitivity to human nature was comprehensive. But his primary concern—reflected in his early theology—was his position before God.

The theses, which can be read in ten minutes, begin in the fairly simple, current. ecclesiastical Latin:

Out of love and zeal for truth and the desire to bring it to light, the following theses will be publicly discussed at Wittenberg under the chairmanship of the Reverend Father Martin Luther, Master of Arts and Sacred Theology and regularly appointed lecturer on these subjects at that place. He requests that those who cannot be present to debate orally with us will do so by letter. In the name of Our Lord Jesus Christ, Amen.

1. When our Lord and Master Jesus Christ said, "Repent" (Matt. 4:17), he willed the entire life of believers to be one of repentance.

2. This word cannot be understood as referring to the sacrament of penance, that is, confession and satisfaction, as administered by the clergy.

3. Yet it does not mean solely inner repentance; such inner repentance is worthless unless it produces various mortifications of the flesh.

These first three theses plunge us deep into theology. The first proposes some kind of conversion and asceticism as the basis for a Christian life. The second says this cannot be achieved by rites or symbolic actions monitored by canonical authority. The third states that neither can this conversion remain purely private. Thus the way is prepared for what amounts to an *a fortiori* argument—if the Church's sacraments did not suffice to bring about the necessary conversion, it was even less likely that this conversion would be achieved through indulgences. Much of the document is written in technical Latin and can only be understood if the theology is grasped. But it penetrated to the heart of problems which, in a variety of guises, then confronted Christendom.

The Pope summoned Luther to Rome to answer for his theses, but the Elector of Saxony persuaded Leo x not to press the summons, and it was not until 1519 that Luther was forced to deny the divine authority of the Church. In the summer of that year, debating with the theologian, John Eck, Luther admitted that the views he held were the same as those of John Huss, condemned as heretical a century earlier. By 1520 Luther had published three pamphlets strongly attacking the position of the Church: *An Address to the Nobility of the German Nation*, in which he stated that the clergy should be deprived of their special privileges and the German princes should liberate Germany from foreign control—this was perhaps the most influential political tract of the century in Germany; *On the Babylonian Captivity of the Church of God*, attacking the sacramental system of the Church; *On the Freedom of a Christian Man*, the essence of Lutheranism—without God's help and faith man is helpless.

The Pope was now alarmed and in June, 1520, banned Luther's works. Luther responded by burning the papal bull. The following January the Holy Roman Emperor, Charles v, called a diet at Worms to decide what to do about Luther. A heated debate ensued—Charles, in loyalty to the Church, was ready to place Luther under the Ban of the Empire, but most of the German princes supported Luther. To settle the issue Luther was summoned to the Diet where he made his defiant stand:

Unless I am convicted by Scripture and plain reason (for I do not accept the authority of popes and councils, since they have often erred and contradicted each other), my conscience is captive to the Word of God. I cannot and I will not recant anything, for to go against conscience is neither right nor safe. God help me. Amen.

Luther confronting Leo X, with the Bible, claiming it held greater authority than the pope.

The Peasants' Revolt. Mistakenly encouraged by Luther's attacks on the Church the peasants rose up not only against the clergy but also against the nobility.

After the Diet dispersed, Charles had to wait a month before issuing the Edict of Worms, placing Luther under the Ban of the Empire. But in defying Rome, Luther had firmly secured the support of most of the German princes, who now confiscated the Church's lands and revenues in their lands and abolished Catholic worship. His words were also heard by the peasants who took them as advocating social as well as religious change. This illusion was shortlived as the inherent conflict of class interests soon became apparent.

What gave the leadership of the Reformation to Luther rather than to another was his dynamism, his spiritual insight, intellectual understanding of theology and his courage. His vivid translation of the Scriptures into German (fully discussed on page 39) added enormously to his influence. The simplicity of Luther's insight makes it difficult to understand how it could have been a vehicle of such power. This power came simply from the insight conveyed by St. Paul's words: "The just live by faith." Luther's works show hundreds of pages written on this theme. We are unable to do anything that is good through human power alone. Every action which is ultimately good is so because of divine aid. God's grace gives man faith, enabling him to live as a Christian and to keep the moral law which alone he is unable to do. Faith in Christ is the only key to man's salvation.

Although conceptually Luther offered nothing new, he had recognized the inherent value of the laity—"the priesthood of all believers"—and individual faith. Thus Luther became the prophet of the common man, and it was to that common man that he directed his fundamental message. Although he wrote in Latin for his intellectual equals, he would translate a particular extract into German whenever he felt the public could benefit by it.

The peasants felt Luther to be instinctively on their side, but when the Peasants' Revolt broke out in 1524, and was directed not only against the Catholic clergy but also against the temporal lords, many of whom were Lutheran, Luther foresaw a political split within his religion. Appalled by the uprising, he wrote his vehement pamphlet, *Against the Murdering, Thieving Hordes of Peasants*, urging the princes to put down the revolt:

> Therefore, let everyone who can, smite, slay, and stab, secretly or openly, remembering that nothing can be more poisonous, hurtful or devilish than a rebel.

The revolt was crushed in 1525 with the massacre of perhaps fifty thousand people. The peasants felt betrayed by their prophet and abandoned him to

Germany depicted as an ass ridden by Rome while Catholic Europe further hampers her progress.

Luther and Melanchthon, his faithful assistant, by Lukas Cranach whose paintings reflected the growing secularism in art.

follow new revolutionary sects which developed, such as the Anabaptists.

After the Reformation was underway, Luther mourned the disappearance of certain good qualities, habits and conventions of society. He found he could not start new schools as easily as he had hoped, and meanwhile the educational work carried on by the religious orders had declined. Things seemed worse, not better. However, he still believed he was right to have followed his conscience. It was necessary to free men from a fundamentally inadequate Church.

In many ways Luther was essentially a medieval man, interpreting every event as God-sent:

> The people everywhere are restless and their eyes are open. They can and will no longer submit to oppression by force. It is the Lord who is directing all this and who is concealing this threat and imminent peril from the princes. It is He who will bring it all to pass through their blindness and their violence; it looks to me as though Germany will be drenched with blood

That was in 1522, two years before the Peasants' Revolt. As a public statement it was inflammatory. When it came to the need for political finesse Luther was entirely without judgment. To exercise his insight in the public arena in this way brought harm, but prophets are always dangerous people.

The final four of the *Ninety-Five Theses* give us the key to Luther's success as well as to his failure. He never forebore to speak the truth as he felt and saw it:

> 92. Away then with all those prophets who say to the people of Christ, "Peace, peace" and there is no peace! (Jer. 6:14)
>
> 93. Blessed be all those prophets who say to the people of Christ, "Cross, cross" and there is no cross!
>
> 94. Christians should be exhorted to be diligent in following Christ, their head, through penalties, death and hell.
>
> 95. And thus be confident of entering into heaven through many tribulations rather than through the false security of peace. (Acts 14:22)

Although Luther had hoped to reform the Church and recall men to the pristine values of Christianity, his defiance at Wittenberg had split the Church asunder. The year before his death, the Council of Trent first assembled in an attempt to heal the rift. However, it only confirmed Christendom's divided allegiance between those who accepted papal authority and those who rejected it.

JOHN M. TODD, FRANCESCA RONAN

1517–1519 Sultan and Shah contend for western Asia

While Europe was torn by religious dissension, Turkish conquest began anew under the energetic Selim I (1512–20), who deposed his father. Selim, surnamed "the Grim," was forced to overcome the Persian threat in order to have a free hand elsewhere. After suppressing the Shi'ites in the Ottoman Empire, as he thought them natural allies of their coreligionists in Persia, Selim gathered a large army in 1515 and invaded the territory of Shah Ismael. By forced marches, which nearly led to mutiny among his men, he surprised the Persians at Chaldiran (1514). He occupied Tabriz and annexed Kurdistan and the areas of eastern Anatolia that had been previously lost to Ismael. Then moving southward overland toward Egypt, and taking Mesopotamia on the way, he attacked the Mameluke Sultan of Egypt's army at Aleppo in 1516, and his victory brought the Turks Syria. Selim entered Cairo in the following year and all Egypt became part of the Ottoman Empire; even the heartland of Arabia acknowledged Ottoman suzerainty. Selim was also appointed Caliph by the last of the Abbasid caliphs—whose enjoyment of the title had been purely nominal.

Sultan Selim I, conqueror of Egypt, with Piri Pasha.

The papacy was thoroughly alarmed at this rapid expansion of Turkish power, and in 1517, Leo X ordered a five-year peace in Christendom in order to attack Selim's western flank. But the Reformation had interrupted Leo's plans and finally scotched any hope of a united Christendom facing the Turks. That the Turkish conquest of Syria and Egypt posed an immediate threat to Christendom became clear two years later, when Selim began preparing a large fleet and army to attack Rhodes, the home of the Hospitallers. The energetic hostility of the Order of St. John of Jerusalem toward the Turks had caused fury in Constantinople and had already led to an attempt to conquer the island in 1480. It was only the death of Selim in 1520 that prevented an all-out attack on Rhodes. The reign of Selim had been a highly successful one for the Ottoman Empire; that of his successor, Suleiman the Magnificent, was to be no less so.

Persia

By 1510, Ismael's authority was firmly established throughout Persia. His speedy rise to power was undoubtedly helped by his descent from the family of the prophet Mohammed, which was always a cause of popularity among Shiite Moslems. In 1510, Ismael invaded Khurasan, which had recently been conquered by the troublesome Uzbek Shaibani, an ambitious and ruthless ruler. Shaibani had, by his capture of Samarkand and Bukhara, already set in motion the series of events that led to the establishment of the Mogul dynasty in India. Ismael claimed that Khurasan was his by "hereditary right," to which Shaibani replied through his ambassadors that he recognized no such right and that the word hereditary had no meaning. Shaibani had a large army, perhaps as many as 28,000 men, but the Uzbeks, like most nomads, fought in small units, which made discipline difficult. Ismael, with an army of around 17,000 men, succeeded in ambushing the Uzbeks near Merv. In the scattered fighting that followed, Shaibani was killed.

The hostility that had existed between the Turkoman dynasty of the White Sheep and the Ottoman Empire in the fifteenth century did not disappear when Ismael overthrew the White Sheep. Indeed it intensified. During his early years as ruler, Ismael succeeded in incorporating large areas of Ottoman territory. The succession of Selim to the Ottoman throne made matters more difficult, because Selim was as fanatical in his orthodox Sunni beliefs as Ismael was in his Shiite views. Ismael was in communication with Hungary, Portugal and—before it fell to the Ottomans—Egypt, and hoped to create a grand alliance against the Turks. Selim's reaction was to massacre his Shiite subjects, whom he regarded as a potential fifth column. About 40,000, roughly half the Shiite population of the Ottoman Empire, are believed to have died.

The massacre infuriated Ismael, but as he did nothing about it, Selim wrote him provocative letters accusing him of occupying Ottoman territory and also of being an atheist. Ismael replied, refuting both charges. He did not want a war; but the conciliatory tone of his letter was damaged by his suggestion that the Sultan's letter must have been written under the influence of opium—Selim was known to be an addict. The Sultan, determined to overcome the Shiite monarch, led an army of 120,000 men into Ismael's territory. The Shah laid waste the country through which Selim would have to travel and harrassed the Turkish army, while avoiding a pitched battle. But Selim wanted to force the issue, because Ismael's army was much smaller and more poorly equipped than his own. Eventually he succeeded in forcing the Persians into battle. The Turkish artillery played havoc with Ismael's cavalry. As a result of this defeat and of the subsequent campaign, Kurdistan, Georgia and parts of eastern Anatolia were lost. However, despite isolated border battles during the following years, the Turks did not invade Persia again until after Ismael's death as their attention was occupied elsewhere.

Because of his defeat Ismael was unable to raise a substantial army to fight the Turks in his later years. He was, however, able to recover Georgia, and continued to hope for an alliance with Christian states against them. Dom Affonso de Albuquerque, the governor of Portuguese India, suggested that a combination of Portuguese sea power and Persian land forces would be able to conquer Egypt, but Ismael was suspicious of Portuguese intentions. As a result, no alliance developed before Ismael's death in 1524.

The Moguls in India

Both Selim and Ismael were remarkable rulers, but the outstanding emperor of the early sixteenth century was perhaps Baber (1483–1530), the founder of the Mogul dynasty in India. At the age of twelve Baber succeeded to the throne of the tiny Kingdom of Farghana in the mountains of Turkeshar, northeast of Bukhara. He showed his ambition early by conquering the city of Bukhara before he came of age. But his ambitions were upset by the invasion of the Uzbeks under Shaibani, who conquered both Bukhara and Farghana. In the following years Baber struggled to recover

Baber holding court.

while a new power emerges in India

his lost kingdom, and it was only by courageous military leadership that he survived plots, mutinies and frequent defeats in battle by generals stronger than he.

As hopes of regaining his kingdom faded, Baber turned his attention elsewhere. He led his army southward across the snow-capped Hindu Kush to capture Kabul, the capital of modern Afghanistan, and Kandahar. He found himself increasingly drawn toward India, much as his ancestor Timur had been a century earlier. Northern India lacked any powerful ruler, as the Afghan Lodi dynasty, although it claimed sovereignty over the whole area, was widely ignored by the other Afghan rulers. It was one of these who invited Baber to attack Delhi. The Afghan prince hoped that Baber would set him on the throne of Delhi in return for plunder, and then go back to his warring in Afghanistan. Baber's ideas were different. Unlike Timur, he wanted to establish a permanent empire. Sultan Ibrahim of Delhi gathered a large army but, despite his numerical superiority, was beaten by Baber at Panipat in 1526. Baber marched on to Delhi. His power at this stage was no greater than Ibrahim's had been, and now the Rajputs of Chitor, who wanted to set up a Hindu empire in Delhi, attacked him. When the battle was joined, Baber won another decisive victory. During the following years, until his death in 1530, he tried to stabilize his rule over northern India and to crush opposition to the Moguls. He thought it more important to establish his dynasty's power firmly than to develop the institutions and forms of government. By the time of his death, Baber had established his mastery over the whole of north India.

Portrait of Basil III.

St. Sophia Cathedral in the city of Novgorod.

Russia

Although Russia was to avoid the religious difficulties that affected most Western countries during the Reformation era, it had comparable problems of its own. From about 1470, the Russian Church was troubled by a group of Judaizing heretics, who denied many specifically Christian beliefs. It was only after Ivan III intervened energetically against the heresy that it died out. More serious than heresy was the problem of Church property. As in many Western countries, Russia's rulers found that the Church's wealth presented severe problems for the authority of the state. The land of some boyars had been expropriated during the late fifteenth century and these lands had been turned into *pomestya* (peasant small holdings). Toward the end of Ivan's reign substantial amounts of Church property around Novgorod were also expropriated. In a Church council in 1503, a motion was proposed to remove property from all monasteries, and it was only with difficulty that the Church establishment overcame these proposals, which had been inspired by Ivan. Throughout the reign of Ivan, the Church was becoming an instrument of state policy, as the Byzantine Church had been and as many Western "national" Churches were to become during the sixteenth century—for example in England and France. An antiheretical work held that "in authority the Tsar is like unto God almighty." Although Ivan's greatest work was in extending the authority of Moscow over the surrounding region and overthrowing Mongol overlordship, he was also the founder of the tradition of tsarist autocracy.

After Ivan's death in 1505, his eldest son Basil (Vasili) III became Prince of Moscow. Basil continued his father's expansionist policy by annexing the regions of Great Russia that his father had left unconquered. More dangerous was Basil's militant approach to Poland, but here too he was successful, owing to Poland's need to protect itself against the threat of war from Maximilian and the Teutonic Knights. While Sigismund of Poland was patching up a hasty treaty with the former and terrorizing the latter into cowed submission, Basil was able to seize the city of Smolensk in 1514.

Like his father, Basil was deeply suspicious of the power of members of the royal family and of the boyars. He was openly contemptuous of his three younger brothers, asking "Who will rule after me in Russia and in my towns and provinces? Shall I give (them) to my brothers? They cannot even control their own possessions." But in fact he was sufficiently worried by his brothers to fill their courts with spies and to forbid them to marry until his wife had given birth to two sons. Like many other rulers, he distrusted the power of the great nobility. He appointed low-born men as his advisers and, secure in the knowledge that they owed their power entirely to him, he gave them considerable authority and listened to their advice rather than to that of the boyars.

Basil's major problem was, in fact, the succession. His first wife was barren, but it was not until 1525 that he was able to persuade the Church to annul the marriage. He then married Helen Glinski, daughter of Michael Glinski, a Lithuanian noble who had helped him in the conquest of Smolensk. Five years later Helen bore him a son, the future Ivan the Terrible. But the death of Basil in 1533 left a serious problem as there was no individual who could be trusted to rule the enlarged possessions of the dynasty for the three-year-old Grand Prince.

The succession was not a problem confined to the Russian, Persian and Mogul empires. In Germany the Emperor Maximilian died on January 12, 1519. The election of his successor was to provide the first great clash in the protracted rivalry between the Hapsburg and the Valois dynasties.

u iuste pois veritable balance

The Election of Charles V

1519

The death of Maximilian I *left seven electors of the Holy Roman Empire with the task of selecting his successor. After much discussion and considerable bribery, they chose Charles, Maximilian's grandson, who ruled as Charles* V. *One of his first acts was to confront the problem of Martin Luther. By his support of the traditional Church and denouncing of Luther, Charles doomed Germany to religious dissent and a political instability that lasted until the advent of Bismarck*

The Holy Roman Emperor Maximilian I, knight errant, eccentric and grand old man of European politics, died on January 12, 1519. By January 30, couriers had brought the momentous news to all the courts of Europe: to Pope Leo x in Rome; to the young and ambitious French King Francis I in Paris; to Henry VIII and Cardinal Wolsey at Greenwich Palace; and last of all, to Maximilian's eighteen-year-old grandson and heir Charles at the Catalonian town of Lerida in Spain. Even before the Emperor's body was laid to rest beneath its splendid monument at Innsbruck, his death sparked off a flurry of speculation, excitement and intense diplomatic activity.

The issue that now engrossed the attentions of kings, courtiers, bishops and statesmen from the Baltic to the Mediterranean was the choice of Maximilian's successor as Holy Roman Emperor of the German nation. Unique among the crowns of Europe, the Emperor's title was conferred not by inheritance but by election. By tradition the choice now lay in the hands of seven electors—the prince-archbishops of Mainz, Cologne and Trier, the King of Bohemia (modern Czechoslovakia) and the secular electors of Brandenburg, Saxony and the Rhineland Palatinate.

The imperial title, like the Empire itself, was a historical curiosity, an anomaly that two centuries later prompted Voltaire's famous phrase that the Holy Roman Empire was neither holy, Roman nor an empire. Founded by Charlemagne on Christmas Day, 800, the Empire was based originally on two ideas: the revival of the old Roman Empire under a monarch strong enough to unite the greater part of Western Europe; and the notion that the Emperor enjoyed a divine mandate to propagate the Christian faith and protect the Church. By the beginning of the sixteenth century both these ideas had undergone a radical change. The boundaries of the Empire had shrunk so that they included only the German-speaking peoples of what is now Germany, Austria, Holland and parts of Poland and Czechoslovakia. The cantons of Switzerland and the Duchy of Milan were nominally part of the Empire also, but at Maximilian's death the Swiss were fiercely independent and Milan had been overrun by the French.

Because the imperial title was elective rather than hereditary the German princes had been able to secure a great measure of independence within their various duchies, margravates, archbishoprics and counties. To maintain himself, Maximilian relied not on the wealth of the Empire but on the fact that he, too, was a territorial prince in his own right. As head of the Hapsburg dynasty he held most of Austria and scattered estates throughout southern Germany. Maximilian thus spent most of his colorful career attempting to rule an empire with the resources of a duchy. In this sense he was transparently unsuccessful. His campaigns to recover Milan and Venice for the Empire ended in expensive failure and he died poor as a church mouse.

Why, then, was there so much excitement throughout Europe in 1519 to see who would succeed him in the thankless role of Holy Roman Emperor? The answer is that the imperial title was the key to the titanic struggle about to begin between Europe's two super-powers, Francis I of France and Maximilian's own grandson, Charles, King of Spain and Duke of Burgundy.

In the seventy years since the French had avenged Agincourt and driven the English back across the Channel, France had emerged as the most powerful kingdom of Europe. By the end of the fifteenth century her kings were strong enough to embark on a policy of conquest in Italy. In 1515, Francis had routed the hitherto invincible Swiss mercenaries at the Battle of Marignano and secured the rich and strategically placed Duchy of Milan.

Charles V, by van Orly. Charles inherited the greatest conglomeration of territories to be ruled by one man since the Roman Empire.

Opposite Allegory of the balance of power in Europe at the accession of Charles V, by Guy d'Amiens. The wars between Charles and Francis I preserved this balance in Europe.

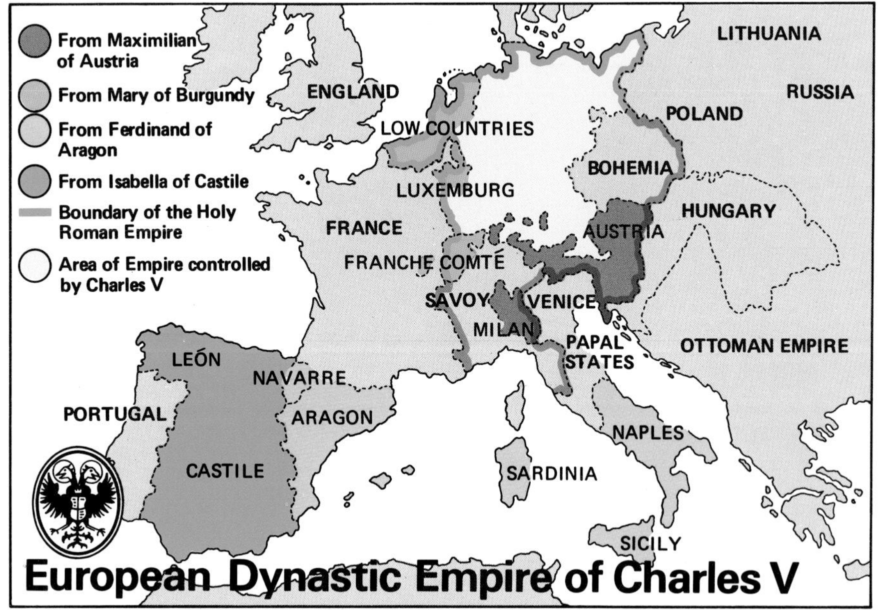

European Dynastic Empire of Charles V

Maximilian I, who built up the Hapsburg dominions by dynastic marriages rather than by force.

Charles, the only European monarch strong enough to prevent the French from overrunning the rest of Italy, owed his position entirely to the matrimonial schemes of his grandfather. Maximilian himself married Mary of Burgundy in 1477, and on her death the Burgundian Low Countries, Luxemburg and Franche Comté passed to their infant son, Philip. In 1496 Maximilian succeeded in marrying Philip to Joan, daughter of the Spanish monarchs Ferdinand and Isabella. Four years later their first son Charles was born. As a boy of six he succeeded to his Burgundian inheritance and in 1516 to his mother's inheritance of Spain, Sicily, Naples and Spanish America. On Maximilian's death in 1519 he stood also to inherit the Hapsburg lands in Austria and Germany. It was the greatest conglomeration of territories to be ruled by one man since the Roman Empire, and the only one in history to be created not by force of arms but by the bonds of marriage.

But the very extent of Charles' dominions posed a vital problem. How could so many different peoples in widely separated lands be welded into a single, unified state? The imperial title offered the only practical solution. Though it had declined in terms of real power, the name of Emperor still rang with a magic that no mere king's title could match—a magic that could bind the Tyrolese peasant, the Flemish merchant and the Spanish grandee to a common loyalty and obedience. To the more sanguine of Charles' advisers it proffered the dazzling prospect of transforming the sad rump of a make-believe German empire into a universal lordship of all Christendom. To the most hardened realist it afforded at least the opportunity to control the corridor of German territory that divided Hapsburg Burgundy from Hapsburg Austria. In any event the coming imperial election offered a prize that Charles could simply not afford to lose.

From Francis' viewpoint it was a prize he could not afford to let Charles win. On three sides his kingdom was hemmed in by territories that already belonged to Charles—Flanders to the north, Franche Comté to the west and Spain to the south. To the southeast lay the Duchy of Milan, now in French hands but nominally still a fief of the Empire. Milan was the key to the strategic domination of northern Italy and an obvious source of friction if Charles also secured the imperial title. The other flashpoint was the ancient Duchy of Burgundy which had once belonged to Charles' great-grandfather, Charles the Bold, but had been overrun by the French on his death in 1477. The young Charles had spent the first seventeen years of his life at the Burgundian court and was taught to regard the recovery of his lost inheritance as an article of faith.

For both monarchs, therefore, the imperial election of 1519 involved not only the leadership of the German confederation, but also the far wider issues of safeguarding the possessions of the Hapsburg and Valois houses; of supremacy in Italy; and of the leadership of Western Europe.

Even before Maximilian's death, Francis had declared his intention of standing as a candidate for the election. "He goeth about covertly and layeth many baits to attain the Empire," one diplomat had reported. The principal bait was money. At a requiem Mass for the departed Emperor, held at Notre Dame in February, 1519, Francis told Sir Thomas Boleyn, "I will spend three millions of gold but be Emperor." Nor were the seven electors, whisked so unexpectedly from obscurity to the forefront of the European scene, averse to the clink of French gold. The Margrave of Brandenburg, known to some as "the father of all greed," succumbed first, pledging not only his vote but that of his brother, the Archbishop of Cologne. The Archbishop of Trier, too, canvassed openly for Francis and even the Elector Palatine, who had grown up at the court of Burgundy with Charles, was said to be wavering.

Until the beginning of May, the tide ran strongly in Francis' favor. Every government in Europe assured him of support. Even Pope Leo X, who had good reasons for fearing the success of either candidate, felt that Francis was the lesser evil.

But at the beginning of May, 1519, three new developments emerged, one an interesting sideshow, the other two crucial to the outcome. The sideshow was the candidacy of King Henry VIII of England, who allowed himself to be gulled into thinking he stood a chance as a compromise candidate and dispatched his most seasoned diplomat, Richard Pace, to the election too late and with too little money. Far more influential than the unfortunate Pace was the powerful current of popular, national German sentiment that he reported to be now running in Charles' favor. Paradoxically it was Charles' weakness and Francis' overconfidence that wrought the change. Although he was no more German than Francis and had never set foot in Germany, Charles was the people's choice, acclaimed by the many who remembered with affection his popular, affable, German grandfather,

Maximilian. The electors themselves were influenced also by the feeling that German interests were being manipulated by an alliance between a French king and an Italian pope. Perhaps the unknown, untried Hapsburg with his far-flung dominions would be less likely or able to interfere with the government of the German princes than the victor of Marignano. Leo himself sensed the way things were going and made an unsuccessful bid to persuade Frederick, Elector of Saxony, to present himself as a candidate.

However, there is little doubt that the final vote, which took place at Frankfurt on June 28, was heavily weighted by Charles' outright victory in the bribery stakes. Backed by the famous Augsburg banking house of Fugger, who refused to honor Francis' bills, Charles' agents lavished some 850,000 florins in support of the Hapsburg claim. Charles was unanimously elected. Even Brandenburg voted for him "out of very fear" for the consequences if he remained faithful to Francis.

Francis attempted to shrug off his defeat with the remark that he was well pleased not to have the Empire's cares, and forthwith departed for the hunt at Fontainebleau.

From a European viewpoint the results of the election were entirely predictable. Within two years Charles and Francis were at war over Milan, and the pattern was set for the whole of Charles' long reign. In 1525 Charles scored an enormous but temporary victory at the Battle of Pavia when his generals actually captured Francis and packed him off to Madrid as a hostage. A year later Francis bought his freedom and immediately renounced the undertakings he had made under oath. A third war lasted from 1526 to 1529 in the midst of which (1527) Europe was treated to the spectacle of the Emperor's Spanish and German troops laying waste the city of Rome itself. The conflict between Hapsburg and Valois in the end outlasted both the original contestants: when it came to an end in 1559 Francis had been dead for twelve years and Charles for six months. In the meantime the Turks, under the leadership of Suleiman the Magnificent and often with active French encouragement, pressed their advance into the heart of Europe so that by 1529 they besieged Vienna and in 1541 they had captured Buda.

It could be argued that the Hapsburg-Valois wars would have taken place irrespective of Charles' election as Holy Roman Emperor, since the main bone of contention was the clash of dynastic interests in the power vacuum of northern Italy. The same is certainly not true of the tragedy that overtook Germany during Charles' reign.

The main catalyst of this tragedy was Martin Luther who within two years of his protest had become the symbol of a nationwide German revolt against the Roman Church. In June, 1520, Luther's doctrines were condemned by Pope Leo x, and on December 10, he was excommunicated.

By the time he confronted his Emperor at the Diet of Worms in January, 1521, Luther was a national hero. As the papal legate Aleander stated, "nine tenths of Germany shouts for Luther." The revolt against Rome was not simply a religious issue but a deeply felt expression of national resentment against an ecclesiastical system imposed on the German people by a foreign pope who administered the system in the interests not of Germany but of Rome. On a deeper level, the pope was simply the most obvious and identifiable target for a revolutionary movement that had been fermenting in Germany for the past forty years or more.

Pope Paul III reconciling Francis and Charles, by Sebastian Ricci. The Pope succeeded in bringing about a ten-year armistice in 1538.

It was not until a year and four months after his election that Charles v made his state entry into Aachen on October 22, 1520, and received the homage of the electors. On the following day the coronation ceremony took place in the great cathedral of Charlemagne. The solemnity and magnificence of the event were a fitting prelude to the momentous confrontation that took place a few months later, in April 1521, between the young Emperor and the renegade monk. The Diet of Worms has a unique niche in history, not only because of its cataclysmic results but also because it provides such a striking example of how a single individual can determine the course of events. Luther himself had high hopes that Charles would recognize the force of his arguments. In August, 1520, he declared that "God has given us a young and noble ruler to reign over us and has thereby awakened our hearts once more to hope." But Luther was tragically wrong. The truth is that every facet of Charles' make-up conspired to deafen him to Luther's appeal.

As a Burgundian by upbringing, Charles had little understanding of Germany or the German people. By culture, tradition and language the Burgundian court belonged to the French rather than the German sphere of influence. Charles was thus ill prepared to grasp or to sympathize with the links between Luther's doctrinal revolt and the national aspirations of the German people.

As a Hapsburg by birth, Charles was also dedicated to the maintenance of his inheritance. Throughout his career German interests would take

Procession headed by Pope Clement VII and Charles. Charles' allegiance to the papacy and his inability to understand the full nature of the Lutheran revolt was to plunge Germany into civil war.

Coronation of Charles V as Holy Roman Emperor, in maiolica.

Francis receives Charles and Cardinal Alessandro Farnese (later Paul III) in Paris.

second place to Hapsburg interests whenever the two conflicted. In 1521, with Francis I preparing to go to war over Milan, Charles needed the support of Pope Leo X, whose opposition in the recent election had emptied the Hapsburg coffers. Leo had already excommunicated Luther. If Charles were now to support Luther's stand against Rome, he would simply cast the Pope into a new alliance with France.

As Emperor by election, Charles had already conceived an ideal of Empire quite foreign to the limited German confederation that had made up the Holy Roman Empire over the past two hundred and fifty years. The extent of Charles' hereditary non-German dominions in Italy and Burgundy, Spain and the Americas, gave birth to his dream of a universal empire.

This was the message behind the speech that the Emperor delivered in French in reply to Luther on April 19, 1521:

> It is certain that a single monk must err if he stands against the opinion of all Christendom. Otherwise Christendom itself would have erred for more than a thousand years. I have therefore resolved to stake upon this cause all my dominions, my friends, my body and my blood, my life and my soul. . . . From now on I shall regard him (Luther) as a notorious heretic and hope that you, as good Christians, will not be wanting in your duty.

Charles' statement made it clear that there was no room for compromise or understanding with Luther. On May 25, Charles imposed on him the Ban of the Empire.

Luther was saved from the consequences of the ban by the intervention of Frederick of Saxony who had him kidnapped. Luther's protective confinement was symbolic of the next and most disastrous stage in the German Reformation—the alliance between Luther and the German princes. Condemned by an emperor who abandoned Germany soon after the Diet of Worms and spent the next seven years in distant Spain, Luther turned to the territorial princes as the bulwarks of the Protestant confession. In 1523 he wrote the important treatise *Of Earthly Government* in which he distinguished the two realms of spiritual and temporal government, stressing the duty of civil obedience and the wickedness of rebellion against lawful government. This strange alliance with the territorial princes was cemented

by the outbreak of the Peasants' Revolt which swept western and southern Germany between 1524 and 1526. To the insurgents, Luther was the apostle of freedom and revolt against oppressive authority. Abbeys and manors were plundered in the name of the liberty of Christian man. To Luther the peasants were anathema, an awful example of how the true faith could be perverted in hands of the ignorant. Aghast at the anarchy he himself had helped to cause, he expressed his views in a vitriolic broadsheet entitled *Against the Murdering, Thieving Hordes of Peasants* (1525).

The years 1525–26 mark the watershed of the Lutheran Reformation. Luther ceased to speak for the spiritual freedom of the German people, and became instead the advocate of their absolute subjection to the authority of the princes. The logical outcome was the formula agreed at the first Diet of Speier in 1526. Pending the calling of a German national council, the estates resolved that every prince "should so conduct himself with regard to the Edict of Worms as he should answer for it toward God and the Emperor." The Recess of Speier thus enshrined the principle that each territory should follow the religious dictates of its prince (*cuius regio, eius religio*). By and large the rulers of northern Germany, in common with a number of imperial cities in the south, chose Luther while the south remained faithful to the Edict of Worms. Lutheranism, once an expression of German national feeling, now became the instrument of political separatism, representing the interests of the class least sympathetic to German unity.

The Recess of Speier set a pattern that neither Charles v nor his brother Ferdinand (to whom Charles ceded Hapsburg Austria in 1521 and who inherited the crown of Hungary in 1526) were able to break. The French wars and the pressure of the Turks on the eastern frontiers enabled the Protestant princes, organized for self-defense into the Schmalkaldic League, to resist all Charles' efforts to re-impose the unity of the Church and ultimately shattered his vision of universal empire. In 1555, Ferdinand concluded the religious Peace of Augsburg, which sanctioned the principle of *cuius regio, eius religio*. A year later Charles retired, defeated and exhausted to the Spanish monastery of Yuste, bequeathing Italy and Spain to his son Philip and the Empire to Ferdinand.

If personal failure was the price that Charles v paid for the dream of a universal empire, it was a light penalty compared to that suffered by the German people in the century after his death. In 1618 the attempts of another Hapsburg, the Emperor Ferdinand II, to impose Catholicism on his subjects ushered in the Thirty Years War. Before peace was restored in 1648 some ten million Germans, out of a total population of sixteen million, had perished—a death toll greater than that of both World Wars. After the Peace of Westphalia the Emperor was shorn of his authority within the Empire and the princes finally emerged as sovereign rulers.

Though the Empire survived, it was a Hapsburg empire, drawing its strength from the hereditary Hapsburg lands in Austria, Hungary and Bohemia. The Holy Roman Empire of the German nation to which Charles v succeeded in 1519 lived on in name only. It lingered on until 1806 when it was abolished by Emperor Francis II. Fearing that Napoleon would shortly declare himself Holy Roman Emperor, Francis declared the Empire and title "extinct" and restyled himself Francis I, Emperor of Austria.

Napoleon shrewdly remarked that if Charles v had put himself at the head of German Protestantism in 1520 he would have created a united German nation. But Charles, a Hapsburg by birth, a Burgundian by upbringing and a universal emperor by his own aspiration, proved incapable of identifying himself with German interests. At precisely the time when the other major European powers—France, England and Spain—were emerging from the cocoon of the medieval world as fully fledged nation-states, Germany's patchwork of princely states and free cities was given new life by the force of religious dissent. It was left for Napoleon, a Corsican general, to rekindle the spirit of German nationalism nearly three hundred years later; for Bismarck, a Prussian junker, to impose nationhood; and for Hitler, an Austrian misfit, to unleash the holocaust of National Socialism that ended, once again, in the division of Germany. As the British historian A. J. P. Taylor wrote in 1945: "The moment for making a national middle-class Germany was lost in 1521 perhaps forever, certainly for centuries."

ANTHONY CHEETHAM

Jacob Fugger with his accounts. It was the backing of the vast wealth of the Fuggers which enabled Charles to outbribe Francis and buy the support of the electors.

The Old World scrambles to explore and

The Field of Cloth of Gold where Henry VIII and Francis I met but could not agree.

The imperial election campaign had postponed the long-anticipated meeting between the kings of England and France, each of whom had sworn that he would not shave until he had met the other. The arrangements for the meeting were in the hands of Wolsey. The English chancellor had cast himself in the role of the arbiter of Europe and had devised the Peace of London, an agreement which he hoped to get England, France, the Holy Roman Empire, Spain and the papacy to sign. The Field of Cloth of Gold, near Calais, was intended as a "summit meeting" between the two kings to guarantee the peace of Europe. By the summer of 1518, 6,000 English workmen were busy preparing King Henry's quarters—which included a huge banqueting hall—at Guisnes, and the French were no less active at Ardres. Midway between Guisnes and Ardres was the Val d'Or, the spot selected for the meeting. Pavilions and galleries had been erected nearby, overlooking a tournament ground.

More than 5,000 people accompanied Henry on his channel crossing in 1520, and rode with him through the Val d'Or. The two kings, accompanied by the greatest nobles of their realms, rode to opposite edges of the field and then, as trumpets sounded, they galloped forward to the appointed place and, still mounted, embraced three times.

Thus opened the Field of Cloth of Gold, a prelude to three weeks of jousting, banquets, dancing and pageantry that ended with a high Mass, celebrated in the open by Wolsey, with music composed especially for the occasion by the English court composer Robert Fairfax. Many contemporaries considered the program of events to be the eighth wonder of the world, for it appeared to herald the rebirth of chivalry, so dear to the hearts of both kings. Most remarkable of all was the fact that the sovereigns of two countries, which had been enemies from time immemorial, should at last meet on such cordial terms. At the end of the festivities a treaty was signed that proposed marriage between the infant Mary Tudor and the Dauphin, and was intended to end French interference in the affairs of Scotland. Both before and immediately after the Field of Cloth of Gold, Henry VIII met with Charles V at Dover and Gravelines. There is no evidence to convict the English King of duplicity, however, for despite all his efforts, Charles found that he could not draw Henry into an alliance against the French.

Exploration and discovery

The thirty years that followed Columbus' discovery of America were crowded with the achievements of other navigators, crowned in 1521 by Magellan's circumnavigation of the world. Columbus himself made three voyages after his first epoch-making discovery. He established a colony on Hispaniola and discovered the islands of Cuba, Puerto Rico, Antigua, Jamaica and Trinidad. He also explored part of the coast of South America.

Portugal

Despite the excitement caused by Columbus' discoveries, their significance was not realized until 1501, when Amerigo Vespucci (1451–1512), an Italian who had led an Italian-financed expedition in 1499, undertook a voyage for the King of Portugal, which convinced him that the Brazilian coast was part of a "new world"—and not an outlying portion of Asia. By 1507 it was obvious that Vespucci was right, and in that year the German geographer Martin Waldseemüller (1470–1520) proposed in his *Cosmographiae Introductio* that the new continent be named America after Vespucci.

Despite Spain's lead in discovering America, the Portuguese were generally the pace setters. Bartholomew Dias' achievement in rounding the Cape of Good Hope was followed up ten years later by his compatriot Vasco da Gama (1460–1524), who retraced Dias' steps in the search for a sea route to India. He reached Calicut on the Indian coast in May, 1498, thus fulfilling the ambitions of Prince Henry the Navigator. A year after Vasco da Gama's return, Pedro Alvarez Cabral (1467–1526) assembled a fleet and established regular trade with Portugal's newly discovered outposts. He sailed first to Brazil, where he stayed for ten days, and then made for the Cape of Good Hope and the Indian Ocean. Loading his thirteen ships with pepper and other spices in Malabar, he brought them safely home to Portugal. By 1503—thanks to the new sea-route—the price of pepper in Lisbon had dropped to a fifth of what it was in Venice.

Important discoveries were being made almost every year. In 1500, for example, Dias discovered Madagascar. In 1502, St. Helena was discovered, and in 1506, Tristan da Cunha. By 1512, a Portuguese expedition had reached Canton. Colonies were founded in Africa and along the coast of India. Da Gama set up a factory in 1502 on India's Malabar coast, impressed by the fact that the natives were Christians—albeit heretical Christians who had to be converted to the true faith. In 1510, a colony was started at Goa which remained Portuguese territory until it was seized by India in 1961. The potential value of African labor in the hugely rich colonies of the New World was recognized as early as 1503, when a shipload of African slaves were sent to Brazil.

The Portuguese did not regard conquest in India as their main aim, but they soon found that their overseas factories and settlements needed administering. Dom Afonso de Albuquerque (1453–1515) was responsible both for the formulation of Portuguese policy in India and for its execution. He saw the possibility of using European possessions in the East for an attack on the Ottoman Empire, although he was never able to bring these ambitions to fulfillment.

A sixteenth-century mariner's compass, one of the earliest in existence.

Spain's American discoveries

Both Spanish and Portuguese explorers in the New World continued to investigate the coasts, estuaries and islands of America during this period. In both countries the crown attempted to keep a firm hold on all exploration efforts, and on the benefits that flowed from them. This often proved to be difficult, as colonists strove to free themselves from the restraints placed on them by the home government. The difficulties of the American Revolution of 1776 were merely a continuation of problems as old as colonialism itself. A few exploratory journeys were made to the north, and Florida was discovered in 1512, but the main effort was in South and Central America. Here Spain set the pace. Unlike Portugal, whose main interest in exploration was to build up trade, the Spaniards sought to found colonies. On his second voyage, Columbus founded a township at Isabela in Hispaniola, but this settlement was quickly abandoned, and in 1497 the settlers founded a new township, Santo

colonize the New

A woodcut of Columbus' voyages showing natives practicing cannibalism.

Domingo. From the beginning, shortage of labor was a major problem and the Spaniards—after they had wiped out the native Indian population—solved the problem in the same way as the Portuguese, by importing Negro slaves from Africa.

A settlement was begun in Jamaica in 1509, in Cuba in 1511, and in Puerto Rico in 1512, although in the last there was formidable resistance from the native population. Many of these early settlements provoked quarrels with the Spanish government, and Columbus was quickly replaced as governor. But the quarrels between colonial governments and their European overlords remained a constant feature of the colonial experience. The Church saw the natives as material for conversion, but the King insisted that the natives were not to be converted by force. In secular matters, too, the crown attempted to regulate the behavior of the *conquistadores* by the Law of Burgos in 1512, which insisted that the Indians were free men and not slaves, an insistence that was frequently ignored. Although mainland settlement was encouraged by Ferdinand and Isabella, it was at first not particularly successful, and in 1509 more than a thousand men were lost in an attempt to settle in Colombia.

Widening the world's boundaries

Spanish exploration continued, partly in an attempt to find gold, partly to find the western route to India and partly to find new regions to colonize. In 1499, Vicente Pinzon, a former associate of Columbus, had explored the coast of Brazil, still hunting for the way to the Indies. Many other voyages were made. On September 26, 1513, the ambitious Vasco Nuñez de Balboa (1476–1519), crossed the Isthmus of Panama in a search for gold and found himself looking into the Pacific Ocean. The discovery of the Pacific, so close to the Atlantic, encouraged false hopes of an easy route to the Indies; as a result, Spanish exploratory efforts were concentrated on the Caribbean and Central America, and this led to the speedy subjugation of the great native mainland empires.

Ferdinand Magellan.

Six years after Balboa's view of the Pacific, a more ambitious attempt was made to broaden the frontiers of man's knowledge of the world in which he lived. Ferdinand Magellan (c. 1480–1521), a Portuguese mariner of considerable experience, received backing from Charles v to attempt to find a western route to the Indies by sailing a southwestern course. Magellan hoped to reach the Molucca Islands in the Pacific and then return by way of the Cape of Good Hope. Charles supplied Magellan with five ships, which left Seville in August, 1519. It was not until October, 1520, that the remaining four ships—one had already returned to Spain—passed from the southern Atlantic into the Pacific—so-called because of its apparent peacefulness—through the "Magellan" Strait. Like so many other explorers at the time Magellan consistently underestimated the distances he would have to cover. It soon became clear that, because of the size of the Pacific, the African route to the Indies would remain quicker than the American one. Magellan himself was killed during a native war in the Moluccas. In October, 1522, a single ship returned to Seville, but it was well-laden with spices.

Expeditions such as this raised problems in interpreting the 1494 Treaty of Tordesillas, by which the line of demarcation between Spanish and Portuguese spheres of influence had been moved further west. The treaty was enormously in Portugal's favor, as the Spaniards, confused by Columbus' discoveries, thought that they had found the western route to the Indies. As a result they had relinquished the Cape route and Brazil. Much more serious was the problem of how other countries could participate in the wealth of the New World and the new trade. Spain and Portugal were not uniquely qualified to take advantage of the discoveries that they had made. England, France and—to a lesser extent, because it was still under Spanish rule—the Netherlands all wanted a share. John Cabot, a Genoese living in England, persuaded Henry VII that he was capable of reaching the "island of Brazil," and in 1497 he sailed westward under royal instructions to "discover and settle new lands across the Atlantic." Cabot's voyage was made in defiance of Pope Alexander VI's bull of 1493, which reserved the new continent for Spain and Portugal. The intrepid Genoese reached Cape Breton Island and sailed south along the coast of Newfoundland. Cabot was convinced that he had found "the land of the Grand Khan," but English commercial interest in Cabot's ventures faded as soon as it became clear that there was no spice trade in the region. The French were a little behind the English. Jacques Cartier (1491–1557) explored the Gulf of St. Lawrence in 1534, and returned in the following year to travel up the St. Lawrence river. But although slower in starting, the French were less easily distracted than the English. The problem of the division of the New World remained. Political and religious differences were to exacerbate it as the century wore on. But for the present the Spanish were free to colonize their possessions.

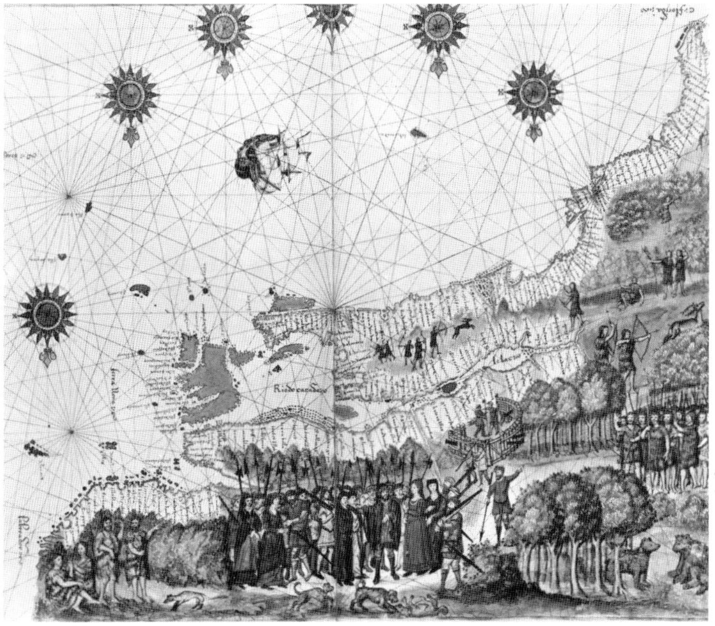

Jacques Cartier's map of the west coast of America and Canada. Florida is in the top right-hand corner.

The Conquest of Mexico 1521

Like many a Spanish youth of his generation, Hernando Cortes was stirred by tales of the New World being explored and colonized by his countrymen. At the age of nineteen, he reached the Antilles; fifteen years later he was the wealthy proprietor of several estates in Cuba. But the rumors of fabulously rich kingdoms—always just beyond the next island or over the next mountain—were persistent, and early in 1519 Cortes set out at the head of an expedition to Mexico. By an incredible combination of luck, ingenuity and courage, Cortes and his small force overwhelmed the awesome Aztec Empire. Horses and firearms—both unknown to the natives—were the keys to Cortes' success; and this easy triumph of European skill and technology over Indian brute force set the pattern for succeeding generations of conquerors—and foredoomed America's native population.

At the dawn of the sixteenth century, Western civilization stood on the threshold of a new age—an age of discovery and challenge, of bursting frontiers and distant, undreamed-of horizons that has had no parallel until our own day. America had been discovered, but the continent remained virtually unexplored.

The pattern was to change in 1519, with the appearance on those shores of a man of very different stamp from any who had gone before him. His name was Hernando Cortes and in less than three years—through a combination of brilliant leadership, superhuman courage and almost incredible good luck—he was to achieve the downfall of the Mexican Empire and of its Emperor Montezuma. His story is one of special significance, for it marks the first direct confrontation, in all their power and might, of the Old World and the New.

Cortes, the son of a humble country squire of Extremadura in western Spain, had left home at the age of sixteen to seek his fortune. Three years later he arrived in Hispaniola. In the years that followed he acquired several large estates in Cuba and became, by local standards, a rich man.

Despite its pleasures, life in Cuba ultimately began to pall, and in 1518, Cortes talked, intrigued and bribed his way into the command of a new expedition to the west. On February 10 of the following year the expedition set sail. It had two main objectives, one material and one spiritual. The material one, as always, was gold—a subject never very far from the minds of the conquistadors. But the spiritual purpose was equally real and even more important; the conquistadors might be despoilers, but they were missionaries as well.

The Spanish commander's resources were small—eleven ships, carrying less than seven hundred men—but he possessed two secret weapons unknown to the American natives: firearms, including several small cannon, and sixteen horses. Cortes used both weapons in his first clash with the mainlanders. In a battle fought near Tabasco in southeastern Mexico, terrified Maya Indians bravely stood their ground against the cannon, but the horses proved too much for them. At the outset they actually imagined horse and rider to be a single animal—some monstrous centaur bearing down upon them—and they soon fled. Cortes, striding over to a nearby tree, struck it a great blow with his sword and claimed the whole territory for Spain. The conquest of Mexico was under way.

The next morning, the Tabascans sent peace emissaries to the Spanish camp bearing rich gifts for their conquerors. Among these gifts was a young native maiden named Marina. This girl, whom Bernal Diaz describes as good-looking and intelligent, was probably the greatest godsend that Cortes ever received—not because she eventually became the conquistador's mistress and the mother of his child, but because she spoke both Mexican and Maya. Cortes already had a Spanish-Maya interpreter, so that from the moment Marina joined him, his language problems were at an end.

Other problems were only just beginning, however. The Spaniards' next landfall, some two hundred miles north of Tabasco, lay within the frontiers of the warlike Aztec Empire of Montezuma.

When the Aztecs went to war they did so not to kill but to take prisoners for sacrifice—and they could never take enough. During the four-day consecration of the great temple at Tenochtitlan, no less than 80,000 victims met their deaths on the sacrificial altars. Throughout the carnage, the method of dispatch never varied: the victim's breast was ripped open with an obsidian knife and the still-palpitating heart was torn out and offered to the gods.

Among these gods was one named Quetzalcoatl, the Feathered Serpent. A recounting of his legend reveals a fantastic series of coincidences that makes the history of the conquest sound more like a fairy tale. Long ago—ran the legend—Quetzalcoatl had

Hernando Cortes, the conqueror of Mexico; by N. Medellin.

Opposite Xochipilli, the Aztec god of poetry, music, theater and dancing.

A view from the *Florentine Codex*. In the background an Indian sights the Spanish ships; left, the Spaniards unload supplies; right, questioning an Indian.

Mask of the sun god, Toratiun.

come down to earth in human form, white-skinned and black-bearded; then after twenty years he had sailed away to the east. It was said that he would return one day, dressed in black, to reestablish his rule. His homecoming would occur in a "One-reed Year," and would bring much tribulation and suffering in its train. According to the Aztec calendar, a "One-reed Year" fell only once in every fifty-two of our years. There had been one in 1415, and another in 1467; the next fell in 1519.

Thus, Montezuma had reason to be anxious even before he learned of the coming of Cortes—and when his spies reported sighting a band of mysterious strangers, led by a man with an unusually pale face and a black beard—and dressed in black from head to foot—the Emperor's direst suspicions seemed confirmed.

Believing that there was a faint chance that "Quetzalcoatl" might be bribed not to come to the capital, Montezuma sent ambassadors down to the coast with propitiatory gifts. The move was a fatal one. These gifts, every one of which was of gold, convinced Cortes that he was indeed on the threshold of El Dorado; and he resolved to lead the puny force under his command against Montezuma's huge empire. Cortes knew that the authorities in Cuba would never countenance so dangerous an enterprise before he established a secure and independent colony on the mainland. Therefore, on the very spot where he had first received the Aztec ambassadors, the conquistador founded a new Spanish colony. In honor of his Good Friday landing he named the settlement Villa Rica de Vera Cruz—the Rich Town of the True Cross—thus neatly reflecting the two preoccupations of the Spanish colonial mind—gold and the Gospel.

While preparations were being made for the great march to the interior, another group of Indian emissaries arrived at Vera Cruz. These friendly members of the Totonac tribe invited Cortes and his men to visit their city of Cempoala, twenty-odd miles to the northwest. Explaining that they had recently been conquered by the Aztecs and were presently being crushed by the savage tribute wrung from them by their hated overlords, the Totonacs asked to accompany the Spaniards on their campaign. Cortes accepted their invitation and agreed to take them with him on the condition that they give up their own predilection for human sacrifice and embrace the Cross.

Before setting forth, Cortes made a decision that, for sheer cold-blooded courage, must rank as one of the most remarkable of his life: he bribed a few of his sailors to puncture the hulls of his ships with holes and then, on the pretext that they were worm-eaten and unseaworthy, deliberately run them aground. Henceforth, whatever happened, there could be no retreat.

Thus, in August, 1519, this extraordinary young man set off without maps across an unknown country, against an empire of apparently limitless power, wealth and savagery, never knowing what lay beyond the next hill except that he would probably be encountering armies many times stronger than his and almost certainly hostile. On this trek, Cortes was accompanied by about five hundred Spanish musketeers (a sizable garrison had been left behind at Vera Cruz), thirteen horses, a few pieces of light artillery and perhaps a thousand Totonac irregulars.

Now there was hard fighting in store for them. The people of Tlaxcala, a town located roughly halfway between Vera Cruz and Tenochtitlan, rejected the Spaniards' peace overtures and put up an impassioned and heroic resistance. Only after three weeks and four major battles (in which they suffered immense losses) did the Tlaxcalans admit defeat and allow Cortes into their capital. Then, however, they too offered him their friendship—and proved as good as their word. Henceforth, they became his most trusted allies, and a large number of them accompanied Cortes on the next stage of his journey, which brought him to the holy city of Cholula.

Although the natives offered no overt opposition as the Spaniards entered Cholula, the conquistadors were immediately suspicious. Many of the streets had been barricaded, and piles of stones were visible on the rooftops. Most ominous of all, there were no women or children anywhere. It was the faithful Marina who first discovered the truth: the Cholulans intended to ambush Cortes' entire army the next day and to carry it off to Montezuma for sacrifice. Cortes laid his plans quickly but carefully. Early the following morning he gathered all the Cholulans he could muster within the Spanish stockade. Then, through Marina, he told them that he knew all that was in their hearts—and pronounced sentence. As he did so, Spanish musketeers opened fire from the surrounding rooftops; by Cortes' own admission, more than 3,000 men died in the next two hours. It was a massacre, and he has been bitterly condemned for ordering it. Yet it is difficult to see what else Cortes could have done. He was not normally a bloodthirsty man—never once in the whole campaign did he resort to force unnecessarily.

The journey from Cholula to the capital—a fifty-mile-long march that led the conquistadors up between the twin volcanoes that guard the southeastern approaches to the city and over a pass 12,000 feet high—must have been the most grueling of all, On the other side of the pass, the road began to descend, and the Spaniards suddenly found themselves gazing down on a huge lake that sparkled in the sun. In the midst of that lake, linked to its shores by three slender causeways, was the city of Tenochtitlan.

On November 8, 1519, Hernando Cortes led four hundred tired and bedraggled soldiers along the southern causeway into the Aztec capital. Another, different procession approached from the opposite direction: the Emperor himself, in his golden palanquin, was riding out to meet his god. The scene must have been a strange one.

> The great Montezuma descended from his litter, and the other great chieftains supported him beneath a marvelously rich canopy of green feathers, decorated with gold, silver and pearls . . . And there were other great lords who walked before the great Montezuma, laying down cloaks so that his feet should not touch the earth. Not one dared to raise his eyes towards him.

Dismounting from his horse, Cortes strode smiling toward the Emperor—and now for the first time, the Old World and the New stood face to face.

This first encounter with Montezuma made a deep impression on the Spaniards—as did the Emperor's address of welcome, in which he greeted Cortes as a king and a god, spoke of promises and prophecies and seemed virtually to be offering the Spanish leader the throne of Mexico. Despite Montezuma's effusive greeting, Cortes remained on his guard; although he was being treated as an honored guest, he had not forgotten that he was on an island fortress in a distant land, with only a handful of men and no lines of communication to the outside world. He followed Montezuma to a great palace that had been prepared for his reception.

At the age of fifty-two, Montezuma was tall and slim, with fine eyes and, as Bernal Diaz put it, "an expression that was at once tender and grave." In the weeks that followed, the Spaniards grew to love and respect the Aztec ruler, not only for his prodigious generosity but even more for his extraordinary natural grace and charm. Montezuma soon knew the conquistadors by name, and they in turn treated him in a manner befitting his rank. Cortes had, meanwhile, told Montezuma of his own Emperor, Charles v—the sovereign to whom the Aztecs were henceforth obliged to acknowledge their allegiance. They seemed to accept this condition readily enough; it was when the conversation turned to religion that Montezuma's jaw seemed to tighten. Nonetheless, he willingly agreed to Cortes' request to be allowed to visit the great temple.

That visit was a nightmare that none of the members of Cortes' party ever forgot. "The walls of the shrines," wrote Bernal Diaz, "were so caked with blood, and the floor so bathed in it, that the stench was worse than that of any slaughterhouse in Spain." In the topmost sanctuary, before the idols, lay five human hearts, still warm and steaming; around the altar, their long hair matted with gore, stood the priests who performed the sacrifices and who afterwards ceremonially ate the limbs of their victims.

Montezuma, who seemed unable to comprehend his guests' revulsion, remained gentle and dignified amid those charnel horrors. Cortes saw that however ready the Aztec ruler might be to pay lip-service to the throne of Spain, he had no intention of forsaking his old gods. Somehow his authority would have to be undermined, while the Spaniards' own security was increased. Cortes therefore took a step that, in so precarious a position, few but he would have dared—he made Montezuma his hostage. As Cortes was careful to explain when he broke the news to Montezuma, the Emperor was not a prisoner. His "captivity" would amount to nothing more than a change of residence; the day-to-day business of government would still be in the Emperor's hands alone.

By the beginning of the year 1520 the conquest of Mexico might have seemed over. But suddenly Cortes' luck changed: the Spanish authorities in Cuba, infuriated by his insubordination and frantic with jealousy at his successes, dispatched a punitive expedition which Cortes destroyed.

Meanwhile, disaster had struck in the capital. In May, during an annual religious festival, Alvarado had suddenly suspected a plot against his garrison. Losing his head, he and his men had charged into the temple precinct, killing every Indian present.

An Aztec priest's knife, with a handle of wood set with mosaic.

Fighting in Tenochtitlan. Spanish cavalry and infantry with their Indian allies attack the temple.

Spanish gunman firing a crude arquebus; from the *Florentine Codex*.

Right A friar describes the ceremonial of the province of Mexico to the Viceroy, De Mendoza, while native priests look on.

More than a thousand natives, including the flower of the young Aztec nobility, were slaughtered, and within an hour the whole city was up in arms. Since that time the Spaniards had been blockaded in their palace. Thanks to Montezuma's intervention there had been no further bloodshed—but Montezuma's influence was waning. An opposition party, resolved to rid Mexico of the Spaniards once and for all, had arisen. And on the very evening that Cortes returned to the capital, a specially convened Aztec Council of State had deposed the Emperor from his throne and selected his nephew Cuauhtémoc as his successor.

By morning the atmosphere had changed from passive sullenness to active hostility. For four days the Spaniards defended themselves as best they could against incessant Indian attacks, but on the fifth, seeing that the situation was hopeless, Cortes sent to Montezuma and asked him to negotiate a truce. The Spanish envoy found the ex-Emperor sunk in despair. There was nothing he could do, he claimed—his friendship for Cortes had cost him his crown, and his people would no longer listen to him. He agreed to make one final effort, however, and for the last time he donned his robes of state and stepped out onto the terrace above the great square.

As Montezuma emerged, the howling mob below fell silent in a spontaneous surge of sympathy for the deposed monarch. Then, suddenly, a volley of stones was launched at the Emperor. One of them struck Montezuma on the head, and he fell to the ground. The Spaniards carried him to his quarters, and Cortes himself hastened to the battered ruler's side. The wound did not seem particularly grave, but Montezuma had apparently lost the will to live. By nightfall he was dead.

Montezuma had been a noble and a tragic figure. He had foreseen, in a way that Cortes had not, that the fall of his empire was to be inevitable and total. Although mistaken in his belief that Cortes was a god, Montezuma could no more have prevented the conquest than if it had been divinely ordained.

His friendship with Cortes—for whose sake he ultimately gave both his throne and his life—was founded not on cowardice but on wisdom, for he had understood that violence could not prevail. Little more than a year after his death, Montezuma's premonitions were to be proved correct.

Cortes' last hope of remaining in the city perished with Montezuma. He knew that he must retreat—and fast. That night, when the crowds had dispersed, he and his soldiers slipped silently from their quarters and began their march along the western causeway (which was shorter than the southern one, and promised to be less well guarded). The Aztecs had not been deceived, however. The silence was suddenly shattered by the blast of a conch-shell trumpet. Suddenly the waters on each side of the causeway were alive with war-canoes, whose occupants showered arrows on the retreating Spaniards. In the chaos and carnage that followed, Cortes lost more than half his soldiers—many of whom died not from wounds but by drowning, weighed down by the pocketfuls of Aztec gold that they had been unable to resist carrying off with them. That dreadful night, June 30, 1520, was afterwards known as the *Noche Triste*—the Night of Sorrow.

Spanish sufferings did not end when what was left of the shattered column reached dry land. It was another two hundred miles and twelve agonizing days—during which the survivors were atttacked by a huge Aztec army at Otumba and, miraculously, routed it—before they at last reached Tlaxcala and safety.

Few other commanders, after such a debâcle,

The title-page of the *Codex Mendoza*.

would have dreamed of continuing the campaign, but Cortes was still determined to reenter the capital in triumph. He immediately set about the task of rebuilding his soldiers' strength and morale and collecting reinforcements. The *Noche Triste* had taught Cortes that he could never trust the causeways again. Therefore, at Tlaxcala, two hundred miles from the sea and 7,000 feet above it, he began to construct a fleet of thirteen shallow-draft brigantines, specially designed so that they could be dismantled into easily portable sections and reassembled on the shores of the lake surrounding Tenochtitlan. By Christmas all was ready; and on December 28 Cortes led some 550 Spaniards—roughly the same number as had accompanied him on his first expedition, but this time augmented by some 10,000 Indian allies and forty horses—back into the valley of Mexico. A base camp was set up at Texcoco, on the eastern shore of the lake, and while the brigantines were being prepared for action, the Spanish leader sent messages across the water to the new Emperor, Cuauhtémoc, calling on him to surrender.

As Spanish strength had grown, so the Aztecs' had declined. Their capital had suddenly been struck by a new and dreadful scourge almost certainly introduced by the invaders—smallpox. Having no hereditary resistance to it, the Indians had perished by the thousands.

The final assault on the Aztec capital began in April, 1521. Victory proved far more elusive than the Spaniards had expected. The brigantines were invaluable, but they could not be everywhere at once, and attack after attack was driven back across the causeways. At last Cortes saw that there was only one solution—the slow, systematic annihilation of the city—and he therefore ordered his men to destroy the houses and the streets one by one, using the rubble to fill in the canals. The Aztecs fought on, but by the end of July the southern half of their city was a heap of ruins. The southern and western spearheads of the Spanish attack, led by Cortes and Alvarado respectively, met in the great marketplace of Tlatelolco. Bernal Diaz again described the scene:

> On the way we passed through a small square, where there were wooden poles on which they had impaled the heads of many of our Spaniards whom they had killed and sacrificed during the recent battles. Their hair and beards had grown much longer than they were in life; which I never would have believed if I had not seen it.

Next to the marketplace was the high temple through which Montezuma had guided Cortes less than two years before. A party of Spaniards climbed to its top, set the shrines on fire, cast the idols down the steps and planted their banners. When the Aztecs saw the eagles of Spain fluttering from their highest pyramid, they knew that they had lost—yet the twenty-six-year-old Cuauhtémoc refused to surrender. Instead he made a valiant effort to escape to the mainland to continue his resistance from there, and it was only when the fastest of the brigantines overtook him that he finally gave himself up.

Bernal Diaz summed up the siege of Tenochtitlan:

The death of the Aztec Emperor, Montezuma, from the *Codex Mendoza*.

> During the whole ninety-three days of the siege there was the unceasing noise of their accursed drums and trumpets, and their melancholy battle-drums in the shrines and on the temple-towers. But after Cuauhtémoc's capture all of us soldiers became deaf—as if all the bells in a belfry had been ringing together and then suddenly stopped.

Thus, on the evening of August 13, 1521, the city of Tenochtitlan finally fell—and with it fell the Aztec Empire. Men still argue over the rights and wrongs of the conquest, some maintaining that imperialist aggression can never be condoned, others, insisting that Mexico was enriched by her Spanish colonial experience, and that Cortes was justified in eliminating the bloodiest civilization the world has known.

There is no statue of the conqueror in modern Mexico City, but in the Square of the Three Cultures, the spot where Cuauhtémoc acknowledged the end of his empire, a marble plaque provides what is perhaps the wisest epilogue of all:

It was neither a victory nor a defeat. It was the painful birth of that commingled people that is the Mexico of today.

JOHN JULIUS NORWICH

1521–1522 The German Reformation sweeps across

The Emperor Charles V and the German princes at the Diet of Augsburg.

Rome's reaction to Luther's theses was a swift one—it had to be, because Luther's arguments were quickly translated and made known to a large audience by printers. Luther was inhibited from preaching in February, 1518, and later in the same year had an unsatisfactory interview with the Italian cardinal, Thomas Cajetan (1469–1534), who tried to get him to abandon his views. Because of the forthcoming imperial election the Pope had to avoid angering Luther's protector, the Elector of Saxony.

After Charles' election, the ecclesiastical machine was free to function more effectively, but by then it was too late to kill Lutheranism. Luther's inhibition did not prevent him from pouring forth pamphlets, and his more extreme disciples, such as Karlstadt (1480–1541), did likewise. By 1521, when Luther was excommunicated, he had become the figurehead of a movement that could only be stopped by force. In that year, Luther had appeared at the Diet of Worms to explain his views, which were swiftly condemned, and he retired into seclusion, devoting his energies to translating the New Testament.

Luther's conservative reaction to the Peasants' Revolt probably added to his popularity with the princes, whose authority he so energetically defended. In the north in particular, the princes turned toward Lutheranism and much Church land was secularized. In 1525, for example, the Grand Master of the Teutonic Order, Albert of Brandenburg (1490–1568), decided to marry and to secularize the property of the order. He surrendered the lands of the Knights to his feudal overlord, the King of Poland, and received them back as an hereditary duchy.

The Empire was becoming rapidly polarized into two conflicting groups that were divided by religion, and although Charles v summoned diet after diet to deal with the situation, none was able to agree on any solution. At the Diet of Speier of 1529 the term "Protestantism" was born when the Lutheran minority led by the Elector of Saxony protested against the attempts of the Catholic majority to push through their ideas. In the following year at the Diet of Augsburg the Catholic-Protestant split was recognized by both sides as being unhealable. The document put forward by the Lutherans to explain their beliefs, the Confession of Augsburg, gradually came to be accepted as the Lutheran rule of faith. The idea of the unity of Protestantism was dealt a severe blow, however, as the Lutherans, guided by Philip Melanchthon (1497–1560), were unable to agree with the ideas of another influential Protestant group, the Zwinglians, who were then led by Martin Bucer.

Peasant revolts

In June, 1524, warfare had broken out in the west of Germany as peasants living on the estate of the Count von Lupfen in the Black Forest took up arms to abolish serfdom, feudal services and enclosures and the payment of tithes. The movement spread rapidly into the Rhineland, Swabia and Franconia and later reached Bavaria, the Tyrol and Alsace. Manifestoes were drawn up which lent an air of respectability to the looting and slaughter that followed. Thomas Münzer, a priest from Saxony who signed orders "The Sword of the Lord and Gideon," attempted to impose some sort of order on the rebels. But after several initial successes, the peasant army was encircled at Frankenhausen, and in May, 1525, Münzer was executed. Martin Luther, who had disowned the rebels' challenge to secular authority, preached against their political attitude.

Zwingli

Shortly after Luther published his theses in Wittenberg, a very different sort of reformer began to revitalize the life of Zurich. After studying at Vienna University, where he was disciplined for rowdyism, Ulrich Zwingli (1484–1531) took holy orders and developed his own approach to Humanism. The publication of Erasmus' Greek New Testament added a new dimension to Zwingli's theology, and by the time that he was appointed priest of the Great Minster at Zurich, he had grounded his faith on the Bible.

Despite his weak voice, Zwingli was a remarkable preacher. He denounced the sale of indulgences, fasting, the celibacy of the clergy and the use of mercenary armies (in which so many men from the Swiss cantons served). His 1523 dispute with the Bishop of Constance led Zwingli to draw up a set of fundamental articles of religion and to promote disputations about them. Zwingli converted the citizens of Zurich who demonstrated their faith by removing all images from their churches and refusing to accept episcopal jurisdiction. In Zurich and the other Swiss cities the Humanist-influenced citizens seemed to have been drawn toward the ideal of a Christian commonwealth, which preachers like Zwingli were expounding. In 1525, Zwingli completed his liturgical reforms, supplanting the Latin Mass with a service that stressed the commemorative nature of the Lord's Supper.

A peasant in revolt waves the banner of freedom.

Ulrich Zwingli, who converted Zurich to Protestantism.

As leader of Zurich, Zwingli envisioned his city as the cornerstone of a wide evangelical confederation. But for some years Zurich was the only Protestant canton, as the other confederates preferred to wait for a general council to settle the dispute between the various Protestant groups and the papacy. It was not until 1529 that Bern accepted the Reformation, but after that reformed ideas spread rapidly. In 1529, Zwingli was able to found the Christian Civic League as a first step toward achieving that goal. Bern, Basel and Constance joined the league immediately and Strasbourg joined a short time later. In the same year the League went to war with the Catholic forest cantons, which were defeated and forced to abandon their alliance with Austria. In 1529 also, Zwingli journeyed to Marburg at the invitation of Philip of Hesse, one of the leading Protestant princes, and took part in a disputation with Luther. Philip hoped to effect a reconciliation between the two reformers, but the chasm proved to be too deep and the Diet of Augsburg the following year killed all chance of agreement.

Zwingli's militancy provoked a second war with the Catholic cantons in 1531, and at the decisive Battle of Kappel he was killed. The subsequent peace treaty divided the Swiss federation into Protestant cantons—principally Zurich, Bern, Geneva and Basel—and Catholic cantons—notably Lucerne and Freiburg—a division that was to persist. As a Catholic soldier noted at Kappel, Zwingli was a "rotten heretic, but a good confederate."

The Reformation reaches Scandinavia

By comparison, the Protestant Reformation made rapid strides in Scandinavia. The kings of Denmark still claimed to rule the three Scandinavian kingdoms under the terms of the Union of Kalmar (1396), but opposition to Danish rule in Sweden had become persistent. The Danish kings imposed a heavy tribute on the Swedish nobles in an effort to force the Swedes to recognize their claim to that country's throne. Christian II, who succeeded to the Danish throne in 1513, was determined to press his claim by force. He defeated a Swedish peasant army on the ice of Lake Asunden in January of 1520. Sten Sture, the leader of Swedish resistance, perished in the battle, but his widow, Christina, defended Stockholm for eight months before surrendering. Christian promised the city an amnesty, but after his hurried coronation he summoned an assembly to Stockholm Castle and, with the assistance of the Swedish Archbishop Gustavus Trolle, took action against Christina Sture, many nobles, two bishops and the chief burgesses of the city. Trolle was anxious to avenge himself on the nationalist party (which had tried to depose him in 1517) by extracting a heavy fine—but Christian was out for blood. On November 8, 1520, after a mock-trial for heresy, some ninety leading Swedes were executed in the city's marketplace. The event, known as the "Stockholm bloodbath," earned its instigator the name "Christian the Tyrant."

Sweden was rescued from tyranny by Gustavus Vasa, a rebel whose father and other relations had been slaughtered at Stockholm. A year before the bloodbath, Vasa had launched a campaign to sever Sweden from the Union of Kalmar. Although he had fallen into Christian II's hands, he had managed to escape.

But in January, 1521, Vasa returned to the province of Dalarna—long a center of nationalist resistance—and was promptly elected to lead the peasant army that began the reduction of castles in Danish hands. Increasing numbers of prominent Swedes came over to Gustavus, but Stockholm held out. Fortunately for Gustavus, a rebellion—provoked by Christian's heavy taxation and his quarrel with the Church—broke out in Denmark at this point, and the King was deposed in favor of his uncle Frederick. In June, 1523, a fully representative *Rikstag* unanimously elected Vasa King of Sweden.

Gustavus was the creator of modern Sweden. For years the independence of his state had to be vigorously defended against its Scandinavian and Baltic neighbors—and even against the Emperor Charles V.

Even before Gustavus Vasa became King there had been attempts to set up an independent national Church in Sweden, and from about 1520 the process of Lutheranization of the Church was gradual. It was to a considerable extent linked with nationalist ideas. The leading reformer, Olaus Petri (1493–1552), had been a pupil of Luther's at Wittenberg University and graduated in 1518. In 1523, Petri married, and in the controversy that followed, it became clear that Gustavus favored the reform party. In 1527, the preaching of Lutheran ideas was permitted by the Diet of Västerås, and in the following year the King began to confiscate some of the property of the Church. In 1532, Laurentius Petri (1499–1573), Olaus' younger brother, was consecrated as Archbishop, and under his influence the move toward Lutheranization was rapid, but the episcopate continued to govern the Church and the Latin Mass only gradually gave way to a more Protestant, Swedish liturgy. In Sweden, as in England, the events of the sixteenth century were an attempt to reform the existing Church. In Germany, Switzerland, the Netherlands and Scotland the old order was simply abolished and replaced with a new one.

The Swedish monarchy had always been elective, but Gustavus feared that his cherished work might be endangered by faction, and in 1544 he established the Vasa dynasty. Gustavus left to his successor an independent nation-state, solvent, effectively administered and defended by a superb army. The new Sweden was soon to become an important factor in European politics.

Despite his energetic suppression of revolution in Sweden, Christian II's rule was popular in Denmark, where he attempted to suppress the privileges of the nobility and to get rid of the influence of the aristocracy. His aristocratic enemies, financed by the Hanseatic League, combined in 1523 to depose Christian. His uncle Frederick, Duke of Schleswig-Holstein, was elected King in 1528. In Denmark—unlike Sweden and Norway—the Reformation was a popular movement, and the crown merely legitimized the changes that took place. During the civil war in Denmark in the 1520s and 1530s, which were caused by Christian II's attempts to recover the throne, the Reformation took a firm root. It was, however, only after Frederick's son, Christian III, secured the throne in 1536, that episcopacy was finally abolished. A few years later Christian introduced the Reformation into Norway.

As in other countries where the Reformation triumphed, the enormous increase in the resources available to the crown had a substantial effect on the nation's economy. One of the reasons for the increased importance of the northern European countries during the sixteenth and seventeenth centuries was the increased financial resources of their governments, resulting directly from widespread confiscation of Church land. Among Roman Catholic countries only France and Spain (the latter merely because of its New World mining resources) could compete.

Gustavus Vasa, founder of modern Sweden.

1520

A Bible for the Masses

1522

The astounding thing about the vernacular version of the New Testament that appeared in Germany in the fall of 1522 was not that it was an able and often forceful translation, but that it existed at all. The translator, the controversial Wittenberg monk Martin Luther, had recently been excommunicated by the Pope—who recognized only the Latin Vulgate Bible—and had been banned by Emperor Charles v. *The printer and publishers of "Luther's Bible"—the first complete translation of the New Testament into any vernacular tongue—were therefore taking grave risks in backing the outspoken monk's enterprise. Their gamble paid off handsomely, however; Hans Lufft, Luther's printer, sold nearly 100,000 copies of the monk's Bible. In one bold stroke, Luther had reached the largest lay audience in history—and in so doing, had proved the power of Europe's fledgling popular presses.*

During the last days of September, 1522, an extraordinary book was published in Wittenberg, Saxony, a German town of three thousand inhabitants. The volume's short title, printed in highly ornamental Gothic letters, was *Das Newe Testament Deutzsch—Vuittemberg (The German New Testament—Wittenberg)*. No publication date was given, and the name of the translator was not mentioned. The name of the printer, Melchior Lotter the Younger, and the names of the publishers, the painter Lukas Cranach and his partner Christian Doering, were also omitted. The format, a smallish folio, included twenty-one woodcuts created in the workshop of Lukas Cranach and devoted exclusively to the last section of the book, *Revelation*. The edition appeared in three thousand copies, each priced at half a gulden, approximately the weekly wage of the best-paid craftsmen of the age.

The printing and publishing of this undated vernacular version of the New Testament had been undertaken in great haste and in full secrecy; the translator, the Wittenberg monk and professor Martin Luther, was under the ban of Emperor Charles v—in addition to his excommunication by the Pope. Names had been omitted for fear that the imperial edict, which threatened anyone who assisted the condemned heretic, might be applied to the printers or to the entire community. Despite those fears, the edition, the first full translation of the New Testament from the original Greek into a vernacular tongue, was soon sold out and a reprint with corrections was issued in December of the same year. At the same time, a pirated edition came out in the Swiss city of Basel, the greatest center of printing and publishing in Europe.

During the next several years, Luther published parts of the Old Testament, which he translated from the original Hebrew with the assistance of collaborators. In 1534, the first complete German-language edition of the Bible was printed in Wittenberg by Hans Lufft, who was to serve as the main printer of the work for decades and who as a result became one of the richest men in the town. Luther himself never received any remuneration for the nearly 100,000 copies of the "Luther Bible" that Hans Lufft printed.

In addition to Lufft's editions, authorized and unauthorized versions of Luther's translation abounded. Pirated editions outnumbered legitimate ones by at least four to one. A form of copyright, granted by special privilege of a local prince, was in existence at the time but in Luther's case this protection was valid only for the Dukedom of Saxony—or, to be more precise, for that half of Saxony ruled by the Elector, Luther's patron. In the other half of the country, which was controlled by Luther's enemy Duke George, the monk's books were banned and his Bible was immediately supplanted by another edition. The text of that version, purportedly written by the court-chaplain Emser, was taken without compunction from the Lutheran translation, with some added "corrections." Many other Catholic editions of the time made use of this procedure.

The Holy Roman Empire was without a central authority in the early sixteenth century. The division of the Empire into self-governing principalities—imperial free towns and countless independent possessions held by archbishops, bishops, prince-abbots and mere counts, each eagerly defending his rights or what he called his "liberties"—made it possible to set up printing presses everywhere and to publish almost any book, however dangerous or seditious it might be. Ecclesiastical as well as temporal censorship did indeed exist, but they could be applied only locally; a book suppressed at one place would soon appear at some other place, often in a remote town where the printer was on good terms with his magistrate. This state of affairs, although politically lamentable, accounted for the rapid spread of printing in sixteenth-century Europe. In particular, Bible printing became commonplace, although vernacular versions of the Bible were still

Title of Luther's translation of the New Testament—the first Bible to be translated into German, published in 1522 by Melchior Lotter.

Opposite A woodcut of Luther, 1520, while he was still an Augustinian.

A printing shop in the late-fifteenth century, from a *memento mori*.

regarded as dangerous by ecclesiastical authorities.

Luther himself enjoyed the huge success of his translation and wrote only: "It is easy to plough a field that has been cleared. But no one wants to uproot the forest and tree trunks and put the field in order." He did become irritated, however, when his qualifications as a Biblical scholar were questioned. He retorted: "You are doctors? So am I. You are theologians? So am I. But I can expound the Psalms and the Prophets. You cannot do this. I can translate. You cannot do this." And when incorrectly printed and garbled editions of his work began to appear in rapid succession, he exclaimed: "They do that snip-snap: Money, that's what they are after."

Luther could indeed translate, and in time his work was recognized as the decisive event in the development of the modern German language. During his own lifetime, Luther's Bible became the cornerstone of the Reformation. It was Luther's belief that Scripture should be the sole guide, the supreme authority in matters of faith. This view was in direct opposition to the tenets of the Roman Catholic Church, which, in Luther's words, "places the Pope above Scripture and says he cannot err."

This principle of "*sola scriptura*"—Scripture alone—had been Luther's guide and weapon from the beginning of his rebellion against Church stricture. In 1521, one year before the publication of his New Testament, Luther journeyed to the German city of Worms, where, at the invitation of the Emperor, he defended his views before an assembled Church diet. In his famous final declaration before Charles V and the assembled prelates, Luther declared: "Unless I am convinced by testimony from the Holy Scriptures . . . I am bound by my conscience and the Word of God." The enraged Emperor issued an imperial edict banning Luther as a heretic and rebel against authority. His decree, the most comprehensive edict of general censorship in modern times, also imposed strict supervision of all printed productions, including leaflets, posters, woodcuts and pictures; no one was permitted to "compose, write, print, paint, sell, buy or secretly keep such productions." Luther's answer was the publication of his Bible.

On his return from Worms, Luther was intercepted by the emissaries of his patron, the Elector of Saxony, and brought in secret to Wartburg. There he wrote the first draft of his translation.

A few words must be said about the extraordinary circumstances under which a work of such magnitude and difficulty was undertaken. Luther labored

almonefrÿe athÿn Black Letter
per le feſſe & proſtei Aldus Roman
ueſtibulum fauiſe Aldus Italic

Aldus Manutius

Johann Froben

Geoffroy Tory

Robert Estienne

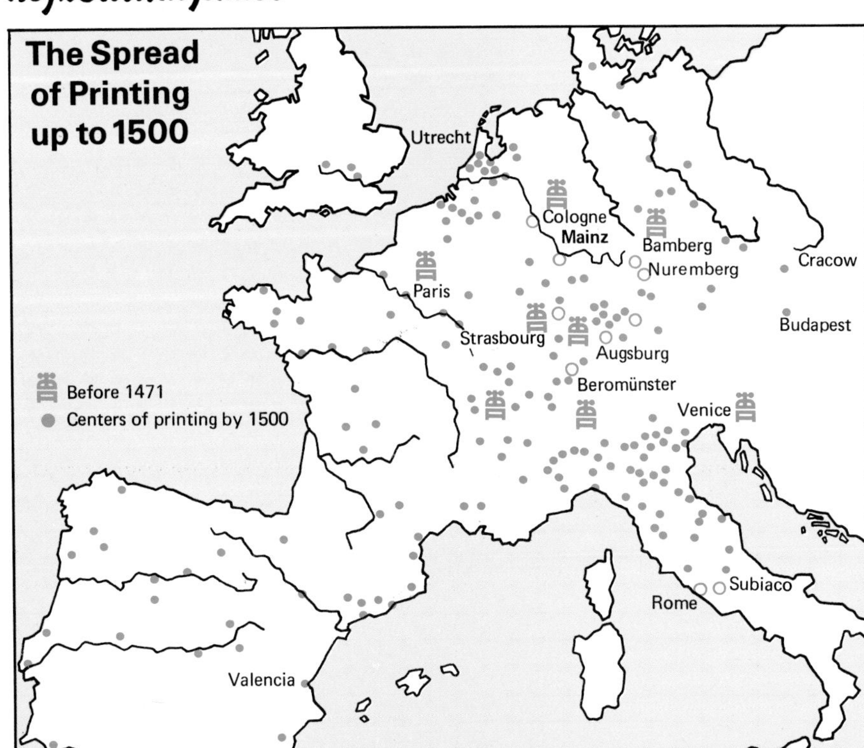

Below right The church at Wittenberg where Luther was reputed to have posted his Ninety-Five Theses on October 31, 1517.

St. Luke painting an icon: a picture from Luther's German edition of the Bible, 1540.

without aid from the outside. He had only a handful of books at hand, and he did not have access to any libraries other than his own meager one. During this period, Luther disguised himself as a Junker. He sported a beard and carried a sword at his side. To the great annoyance of his protector and his entourage, who wanted him to keep quiet, Luther wrote numerous letters and tracts from his hiding-place.

Only during the last weeks of his seclusion did the fugitive start on his great translating task. He had nothing to work with except the Greek New Testament published by Erasmus of Rotterdam eight years earlier, the Latin Vulgate, the only officially recognized version of the Bible (which Luther had known more or less by heart since his monastery days), and perhaps two or three books more. It took the monk no more than ten weeks to finish his translation; a mere copyist would have been pressed just to copy the entire text from an existing original in this amount of time, at the standard rate of ten pages a day. Speed was crucial, for Luther was extremely eager to return to Wittenberg, where serious disturbances had arisen among his followers.

Luther therefore broke out of his prison—in defiance of the express order of his protector—and went to Wittenberg, where he corrected the rough draft of his manuscript with the help of his friend, Philip Melanchthon, a twenty-five-year-old professor at the university who was already recognized as one of the most eminent classical scholars of the age. In the midst of the dissension that was shaking the little town to its foundations, the monk's text went into print on three presses at the same time. Luther's concern over such minutiae as the typography of his volume led him to replace his slovenly former printer with Melchior Lotter, who did his work so well that the list of errata at the end of the first edition of Luther's Bible contained only a handful of minor errors. (There were no major printer's errors like the one contained in the English Bible of 1631. That version, called the "wicked Bible," omitted the word "not" from the Seventh Commandment.)

In the eyes of the Church, Luther's grave and unforgivable error was in undertaking his task in the first place. The Latin text of the Vulgate was the only accepted one, and to translate it into the vernacular was considered an act of willful interpretation, dangerous and possibly heretical. The fight to make the Bible available in the "vulgar tongue" had indeed attached itself to great schismatic movements throughout the centuries of Church history. The Waldensians and Albigensians,

Right Part of a page of Wycliffe's Bible: those who translated the Bible into the vernacular were always suspected of heresy.

Opposite right The title-page of Luther's Latin Bible with his handwritten notes and his signature.

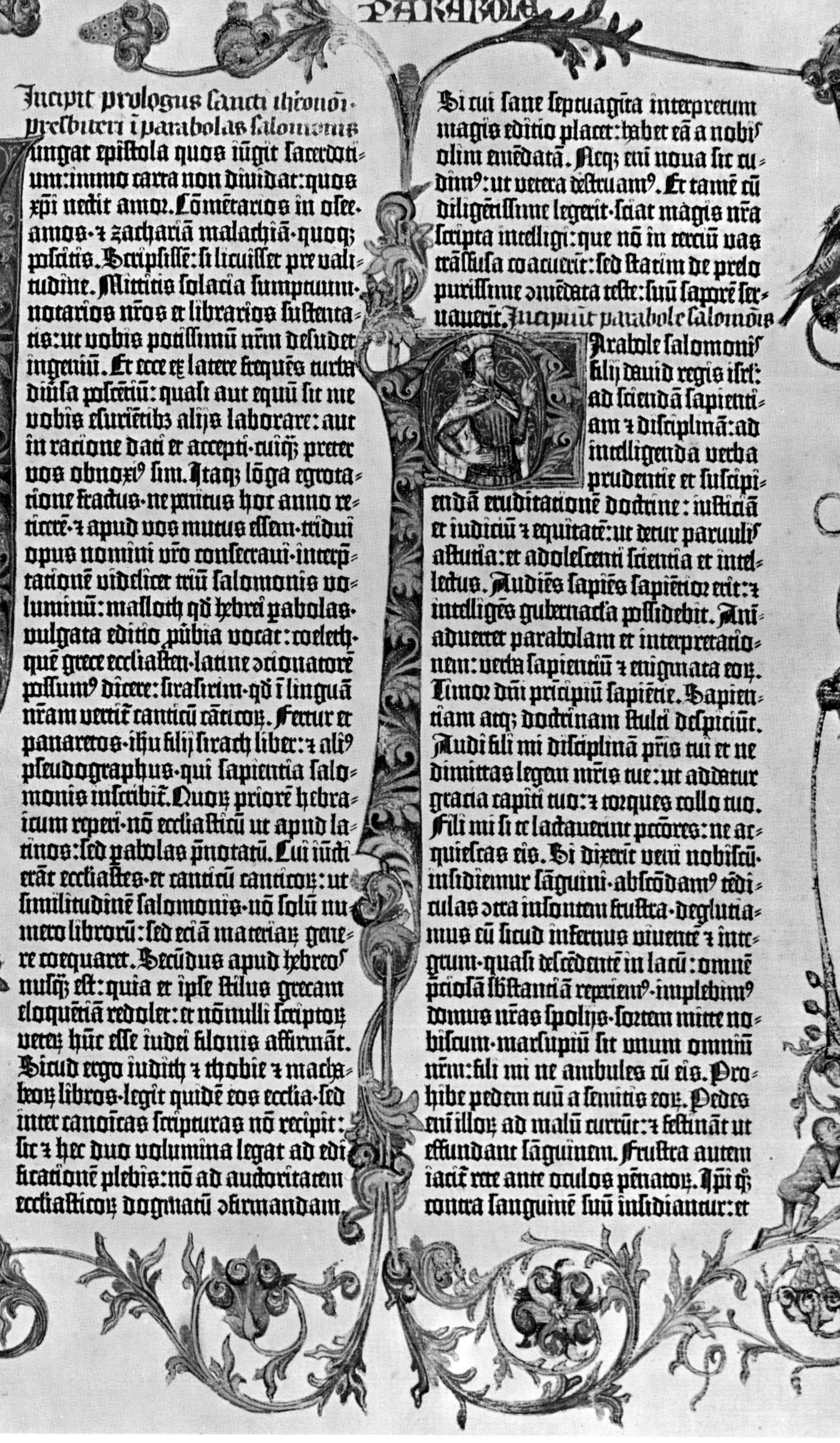

PARABOLE

Incipit prologus sancti iheronimi presbiteri in parabolas salomonis

Iungat epistola quos iungit sacerdotium: immo carta non dividat: quos christi nectit amor. Commentarios in osee. amos. et zachariam malachiam. quoque poscitis. Scripsissem: si licuisset pre valitudine. Mittitis solacia sumptuum. notarios nostros et librarios sustentatis: ut vobis potissimum nostrum desudet ingenium. Et ecce ex latere frequens turba diversa poscentium: quasi aut equum sit me vobis esurientibus aliis laborare: aut in ratione dati et accepti cuiquam preter vos obnoxius sim. Itaque longa egrotatione fractus. ne penitus hoc anno reticerem. et apud vos mutus essem. tridui opus nomini vestro consecravi. interpretationem videlicet trium salomonis voluminum: masloth quod hebrei parabolas. vulgata editio proverbia vocat: coeleth quem grece ecclesiasten. latine concionatorem possumus dicere: sirasirim. quod in linguam nostram vertitur canticum canticorum. Fertur et panaretos. ihesu filii sirach liber: et alius pseudographus. qui sapientia salomonis inscribitur. Quorum priorem hebraicum reperi. non ecclesiasticum ut apud latinos: sed parabolas prenotatum. Cui iuncti erant ecclesiastes. et canticum canticorum: ut similitudinem salomonis. non solum numero librorum: sed etiam materiarum genere coequaret. Secundus apud hebreos nusquam est: quia et ipse stilus grecam eloquentiam redolet: et nonnulli scriptorum veterum hunc esse iudei filonis affirmant. Sicud ergo iudith et thobie et machabeorum libros. legit quidem eos ecclesia. sed inter canonicas scripturas non recipit: sic et hec duo volumina legat ad edificationem plebis: non ad auctoritatem ecclesiasticorum dogmatum confirmandam.

Si cui sane septuaginta interpretum magis editio placet: habet eam a nobis olim emendatam. Neque enim nova sic cudimus: ut vetera destruamus. Et tamen cum diligentissime legerit. sciat magis nostra scripta intelligi: que non in tercium vas transfusa coacuerint: sed statim de prelo purissime commendata teste: suum saporem servaverint. Incipiunt parabole salomonis

Parabole salomonis filii david regis israel: ad sciendam sapientiam et disciplinam: ad intelligenda verba prudentie et suscipiendam eruditationem doctrine: iusticiam et iudicium et equitatem: ut detur parvulis astutia: et adolescenti scientia et intellectus. Audiens sapiens sapientior erit: et intelligens gubernacula possidebit. Animadvertet parabolam et interpretationem: verba sapientum et enigmata eorum. Timor domini principium sapientie. Sapientiam atque doctrinam stulti despiciunt. Audi fili mi disciplinam patris tui et ne dimittas legem matris tue: ut addatur gracia capiti tuo: et torques collo tuo. Fili mi si te lactaverint peccatores: ne acquiescas eis. Si dixerint veni nobiscum. insidiemur sanguini. abscondamus tendiculas contra insontem frustra. deglutiamus eum sicud infernus viventem et integrum. quasi descendentem in lacum: omnem preciosam substantiam reperiemus. implebimus domus nostras spoliis. sortem mitte nobiscum. marsupium sit unum omnium nostrum: fili mi ne ambules cum eis. Prohibe pedem tuum a semitis eorum. Pedes enim illorum ad malum currunt: et festinant ut effundant sanguinem. Frustra autem iacitur rete ante oculos pennatorum. Ipsi quoque contra sanguinem suum insidiantur: et

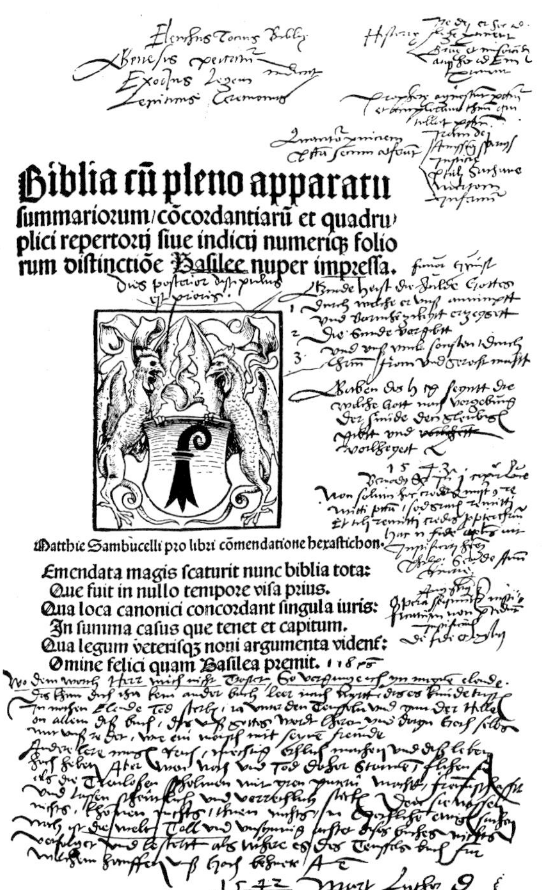

Biblia cū pleno apparatu summariorum/cōcordantiarū et quadruplici repertorij siue indicij numericꝫ foliorum distinctiōe Basilee nuper impressa.

Matthie Sambucelli pro libri cōmendatione hexastichon.

Emendata magis scaturit nunc biblia tota:
Que fuit in nullo tempore visa prius.
Qua loca canonici concordant singula iuris:
In summa casus que tenet et capitum.
Qua legum veterisqꝫ noui argumenta vident:
Omine felici quam Basilea premit.

heretical sects that sprang up in southern France at the end of the twelfth century, had their own translations of the Bible—and both were equally condemned by the Church

The first German translations of the Bible were produced in Bohemia during the fourteenth century. These manuscripts were written in secret and distributed clandestinely under threat of death; to be found in possession of a vernacular Bible was often sufficient evidence to condemn a man to the stake. The smell of burning hangs on each surviving copy of these Bibles. No Albigensian translations have been preserved, but in spite of severe suppression, more than two hundred manuscript versions of Wycliffe's translation, as well as other medieval versions, are still extant.

The publication of each of these editions was a religious, social and political event of the greatest consequence. The masses—the poor to whom Wycliffe sent out his "poor priests"—wanted to have access to the Word of God in their own language. The fifteenth-century Hussite movement presented the Church, and governments as well, the frightening spectacle of a great rising of the common people, under the banner of Biblical inspiration combined with strong national and social aims. Luther was, therefore, initially accused by his adversaries of being a "Bohemian," a "second Huss."

Persecution of religious dissenters was rampant throughout Europe. William Tyndale, the first to translate the Bible into modern idiomatic English,

Vom vrsprung vnd herkunfft des Antichristi.

Above One of a series of woodcuts on the papacy by Cranach.

Below Luther's meeting with Pope Paul III, by Salviati.

Luther's friend and ally Melanchthon, by Dürer.

printed his work at Cologne and Worms in 1524, two years after Luther's New Testament first appeared. Tyndale, whose translation was strongly influenced by Luther's model, perished at the stake. Only a pitiful single fragment of his first edition of the New Testament has been preserved. Later reprints, brought over to England from Antwerp, were publicly burned at Paul's Cross. The list of "Bible-martyrs" is a long one, as is the list of strict prohibitions against the printing or reading of those martyrs' translations. In Spain, all translations in the "vulgar tongue" were placed on the first Index printed by the Inquisition in 1551. Shortly after Luther's death, the Spanish representatives at the Council of Trent described all renderings into the vernacular as "mothers of heresy."

Luther's undertaking had another important meaning, as the crowning achievement of the great Humanist movement. "*Ad fontes*"—back to original sources—had been the watchword of Renaissance scholars. The phrase, applied at first to the Greek and Latin classics, later came to include the greatest monument of antiquity, the Bible. It was known, of course, that the Bible had originally been written in Hebrew and Greek, but only the Latin Vulgate, derived from a translation made by St. Jerome in the fourth century, was officially recognized by the Church. By 1500, scholars had grown dissatisfied with this state of affairs. Italian Jews printed the Hebrew text of the Old Testament, and in 1516 the Dutch scholar Erasmus published his Greek New Testament. The Dutchman's move was a bold and dangerous one, and only the considerable prestige enjoyed by the man universally recognized as Europe's greatest living scholar saved Erasmus from prosecution. As criticism went further, many differences between the original text and the Latin translation were detected, indicating how corrupted the official version of the Bible had become in the course of more than a thousand years.

From the Church's point of view, however, every single word of the Vulgate remained sacrosanct and unalterable; it was still the basis of Church dogma and of the body of usages, including the smallest details of the worship service. Interpretation of ecclesiastical law, based on the Vulgate, was conducted exclusively by the appointed doctors of the Church, and subject to final sanction by the Pope. Any textual criticism was considered an attack on Church tradition, rather than a philosophical exercise. Indeed, the official revision of the old Latin text of the Vulgate itself, reluctantly recognized as inevitable, was only undertaken at the end of the sixteenth century. In some instances, arguments regarding the placement of a single comma in the revised Vulgate raged for years.

Luther was not concerned with commas. He translated the Latin text to the best of his ability and with considerable command of Biblical scholarship. The style and sweep of his language has been admired even by his enemies, and his powerful German has been marveled at—particularly since Luther had been educated, from boyhood onwards, exclusively in Latin. During his long years in the monastery and his first academic career, the monk had been obliged to express himself in that language; how he acquired his rich and flexible German vocabulary therefore remains a mystery. It was only in his thirty-fifth year that Luther suddenly broke out of the prison of an alien language—and into the freedom of his native speech. His little tract entitled "On Indulgences and Grace," which followed immediately upon the steps of his *Ninety-Five Theses*, was Luther's first German-language publication. It was immediately reprinted, and twenty different pirated editions were soon being sold.

Historically speaking, the publication of Luther's Bible marked the first time that the medium of printing had made a profound impact on the masses of the people. With one bold stroke, Luther had reached a public of incomparably larger dimensions than any former revolutionary or reformer had dreamed of. He continued the fight with his well-known pamphlets and books, and it has been estimated that during the first decade of his public struggle, nearly a quarter of the works published in Germany came from his pen.

Despite the futile edict issued by Emperor Charles V at Worms, printing increased by leaps and bounds in those years. In addition to pamphlets, broadsides, tracts and books, pictorial propaganda became a very powerful weapon as well. It was aimed at the still largely illiterate public, a very large proportion of which was converted to Lutheranism by this means of communication. The papal nuncio, who had been sent to Worms to deal swiftly with the heretical Wittenberg monk, wrote home in near-despair. He counseled the Pope that almost nine-tenths of the Empire had become Lutheran, and that the rest cried out against "Roman tyranny." The publication of Luther's Bible was unquestionably the greatest and most lasting achievement of this period, and therefore that date of September, 1522, may be regarded as no less important than those of such well-known historical events as the publication of Luther's *Theses* in 1517 or his stand at the Diet of Worms in 1521.

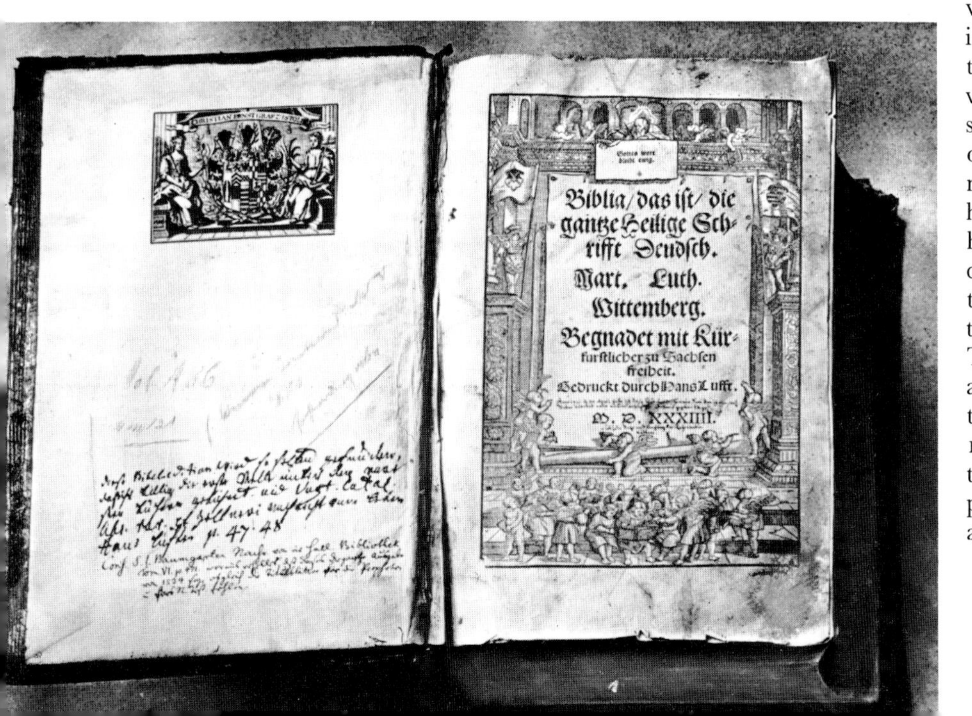

The title-page of the first translation of the Bible into German, 1534. Copies of this edition are usually in bad condition due to its enormous popularity.

Left An engraving of Desiderius Erasmus of Rotterdam, one of the leading Humanists of the sixteenth century, by Albrecht Dürer.

Luther with Melanchthon's version of the Bible in Greek and Hebrew: an illustration by Cranach from Luther's translation of the Bible.

Statistical figures about book sales do not tell the whole picture, however. It is not true, as has been repeatedly said, that the Bible was, for all practical purposes, "unknown" before Luther's version appeared. The Latin text of the Bible had been printed on the presses of Gutenberg and his companions at Mainz, in 1450–55, and many editions had followed. There had even been earlier unauthorized German translations, printed during the fifteenth century. More than a dozen of these works, mostly taken from texts printed in the previous century, were in existence. Extracts from Biblical texts, homilies and commentaries abounded.

Nevertheless, the demand for the whole text, the clear and unfettered Word of God, printed in the language of the people, remained and became irresistible. The older editions, written in Latin or in out-dated and halting vernacular, were not read by the people; they were intended for scholars, well-to-do persons or great libraries, and their cost was forbidding (the price of a single volume amounting in earlier times to the value of a good-sized town house). It is significant that a large number of these books have been preserved in excellent condition. By contrast, very few copies of the early printings of Luther's Bible are still extant, and in most cases these are badly mutilated from constant rereading over the years.

In those countries where the book was admitted, Luther's Bible became the great formative influence over the next centuries. The imposing figures regarding distribution of the Scriptures that were published by the great Bible societies in the nineteenth century pale almost into insignificance if compared with the number of old family Bibles in the sixteenth and seventeenth centuries. These volumes were, more often than not, the only book in the house, the only family possession of value, bequeathed from one generation to the next, and consequently bearing the family tree on the fly-leaf. No statistical figures will tell us how often those editions were read aloud to the whole household, servants included. One could, however, design a map of sixteenth-century Europe that divided the Continent into Bible-reading and non-Bible-reading regions. In central France, for instance, the Catholic Church continued to struggle with the stubborn, Bible-reading Jansenists, long after the Huguenots had been thoroughly eliminated.

Bible reading was not an unmitigated blessing. The Roman Church had reservations about individual interpretations of the Scriptures, and Luther himself was forced to struggle, from the time he printed his first draft, with what he called the "heavenly prophets" who interpreted the text in their own light, according to inspiration they claimed to receive from above. Many sects and movements, such as the Spiritualists and the Anabaptists, evolved during this period. Some of these groups developed valuable versions of their own. Bible reading, no longer restricted to matters of faith and religion, became the basis for studies of social and political developments. It was not displaced until the eighteenth century, when secularization arrived in the wake of the Enlightenment.

RICHARD FRIEDENTHAL

Two great battles, Pavia and Mohacs,

Clement VII crowns Charles V as Emperor, by Vasari.

Despite the increasing importance of its New World empire, Spain concentrated mainly on European politics. In May, 1520, nine months after his election as King of the Romans, Charles appointed his old tutor, Hadrian of Utrecht, the Cardinal Bishop of Tortosa, as regent of Spain and left for Germany. He left Spain in disorder. His two and a half year visit to Spain—he had only arrived in 1517—had given him little time to familiarize himself with the large cities, let alone with the complexities of the constitutions of Spain's integrant parts. Castile was bubbling over with revolutionary enthusiasm and the citizens of Valencia were furious that Charles had not seen fit to visit them. Charles had too much to think about in Germany—not least the outbreak of religious disputes—to pay much attention to Spain's problems. But Hadrian, for all his many talents, was not the man to deal with this situation, which required a firmness that he lacked. Almost as soon as Charles left, rebellion broke out, because it was claimed that ancient privileges had been abrogated by the government. The actual reason was discontent at the way in which foreigners were being appointed to high office in Church and State. Francis I, jealous of Charles' success in the German election, had encouraged the rebels, and took advantage of the rebellion to launch an invasion of Navarre, on behalf of its French ruler, Henri d'Albret. But characteristically, Francis acted too slowly, and by the time the French army arrived the rebellion had collapsed, and the French were easily driven out.

The failure of the revolution and the French invasion attempt helped to rally public opinion in Spain in Charles' favor. It also made inevitable what had been probable for years—war between Francis and Charles. England's Cardinal Wolsey attempted to arbitrate between the two countries, but discovering that Francis was plotting to upset the situation in Scotland, Wolsey made a secret treaty with Charles at Bruges in September, 1521. England and the Empire were to declare war on France. In November war broke out. A joint imperial and papal army—Leo X had abandoned his anti-Hapsburg policy—invaded Milan, which was still occupied by the French.

Charles found himself too busy to rule the whole of his vast dominions, and handed over the government of the Hapsburg possessions in the Tyrol and southwest Germany to his brother Ferdinand, Archduke of Austria. He could well afford to do so as his Italian war was going well. Milan was conquered by Charles' general, Prospero Colonna, and handed back to its duke, Charles' kinsman Francesco Sforza. Better still, the succession of Hadrian of Utrecht as Pope insured continued papal support for the Emperor. By 1523, Venice had joined the anti-French alliance. It was hardly surprising that prominent Frenchmen thought they stood no chance of victory, or that the Constable of France, the powerful Duke of Bourbon, should join Charles. When a French army led by Admiral Bonnivet and the Chevalier Beyard invaded Lombardy in 1524, Bourbon routed it, laid waste Provence and put Marseilles under siege.

But Charles' position was less strong than it appeared. The new Pope surprisingly decided on a policy of neutrality. Charles' Swiss mercenaries returned to Switzerland; financial difficulties forced a reduction in the size of the imperial army in Italy. An attempt to invade France in 1523 failed dismally. Even the English alliance could no longer be relied upon; Wolsey had twice been promised Charles' support for his papal ambitions but when Clement VII was elected Pope, it became clear that Charles could not be trusted. Wolsey was also attempting to arrange a divorce between Henry VIII and his wife Catherine of Aragon, Charles' aunt. As a result, Wolsey began to prepare to change sides. It was only the incompetence of the French generals that prevented imperial power in Italy from collapsing.

The entry of Hadrian VI into Rome, a detail from his tomb. His succession ensured continued papal support for the Emperor.

The Battle of Pavia

It was this incompetence that gave Charles a great victory. Undaunted by his defeats in France, Francis I crossed the Mont Cenis Pass in the winter of 1524–25, easily took Milan and opened the siege of Pavia. In February, 1525, Bourbon led a well-disciplined army of Spaniards and imperialists to Pavia's aid. Outside Pavia on February 24, 1525, Francis I abandoned his strong defensive position north of the town. He attacked the huge imperial army which was maneuvering at the time. However, because of shortage of ammunition he was unable to follow up his early advantage and the imperial garrison in the town was able to fall on his undefended flank. The French and their Swiss allies were routed, and casualties exceeded those inflicted in the Battle of Marignano some ten years before. Roughly 14,000 men were killed, including Richard de la Pole, pretender to the Earldom of Suffolk and the throne of England. Many of the deaths were attributed to the use by the Spanish infantry of muskets for the first time in the history of warfare. Francis was taken prisoner and transported to Madrid, where months later he had to purchase his release by surrendering all claims of the French monarchy to the Duchy of Burgundy.

The Battle of Pavia, a tapestry showing Spanish troops with muskets.

alter the European balance of power

Eastern Europe

The fifteenth century had seen a rise in the power of Poland from a small and obscure kingdom into the dominant Christian power of Eastern Europe. Lithuania had been absorbed, the independent power of the Teutonic Knights crushed and toward the end of the century the kingdoms of Hungary and Bohemia had elected a king from the Polish Jagellionid dynasty. By 1500, the potential areas of expansion had been exhausted. To the east lay a newly confident and expansionist Russia under the rule of Ivan the Great and his son Basil III; to the west lay the lands of the Holy Roman Empire, which offered no hope of expansion, even if it presented no real threat; to the south, the Turks presented a real threat to Hungary as a result of their Balkan expansion. The sixteenth and seventeenth centuries were to destroy the effect of the expansion of the fifteenth century. The Jagellionid Empire was to be torn apart, leaving Bohemia and half of Hungary in the hands of the West and half in the hands of the Turks, while Poland eked out a precarious existence dependent on the good will (or, more usually, the lack of it) of its Russian, Swedish and Prussian neighbors.

After the death of the great Polish ruler Casimir IV in 1492, one son, Jan, succeeded him as King of Poland, and another, Alexander, as Grand Duke of Lithuania. Jan died in 1507 and Alexander in 1506, and the countries were reunited by their brother, Sigismund. For the first twenty years of the sixteenth century, peace on the most dangerous border, that with the Turks, allowed the different Jagellionid kings to follow a common foreign policy. The different kings were able to act in close consort—to follow an unaggressive line. Sultan Bayazid II was of a pacific nature, and Selim was too occupied elsewhere to desire war with Hungary. War with Moscow was almost continuous, but was inconclusive, except for the loss of Smolensk.

As far as Bohemia and Hungary were concerned, the major question was who would succeed Ladislas, the fourth son of Casimir, as King. The leading contenders were members of the Hapsburg family. By the Treaty of Vienna in 1515 the

Sigismund, son of Casimir IV, who reunited Poland and Lithuania.

Emperor Maximilian, spinning his dynastic web, arranged marriages in order to make the Hapsburg succession certain. Maximilian's granddaughter Mary married Ladislas' son and successor Louis, while Ferdinand, brother of Charles V, married Ladislas' daughter Anna. Ladislas died in the following year, and Hapsburg influence, already strong, became dominant.

But neither in Bohemia nor in Hungary were they fully accepted. Bohemia was still disturbed by the Hussite religious disputes which had been the main characteristic of its fifteenth-century history. In Hungary there was strong opposition in some quarters to the idea of Hapsburg, Polish or any foreign succession. The leader of this opposition and the main native candidate for the throne was John Zápolya (1487–1540), who in 1505 had persuaded the national Diet that no foreigner should be eligible for election as King of Hungary. Zápolya's popularity secured his election as governor during the infancy of the young Louis, but this was not accepted throughout Hungary, and the Hapsburg party—which actually held Louis—appointed Istvan Báthory as governor. The fighting between these rivals meant that during the years of peace with Turkey no action was taken to build up Hungary's defenses. Indeed, the highly professional "Black Brigade" was abolished because of the expense of its upkeep.

The death of the Ottoman Sultan Selim and the succession of his son Suleiman in 1520 ended the peace. In 1521, Suleiman attacked Hungary. The fortress of Belgrade, key to the country's Danube defenses, was captured, mainly because no assistance arrived for its garrison. The attack was not carried through as Suleiman decided to throw all his resources against the island of Rhodes, but in 1526 the Turks began to move north again. This was largely due to the fury of Francis I of France at being forced to sign the Treaty of Madrid. He suggested that the Turks attack Hungary, which he saw as a useful way of getting revenge on his Hapsburg enemies.

The Battle of Mohacs

Louis marched to attack the Turkish vanguard, but his army was tiny, as both Zápolya and the Croatian levies had been given contradictory orders. Louis attacked the Turkish vanguard at Mohacs on the Danube, hoping to destroy it before the rest of the Turkish army arrived. He succeeded in driving it back, but the main army was close behind and the Hungarians, including the King, were almost entirely wiped out.

Mohacs was a decisive defeat. It laid open the whole of Hungary to attack by the Turks, and within a few weeks Buda and Pest fell to them. The Hapsburg Archduke Ferdinand of Austria immediately claimed the thrones of Hungary and Bohemia, but Zápolya was able to secure the support of the majority of the Hungarian nobles. A minority elected Ferdinand, and as a result civil war broke out. The civil war gave the Turks an easier task than they would otherwise have had, and over the next few years their invasions brought them control of much of the country.

In 1528, Zápolya made an alliance with Suleiman, and in the following year the Turks invaded Austria and laid siege to Vienna. The onset of winter forced Suleiman to give up the siege, but the respite allowed Zápolya to secure a position of sorts in Hungary. Except in Transylvania, where Zápolya was firmly in control, neither the Turks nor either Christian king could rule effectively. In 1532, Suleiman again invaded Austria, although this time he confined himself to laying waste the countryside rather than attempting the conquest of Vienna. In 1533, the three contenders for Hungary made peace. Ferdinand was allowed to continue to rule the territory he already held, but Zápolya was given most of the rest, subject to Turkish control. In 1538, Ferdinand formally accepted Zápolya as king, and was given the right to succeed him.

Poland and Bohemia meanwhile had troubles caused by the Reformation. The addition of Lutheran ideas to the religious problems of Bohemia made the task of the energetically Roman Catholic King Ferdinand doubly difficult. But he showed far greater firmness than his predecessors. In Poland attempts were made—in particular by the Duke of Prussia—to spread Protestantism, but Lutheran ideas never took firm roots.

The Battle of Mohacs.

1532 Pizarro Conquers Peru

Illegitimate, illiterate, of poor peasant stock, Francisco Pizarro could advance only through force of arms. With courage, determination and unbridled savagery, he led a troop of soldiers down the west coast of South America and discovered and despoiled the incalculably rich Inca Empire. He himself was stabbed to death by followers of a disgruntled colleague and the vast wealth that Spain took from the New World led that nation into costly wars, massive inflation and economic decline.

Francisco Pizarro, who discovered and despoiled the fabulously wealthy Inca Empire.

Opposite The ruins of Macchu Pichu, an Inca fortified city in the mountains near Cuzco built of massive rocks without cement.

In November, 1526, a small band of Spanish adventurers set sail from the newly built port of Panama down the unexplored west coast of South America. Inspired by Hernando Cortes' conquest of the wealthy Aztec Empire five years earlier, they were hunting for a people called the Birú, whose empire, rumor said, was as rich as the Aztec. Following several months of fruitless search, they at last sighted a balsa-wood sailing raft. It proved to be a small Indian trading vessel loaded with wares, including that closest to the Spaniards' hearts—gold. This first recorded contact between the West and the isolated Inca civilization of Birú, or Peru, was the beginning of one of the most brutal invasions in the history of European colonization.

The expedition of 1526–27 was led by two illiterate peasant-born Spaniards from Panama who, in the next eleven years, were to conquer the heartland of the Inca Empire and then fight to the death over the spoils of their victory. Francisco Pizarro and Diego de Almagro, men of extraordinary resilience and courage, were both more than fifty years old when they set out. Pizarro's fanatical determination was to carry the conquest to its inevitable conclusion, as illustrated some time after the exhilarating discovery of the trading ship. With no sign that they were any nearer their goal and having suffered appalling losses through hunger and disease, the expedition landed on a barren, uninhabited island. Morale was at its lowest and most of the party proposed to return to Panama. Pizarro, adamant, drew a line on the sand and invited those of his followers who wanted to continue the expedition to cross it. Thirteen did so, including Diego de Almagro. The now-abbreviated band continued down the coast and discovered their first Inca city at Tumbes. They then returned home with the spoils of the rich civilization they had discovered.

Pizarro had begun life in the humblest circumstances. A native of Extremadura in the west of Spain, he was illegitimate and illiterate. For such a person the only road to self-improvement was through military prowess and Pizarro set out to make his fortune in the New World, where a courageous swordsman could hope to amass undreamed of wealth within a few years. By the age of thirty-five he had become a senior officer in the first Spanish expedition to penetrate the Panamanian forests and reach the Pacific Ocean. He settled in Panama and engaged in raids along the coast to the south. Then, fired by the success of Cortes, Pizarro determined to find a rich Indian empire for himself. His first expedition, in 1524, was a failure. The second, in 1526–27, suffered terrible hardships but returned fortified by the discovery of the Indian trading ship and the wealth of Tumbes. Pizarro now sought backing for a third expedition, which would reach into the heart of the Inca Empire.

He returned to Spain in mid-1528 and was warmly received by King Charles v, who doubtless saw the conquests of Cortes about to be repeated. Pizarro was appointed governor and captain-general of Peru and returned to Panama with his four half-brothers, to find Diego de Almagro furious at having been granted nothing more than the governorship of Tumbes. This was the first note of jealousy between the two that, although resolved this time, developed into acrimony.

On December 27, 1530, Pizarro finally sailed from Panama with about one hundred and eighty men and twenty-seven horses. The expedition began inauspiciously. The Spaniards made slow progress, landing far up the coast from Tumbes, fighting off natives and suffering a plague of ulcers as they marched south along the tropical coastline. When they finally reached Tumbes they found the city sacked, the result of a civil war raging within the Inca Empire. Reinforcements were dispatched to Pizarro and in September, 1532, with a force of sixty-

Atahualpa; the Inca commanded such loyalty that his people came from all corners of the Empire bearing gold and silver as ransom for their captured emperor.

two horsemen and some hundred and six foot soldiers, he struck inland to take on the massed might of the Incas.

The civil war that had razed Tumbes was to prove one of Pizarro's greatest assets in the ensuing struggle, for he was able to play off one branch of the Inca royal family against another, while they, engrossed in dynastic rivalry, totally underestimated the threat posed by the invaders. In the early 1520s one supreme Inca, Huayna-Capac, had ruled some 3,000 miles of territory stretching along the Andes from modern Colombia in the north to central Chile in the south. By 1530 he was dead and civil war was raging between two of his sons—Atahualpa, who controlled most of the imperial army, and Huascar, who held sway in the capital city, Cuzco. This strife encouraged subject tribes to rise against their overlords, for the vast Empire contained many groups, unassimilated into the Inca civilization. Indeed, the Inca Empire was itself a comparatively recent phenomenon. A mere century before the coming of the Spaniards they had been just another tribe living quietly along the Andean mountain chain. By combining military skill, benevolent administration and a cult of ruler-worship, the Incas had expanded dramatically in all directions. Members of the royal family held important positions in an elaborate administrative hierarchy, ruling over peasants who lived in simple thatched huts and collectively farmed corn and potatoes.

Special state storehouses provided food for royal officials, armies on the march, the sick and, in times of famine, the general population. The official Inca religion was sun-worship and the royal family bolstered its authority by claiming descent from the sun. A network of roads radiated from Cuzco to other parts of the Empire. Along them traveled caravans of llamas—the main method of transport since both the horse and wheel were unknown. Nor did the Inca civilization, the culmination of thousands of years of isolated Andean development, possess any form of writing. Messages were transmited by means of the *quipu*—a mnemonic device consisting of rows of colored thread which took on meaning according to the position of knots and colors.

This, then, was the civilization that unfolded before Pizarro when he turned inland toward the Andes. By coincidence his route lay close to Cajamarca, a fertile valley where Atahualpa, having just defeated and captured his brother Huascar, had paused before a triumphal march on Cuzco. Emissaries from the victorious Inca, sent to assess the power of these strange, bearded invaders, invited Pizarro to visit their ruler and he readily accepted. But the Spaniards' enthusiasm vanished when they arrived in Cajamarca, for around the town was encamped Atahualpa's army of between forty to eighty thousand men. The Europeans felt trapped. Putting up a brave front, Pizarro sent thirty-five horsemen for a preliminary audience with the emperor. Passing through rank upon rank of soldiers, they found the Inca surrounded by his chiefs and concubines. He appeared to regard the invaders as an entertaining distraction rather than a serious threat and displayed almost as much interest in the Spaniards' horses as in the men themselves. But he did agree to come and visit Pizarro the following day.

The terrified Spaniards spent the night in furious preparation. They believed that their only chance of survival was to employ the tactic that had served Cortes so well in Mexico—to seize the person of the emperor himself. Commending themselves to God, their weapons ready, the Spaniards concealed themselves in buildings round the square to await the arrival of the Inca. All morning they waited in vain, with no sign of native movement apart from an envoy who came first to tell them that the Inca's retinue would be armed and then that it would not.

Finally, as the sun began to set, Atahualpa headed for the town, lured by a messenger from Pizarro who assured the Inca no harm would befall him. An advance party swept the road before the ruler as he was borne on a gold and silver-plated litter by eighty chiefs in rich blue livery. Gradually the main square of Cajamarca filled with the Inca's men, wearing large gold and silver ceremonial discs

Three illustrations from *Nueva Cronica y Buen Gobierno* showing the progress of the Spanish conquest.

Below An Inca settlement before the arrival of the Spaniards.

Center A Peruvian peasant with llamas. These animals were a fundamental part of Inca life providing transport, food and clothing.

Right The Spaniards confronting Atahualpa, borne by his faithful people.

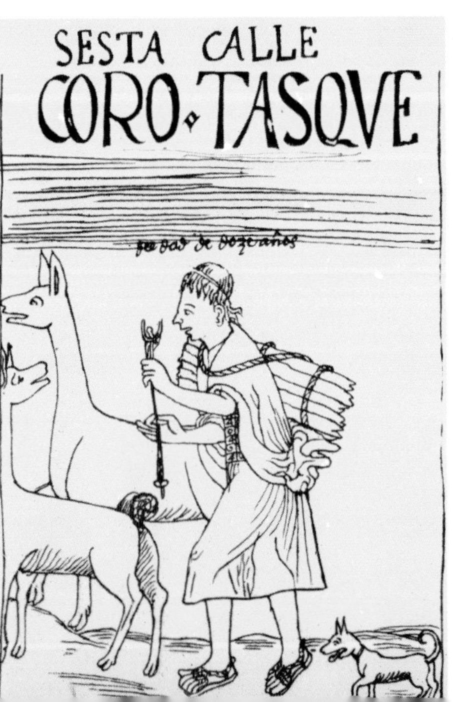

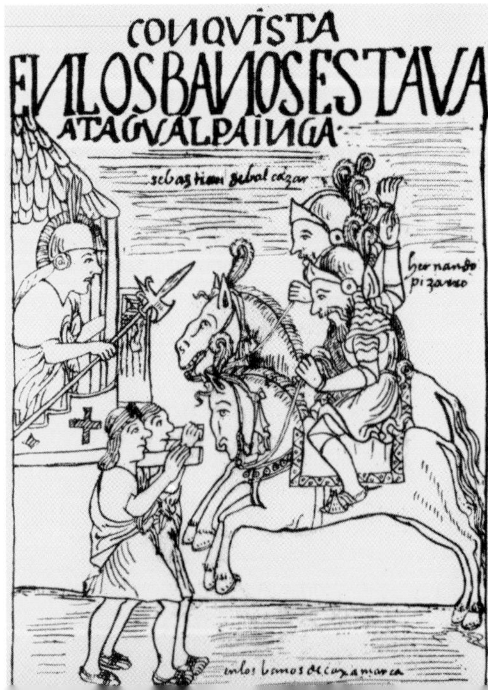

on their heads. The Spaniards remained in hiding, apart from a Dominican friar who launched into a long discourse on the truths of Christianity and the authority of the pope, finally handing Atahualpa a breviary. Atahualpa examined the volume, displaying some curiosity at the strange signs on the pages, then flung it angrily to the ground.

The friar called for vengeance on the desecrator of the holy book and two cannons were fired into the midst of the unarmed Indians—the signal for a concerted attack by the hidden horsemen. Spanish trumpets echoed round the square and the armor-clad riders, sword in hand, spurred their mounts into the midst of the terrified natives. Pizarro made for Atahualpa's litter but the bearers, in devotion to their lord, refused to drop his throne. When their hands were cut off they continued to support the litter with their shoulders, as they were killed others rushed to take their place. Finally a group of horsemen reached the litter, turned it on its side, and tipped the supreme Inca onto the ground. He was hustled away to captivity as the massacre continued. Indians fighting to escape from the square were trampled to death. Within two hours the Spaniards had total control of the town and some 7,000 Indian dead littered its streets.

In captivity, Atahualpa had time to reflect on the folly which had led him into such a position. He had totally underestimated the aims, fighting ability, brutality and mendacity of the invaders. Yet he still saw the Spaniards as gold-hungry plunderers rather than the advance guard of a wave of colonization, and thought he could buy them off. He offered them the contents of a large room piled high with gold artifacts, and twice as much silver, in exchange for his freedom. Pizarro readily agreed. So great was the Inca's authority that a steady stream of natives now arrived in Cajamarca from all corners of the Empire bearing his ransom. Centuries of delicate Andean artistry was melted down into bars, one fifth of which were dispatched to the Spanish crown as its customary due. The remainder were shared by the invaders, according to rank. But far greater wealth lay in Cuzco, more than six hundred miles to the south, and Pizarro was eager to start the march there.

By May, 1533, the ransom had been paid in full but Atahualpa still languished in captivity, despairing of ever being released. He had cause to be dejected for the previous month Diego de Almagro had reached Cajamarca with reinforcements of a hundred and fifty men. Almagro, fresh from the coast, had little sympathy for the captured emperor and demanded his execution, arguing that as long as he remained alive the Spaniards would be threatened by armies attempting his release. Pizarro held out against such a move but finally, crediting false rumors that a vast Inca relief expedition was marching on the town, he panicked and capitulated. Atahualpa was convicted of treason, baptized to avoid being burned at the stake and then garrotted with a piece of rope. His body was half burned, left exposed in the square for a night as a lesson to others and finally given a Christian burial.

The Spaniards now started on the march to Cuzco, through difficult mountain country swarming with enemy troops. Their first major encounter came at Juaja, just over half way, where a large army loyal to Atahualpa had gathered. The Spaniards unhesitatingly employed their supreme tactical maneuver—a vicious cavalry charge into the midst of the enemy. Many natives fled and those that remained were butchered. Pizarro left eighty followers in Juaja to found a municipality and pressed on boldly for Cuzco with a force of one hundred horsemen and thirty foot soldiers. As he neared the capital the Indians' resistance increased. They harried his column, adopting a scorched earth policy and cutting suspension bridges across river valleys.

But whenever the opposing forces met in a pitched battle, superior Spanish military technology won the day. The Indians were terrified of horses, those huge yet easily maneuvered beasts, and their stone-headed clubs and slingshots were no match for Spanish swords and lances. There were few fatalities among the well armored invaders in the initial stages of the conquest, and Pizarro marched onward to

Left Diego de Almagro and Francisco Pizarro, the architects of the Spanish invasion.

Center The headstrong Gonzalo Pizarro fighting a Spanish rival. The discovery of Peru was accompanied by bitter strife within the Spanish forces.

Below Burial of Atahualpa. Despite the Spaniards' promise to release him for ransom the Inca was murdered.

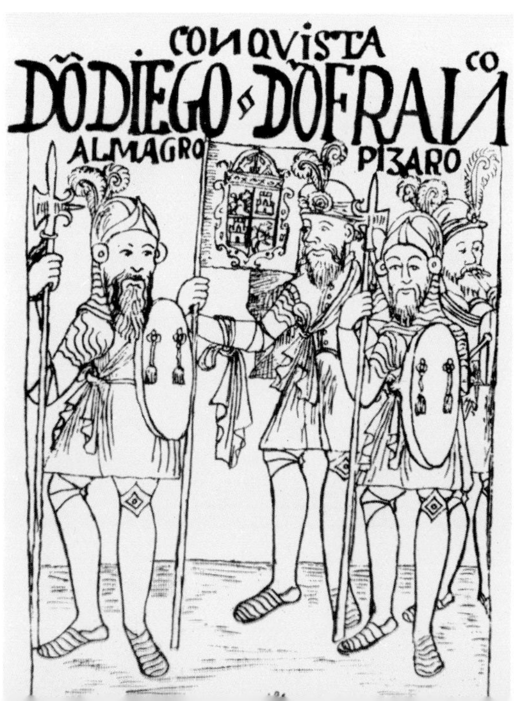

A drawing from Theodor de Bry's *Americae*, illustrating the capture of Atahualpa by Pizarro.

An Inca silver mask. The gold and silver of the Andean civilizations provided the main source of revenue for the Spanish crown and a spur to further conquest.

the outskirts of Cuzco, nestling in its valley 11,500 feet above sea level. Here the Inca army mounted a last stand. The battle ended inconclusively but the Indians lost heart and, slipping away under cover of darkness, left their capital at the mercy of the invaders.

Pizarro entered Cuzco in triumph in November, 1533, after a three-month march from Cajamarca. He was accompanied by a young Inca prince, Manco, a son of Huayna-Capac, opposed to the Atahualpa faction, whom Pizarro installed as a puppet emperor. The Spaniards immediately set about desecrating the city. Imperial palaces housing the mummified bodies of former rulers were commandeered as officers' quarters. Temples, homes, storehouses and tombs were meticulously stripped of precious metals, which were melted down. Everyday utensils and priceless works of art suffered the same fate.

But the occupation and looting of this magnificent city was no sure basis for a permanent hold on the Empire. Even though Manco had thrown in his fortunes with the Spaniards, the Atahualpa branch of the royal family was still in the field, based on the northern stronghold of Quito. During 1534 three Spanish armies converged on Quito: one was led by Pedro de Alvarado, an interloper from the north operating independently of Pizarro's force. As he advanced he inflicted appalling atrocities on local Indian leaders, torturing some, burning others alive and raping their women. To forestall this outsider, Sebastian de Benalcázar, one of Pizarro's men, succeeded in reaching the city first, followed by the indefatigable Diego de Almagro. They reached a settlement with Alvarado, who agreed to return to the coast, while Benalcázar defeated the remaining Inca forces.

But relations between Pizarro and Almagro began to sour once more when news arrived of a Spanish royal decree granting Pizarro governorship of the north and Almagro of the south. The edicts gave no clear demarcation of their respective spheres of influence and both men claimed control of Cuzco. In May, 1535, they met in the Inca capital and reached a temporary settlement: Almagro set out on an expedition to the south, in the hope of finding further riches in Chile; Pizarro returned to Lima, the new European capital he had built in the more equitable climate of the coast, leaving Cuzco in the hands of his headstrong younger brothers, Juan and Gonzalo.

The Chilean expedition merely delayed the clash between Pizarro and Almagro. Meantime the situation in Cuzco deteriorated rapidly, with the young Pizarro brothers subjecting Manco to degrading insults—taking one of his wives, demanding nonexistent treasure and generally undermining his attempts to rebuild the shattered imperial prestige. Manco finally decided on resistance and slipped out of the city one night but was recaptured and shackled in chains. The arrival in January, 1536, of another brother, Hernando, to take over the governorship of Cuzco, promised an improvement in Manco's fortunes. Hernando allowed him to leave the city to perform religious rites. But the insults of the past months had gone too deep and the ruler fled to the Inca army, a hundred thousand strong, massed in the hills around his capital, held by one hundred and ninety Spaniards.

The Indians attacked ferociously on May 6, hurling red hot stones into the thatched roofs of their desecrated capital. The Spaniards were driven

back until they held only two buildings in the main square. They knew that unless they could capture an easily defensible position they were doomed. After a night of prayer, a small party of horsemen broke through the Inca ranks and out of the city. They suddenly swung back, intending to take the strongly-held stone fort of Sacsahuaman, above the city. They were met by a hail of javelins and stones and forced to retreat, taking with them a fatally-wounded Juan Pizarro.

The next night the Spaniards managed to penetrate the battlements of the fort with scaling ladders. A two-day battle ensued. An Indian commander spurred on his men by hurling any who faltered from the top of the castle tower and, when their resistance cracked, he himself leaped to his death. The Spaniards finally took Sacsahuaman but could not hope to hold out for long without reinforcements.

Francisco Pizarro, in Lima, had begun to raise relief parties as soon as he heard of the rebellion. The Indians, however, under their great general, Quizo Yupanqui, had now evolved more successful tactics for dealing with the invaders—ambushing the Spaniards in narrow mountain passes and rolling huge boulders upon them. Of some two hundred men sent to raise the siege of Cuzco, only a handful survived the attack of Quizo's forces. Quizo now resolved to raze Lima and drive the Spaniards into the sea. He failed miserably. The Incas were not used to fighting at such a low altitude and were no match for the Spanish horsemen on the plains surrounding the European city. The native columns were routed and Quizo, at the head of his men, was one of the first to die.

Ironically, the siege of Cuzco was ultimately raised by Diego de Almagro, returning tired and bitter after a fruitless Chilean expedition. He claimed the city as his own in April 1537, and imprisoned Hernando and Gonzalo Pizarro when they attempted to resist him. Gonzalo eventually escaped while Hernando was released following protracted negotiations between the two factions. The two sides squabbled bitterly throughout the year and finally, early in 1538, Hernando Pizarro led an attack on Cuzco. The rival Spanish armies clashed outside the city on April 26 and Diego's forces were routed. He himself was captured, tried and garrotted. But the conflict did not die. His followers remaining in Peru bore a bitter grudge against Francisco Pizarro, remembering his discriminatory attitude toward them. Robbed of the riches of the conquest, they took their revenge—forcing their way into the elderly governor's palace and stabbing him to death on June 26, 1541. Thus the two architects of the Spanish invasion died as they had lived.

Throughout these years of Spaniard against Spaniard, Manco's fortunes had fluctuated. He succeeded in raising a second rebellion but the Spaniards now pouring into Peru proved too strong and he fled to a remote sanctuary, Vilcabamba, its whereabouts undiscovered to this day. In 1544, Manco, the last of the great fighting Inca emperors, was stabbed to death by fugitives from the Almagro faction to whom he had granted shelter. Like his fellow Inca Atahualpa he died a victim of the perfidy, brutality and ruthlessness of Spain's colonialism. These characteristics, coupled with extraordinary bravery and fighting ability, were the hallmark of the invaders who, in the first fifty years of the sixteenth century, laid the foundations of a vast Spanish empire, the length and breadth of South America. After the fall of Peru came the lands to the south. In 1540 Pedro de Valdivia set forth from Cuzco and at his death in 1554 had subdued most of Chile and founded its capital, Santiago. With Portugal holding Brazil, it only remained for the southeast of the continent to fall. Buenos Aires was founded in 1536 and, a prey to Indian attacks, was evacuated five years later. It was left to an expedition from Chile to found the first permanent settlement in Argentina in 1553.

The bullion-laden galleons that sailed from the colonies to Spain throughout these years proved a mixed blessing for the mother country. Initially the gold and silver increased Spain's prosperity and helped finance the costly wars of Charles v and Philip II. But the precious metals led to massive inflation, prices quadrupling during the century. The unsettling effects of the gold, the European wars and the cost of maintaining its vast South American empire, all contributed to Spain's rapid economic decline at the end of the century. The rise of the New World and the fall of the Old were intimately linked.

CHARLES GREGORY

Balboa, discoverer of the Pacific Ocean, throwing Indians to the dogs. Spain's South American conquests were marked by great cruelty.

The Counter-Reformation—Roman

The birth of Protestantism irrevocably changed the face of Christianity. The reaction of the Roman Catholic Church to Protestantism had an effect that was little less great. The papacy and its supporters could not simply ignore the Reformation and anathematize the reformers. The papacy was subject to many of the same pressures that had led to the Reformation, and the reaction of a papacy to those pressures meant that the Roman Catholic Church of the late sixteenth century was no less a new Church than were the various Protestant Churches. Apart from the changes that took place in order to satisfy princes, there was substantial pressure for change from within the Church. Many leading ecclesiastics took part in discussion and debate with Protestants and wanted to make some concessions to them. Just as Philip Melanchthon on the Lutheran side wanted to reach a compromise agreement that would satisfy the honor of both sides, so too did many Roman Catholics such as Cardinal Reginald Pole (1500–58) and Cardinal Gaspar Contarini (1483–1542). Although a conference at Ratisbon managed to reach

Cardinal Reginald Pole.

theological agreement on most of the disputed points—largely by accepting the Lutheran idea of justification by faith, with slight verbal modifications—it was never formally accepted by either side, each of which tried to get further concessions from the other.

Religious orders

But there was a sincere desire for reform among Roman Catholics. Apart from the enormous pressure for the holding of a general council—a demand to which the papacy only gave way eventually on its own terms—there were three main ways in which reforms were carried out in the Roman Catholic Church. The most important was through the foundation of new religious orders. The well-established monastic orders, such as the Benedictines, with their enormous wealth, had been one of the main targets of Protestant anger, and probably more than half of Europe's monasteries were abolished during the sixteenth century, with much of the wealth finding its way into the pockets of princes even in Roman Catholic countries. The friars were no longer active as itinerant preachers, but had settled down into respectability, and they, like the monks, had often given way to the munificence of private benefactors and accepted endowments—despite the precepts of St. Francis. What was needed was an entirely new approach to the requirements of the religious life. Strangely enough it was Italy, where there was little other sign of reforming zeal, that produced most of the new orders. Paolo Giustiniani, a Venetian of noble birth, embraced poverty in 1528, and with a Franciscan friar, Matteo di Bassi, drew up a rule in 1529. The order they founded was the Capuchins (cowled friars). This was heavily influenced by the original Franciscan ideals, and most of its early members were former Franciscans who, distressed at the laxity of the Franciscan Order at the time, sought to return to the vigor of the original rule. The Capuchins were almost suppressed in 1541, when their general became a Protestant, but they survived the crisis. They sought a much more active life than the Franciscans of the time, and were dedicated to working among the sick and needy.

An active desire to do good and to preach the Gospels was a characteristic of most of the other orders founded in the sixteenth century, too. The future apostle of Rome, Philip Neri (1515–95), founded the Congregation of the Oratory in 1540: the Oratorians were in fact not members of a proper religious order at all, as the Oratory was a highly flexible community of secular priests. In 1535, Angela Merici founded the Ursulines, an association of lay women pledged to good works. This was the first active order for women and remained the largest women's teaching order in the Roman Catholic Church. The Ursulines originally lived in their own homes rather than in a nunnery, although this was later changed.

The relative informality of the Ursulines was found among many of the male orders also. A new kind of religious order, the clerks-regular, who were neither monks nor friars, developed. In 1524, a priest from Vicenza, Cajetan (1480–1547), and Gian Pietro Caraffa (1476–1559) Bishop of Chiete (also known as Theate), who later became Pope Paul IV, founded the Theatines.

Pope Paul IV, who as Bishop of Chiete was founder of the Theatines.

The Theatines, despite their apparent similarity to the secular clergy in outward appearance—the only difference in dress was that the Theatines wore white socks instead of black—were sworn to poverty, and their life was one of considerable austerity. The aim of the order was to help the reform of the Church.

The Jesuits

By far the most significant of the new orders was, however, not Italian but Spanish. This was the Society of Jesus, founded by Ignatius Loyola. Loyola (1491–1558) was a Spanish soldier and courtier who underwent conversion in 1521, when recovering from a wound received in battle and wrote his *Spiritual Exercises*. While studying at Paris in 1534, the young Spaniard and his friends renounced worldly possessions and pledged to dedicate their lives to God's Word. They ultimately intended to undertake a barefoot pilgrimage to Jerusalem, but in the interim Loyola's followers worked in Italy. The Jesuit Order was formally recognized by Paul III in 1540. Their Rule involved unquestioning obedience to the pope—and almost from the beginning they served as the Church's shock troops, propagating the faith wherever they were sent. Their task was to reconvert the lands lost to Protestantism and to convert the heathen.

As Spaniards, both Loyola and his compatriot, Francis Xavier, were more at home among the heathen in the Moslem world than among Lutherans in North Germany. Their plans for missions to India, Brazil and the Congo received enthusiastic support from John III of Portugal and in 1542 Xavier set out for Goa. Meanwhile, in Europe the Society of Jesus quickly won a reputation as a teaching order with high standards in both classical studies and theology. The Jesuits established their first college at Padua, but their most famous was the college at Rome which was founded in 1551.

The Jesuits were, however, often unpopular both with the secular clergy and with the long established religious orders. The close relationship between the pope and the Jesuits led to jealousy; the Jesuits were often accused of a tendency to be lax in their moral theology and of overleniency in the confessional; in the mission field they were accused by the secular clergy of accepting converts too easily; in Europe their devotion to the papal monarchy in the Church made princes suspicious of them.

Ignatius Loyola, founder of the Jesuits, spearhead of the Counter-Reformation.

Catholicism's response to the "new religion"

The Roman reaction

Although the papacy did not play a leading part in setting up the new religious orders, it did react to Protestantism after its own fashion. Even before Luther's attack on indulgences, there had been efforts, largely as a result of pressure from secular princes and a few energetic bishops, to bring about reforms. The Lateran Council of 1512 had made gestures in the direction of reform. Adrian VI had attempted to reform the Curia, but his early death and the troubles of the papacy under Clement VII had aborted his efforts. Control over the reformation of reading matter was almost inevitably a preoccupation, at a time when the printing press was transforming the culture of Europe. The Lateran Council sought to control the publication of books by forcing printers to be licensed. This was never successful and later in the century diocesan censors' offices were set up to read books before publication. But, because of the enormous outflow of books from the Protestant lands, Paul IV in 1557 published an Index of Prohibited Books, which was frequently brought up to date thereafter.

Another way in which the Roman Catholic Church sought to fight the tide of heresy was by the resuscitation of the Inquisition. In 1479, the Spanish Inquisition had been set up by Ferdinand and Isabella and the growth of Protestantism made the popes eager to form a similar body in Italy. In 1542, Paul III set up the Congregation of the Index or Holy Office. The influence of the Inquisition was not felt throughout Italy, as Venice insisted on modifications of its status before allowing it to operate, but it was felt in fields of thought far removed from theology, as Galileo's troubles were to show.

The effect of the changes in the Roman Catholic Church was to strengthen the authority of the papacy and to make the local episcopate more dependent on Rome. But it was also a spiritual change.

Thomas Wolsey

Politics could not be kept out of religion altogether, and England was to be lost to the papacy largely because of the papacy's temporal weakness.

Cardinal Wolsey, who dominated English politics for fifteen years, and fell from power when he proved unable to obtain an annulment of Henry's marriage.

In England the Reformation caused a massive struggle for power that went on almost to the end of the century. The first to lose in the power struggle was to be Thomas Wolsey.

By 1520, Wolsey was preeminent in England. His power was symbolized by his two residences, Hampton Court and York Place (later Whitehall), both of which were built out of ecclesiastical revenues and the fat fees that he received as Lord Chancellor. His palaces were the envy of every Englishman, including the King. No Englishman had ever wielded such authority, for Wolsey was both King Henry's chief minister and the pope's legate—an unprecedented combination of powers. His high-handed rule weakened the Church's resistance to subsequent royal demands—and consequently lay people became antipapal, if not also anticlerical.

In 1527, Wolsey had become ensnared in negotiations with the Pope about the validity of Henry's marriage to Catherine of Aragon. Catherine had failed to give Henry a legitimate male heir, and the King was bent on divorce, legally sanctified by Rome. But because Charles V was Catherine's nephew and—unprompted—took her part, the chances of obtaining a favorable ruling from Clement VII, the Emperor's puppet, was remote. For one brief moment, when Clement was seriously ill, Wolsey had hopes of becoming pope himself, but Clement recovered and Wolsey, who knew Henry only too well, realized that he could not remain his chief minister much longer. For all his claims to having influenced events in the courts of Europe, the Cardinal had failed to achieve Henry's wishes. In 1525 he presented the King with Hampton Court and in October, 1529, he gave him York Place as well. Wolsey had fallen from power—and Parliament was as determined as Henry had been to seek revenge. Stripped of all his offices except the Archbishopric of York, Wolsey retired to the north. Within a few months he was arrested as a suspected traitor and he died on the way to London.

Henry VIII was to achieve his divorce by uniting in his own person—as King and Supreme Head of the Church—the same powers that Wolsey had accumulated as Lord Chancellor and cardinal-legate.

Another who was to suffer was Sir Thomas More (1478–1535), who was the voice of conscience in these times, a Humanist and lawyer whom Henry VIII had chosen to succeed Wolsey as Lord Chancellor. More's father had removed Thomas from Oxford when he discovered that his son was learning Greek, a subject that the elder More regarded as one of dangerous modernity. Thomas had been placed at Lincoln's Inn to read law and to prepare himself for the King's service. In his *Utopia*, More condemned the abuse of power and preached toleration, and as Speaker of the House of Commons in 1523 More proved a forceful opponent of Wolsey. His home at Chelsea epitomized the "new learning" in England. Erasmus, an occasional houseguest, noted that "in More's household you would realize that Plato's academy was revived, except that in the Academy the discussions concerned geometry and the power of numbers, whereas the house at Chelsea is a veritable school of Christian religion."

More had accepted the position of Lord Chancellor on the understanding that he would not be required to play a part in Henry's divorce, but by 1532 that issue so dominated politics that Sir Thomas felt obliged to resign. He repeatedly refused to take the oath of supremacy to Henry that was required by statute—although he swore to be loyal to the King and the succession—and as a result he was imprisoned in the Tower of London for a year. At his trial, Sir Thomas denied that Parliament could make the King Supreme Head of the Church, and he was executed as a traitor in July, 1536.

The background against which both More and Wolsey fell was the single issue of Henry's divorce.

The entrance to Wolsey's great palace at Hampton Court.

HRVIII

Henry VIII's "Great Matter"

1533

England's dramatic break with Rome was instigated by the desire of Henry VIII for a legitimate male heir. This required a divorce from the wife he had had for twenty years—now past child-bearing age. When the Pope did not grant the divorce, Henry, building on widespread popular discontent with Church taxes and practices, set in motion the English Reformation. From it would come the establishment of the Church of England, war with Spain (and the Great Armada), and five more wives for Henry. But the only legitimate male heir would be the sickly Edward VI, who succeeded to the throne at age ten and died at age sixteen.

Anne Boleyn had always been brazen, but one February morning in 1533 she surpassed herself. The courtiers of Henry VIII were amazed to see the King's mistress come out of her chamber and cry out to an old admirer that she "had a furious hankering to eat apples, such as she had never had in her life before; and that the King had told her that it was a sign she was pregnant." Then she broke into a fit of hysterical laughter and rushed back into her room. Henry's diagnosis was correct—in early September Anne Boleyn was delivered of a child, Henry's child. This event was to bring about a cataclysmic change in the relations of Church and State in England.

The English Reformation, the portmanteau title given to the changes of 1533, did not of course derive simply from the pregnancy of a pretty young woman. Yet Anne Boleyn's surrender to the amorous advances of Henry VIII did trigger the crucial series of events that severed England's thousand-year allegiance to the Western Church. For the sake of his, as yet, unborn child, Henry was prepared to turn his country upside down, break the traditions of centuries and impose a new faith upon his subjects. In 1533 Henry was forty-two years old—elderly by sixteenth-century standards—and lacked a son who could take control of England after his own death. It was to secure a legitimate male heir that Henry VIII embarked upon the English Reformation.

The roots of Henry's motivation went back to the Wars of the Roses when, for more than thirty years, England had been torn between rival claimants to the throne. Henry's father, the great-grandson of a fugitive Welsh brewer, had literally seized the crown from the battlefield to found a new dynasty, the Tudors, and Henry was determined that this dynasty should continue to provide England with strong male rulers to keep peace within the kingdom.

His father, Henry VII had sired two sons, of whom Henry was the younger. When he was ten his older brother Arthur married Catherine of Aragon, and left her a widow four months later. In 1502 Henry not only succeeded Arthur as heir to the English throne, but also became prospective bridegroom to his brother's widow. This marriage and the difficulties that surrounded it were to provide the principal arguing point of the English Reformation.

Could a man marry his brother's widow? The Bible gave contradictory advice. The Book of Leviticus asserts that: "If a man shall take his brother's wife it is an unclean thing," while Deuteronomy states: "When brethren dwell together and one of them dieth without children, the wife of the deceased shall not marry to another; but his brother shall take her and raise up seed for his brother."

Catherine maintained that the question was academic. Although she had been married in law to the sickly Prince Arthur, the marriage had never been consummated, an assertion confirmed by her duenna. But the politicians on both sides ignored the ladies' protests, maintaining that the marriage *had* been consummated. They referred the matter to the Pope, who declared that despite the affinity between them, Henry and Catherine might wed. He issued a dispensation for the marriage, which was celebrated a few weeks after the young Henry's accession in 1509.

Twenty years later Catherine, now past the age of child bearing, had only been able to produce a daughter, Mary. Henry, desperately seeking a male heir, once again turned to the disputed biblical texts of his youth. There, in Leviticus, he discovered why he had been unable to produce the male heir he longed for: "If a man shall take his brother's wife . . . he hath uncovered his brother's nakedness; they shall be childless." Here, for a pious man, as Henry always was, was the divinely inspired answer: he had been living in sin. The Pope had been mistaken in allowing him to wed his brother's widow and

Anne Boleyn, whose timely surrender to Henry was to alter fundamentally the relations of Church and State in England.

Opposite Detail of Henry and his third Queen, Jane Seymour, and their son Edward. The painting is not from life, as Jane died in childbirth, but is intended to glorify the King and his family.

refusal to aid Henry to secure a legitimate male heir provoked the King to deny the right of the Pope to have any say in the political or spiritual affairs of the realm, thereby initiating the English Reformation.

When Henry was first troubled by what he described as his "great scruple" over his marriage to Catherine, he had several reasons for supposing that the papacy would assist him to carry out his ambitions. For a dozen years his principal minister, Cardinal Thomas Wolsey, had conducted English foreign policy with a regard for papal interests such as had seldom been shown before and was never to be in evidence again. Also, as papal legate to England, Wolsey possessed certain ecclesiastical powers that made it possible for him to allow Henry to remarry without having to refer the matter to Rome.

The established Church in England was, furthermore, badly in need of royal support against heavy attack from many quarters. The resentment many Englishmen felt at the power that the Pope's representatives held over them expressed itself in pamphleteering and even rioting. The Church was England's largest landowner, owning over a third of the country, far more than the King, and it deployed its immense wealth and power in ways that often seemed worldly and self-indulgent. In the north of England the monasteries usually put their resources to honest, charitable uses, but there were many clerics like Wolsey whose fine clothes, high living and arrogant manners were far from spiritual.

Worse still in the eyes of many was the right of the Church to levy taxes on all Englishmen. Tithe—the payment of a proportion of personal income to the local priest—was a tax more fiercely hated than the royal levies to pay for war or defense, if only because royal tax demands were less frequent. The poorest widow had to make the priest a mortuary payment before the body of her husband was laid to rest, and, along with many other financial exactions, payment was enforced by a system of Church courts. A layman sentenced to a fine or imprisonment by a Church court for some ecclesiastical offense could not appeal to the ordinary law courts, while a priest who had fallen foul of the Common Law could appeal to his own Church courts and be tried and judged by his fellow clerics.

Design for triumphal arch to be used at Anne Boleyn's coronation procession. Sketch possibly by Holbein.

God had pronounced judgment by refusing to bless the union with healthy male offspring. Henry should therefore seek a new, theologically acceptable wife and ask the Pope to recognize the mistake by approving a new marriage and affirming the illegality of the old one.

Henry VIII was at this stage of his life a loyal son of the Pope—he had been awarded the title "Defender of the Faith" by the Holy Father for his book attacking the heretical doctrines of Martin Luther—and until his death he was to adhere to a personal faith that was in essence Catholic. But the Pope's

Anthony van Wyngaerde's drawing of Whitehall Palace, viewed from the Thames. After Wolsey's fall Henry confiscated his home, York Place, enlarging it into Whitehall Palace for Anne.

This privilege, known as Benefit of Clergy, rankled, and by the 1520s Englishmen of all classes felt that a change was necessary in the conduct of relations between Church and State. As yet, however, the majority of people did not adhere to radical reformist doctrines such as Martin Luther's. Few could imagine, let alone accept, that England might break with Rome and establish her own Church as certain German states had done. But the need for reform was acknowledged, and the interests of the Pope could be seriously damaged if Henry were not on his side when that reform took place.

Seen from London "the King's great matter" seemed straightforward. However, Rome saw matters differently, for in addition to being the spiritual leader of Christendom, the Pope, Clement VII, was the temporal ruler of the Papal States stretching across central Italy. The interests of those states depended on the balance of power between the three principal European political units, Spain, France and the Holy Roman Empire. The Empire was a fluctuating amalgam of states, controlled by the Hapsburg family, based in Austria, northern Italy, Germany and the Low Countries. In 1520 Charles of Hapsburg, already King of Spain, had become Holy Roman Emperor, and in 1525 had given proof of the power inherent in ruling such large tracts of Europe by not only defeating but also capturing the King of France at the Battle of Pavia. Pope Clement VII, like many of the minor princes of Europe, had effectively become the hostage of the Emperor Charles. There was therefore little chance of Rome consenting to Henry's proposed divorce, for Charles was the loyal nephew of Catherine and would not be prepared to see his aunt cast aside by the King of England.

Cardinal Wolsey's characteristically devious solution to this impasse was to set up at his London home in May, 1527, a secret tribunal before which Henry was called to answer the charge of having, for eighteen years, lived unlawfully with the wife of his deceased brother Arthur. Catherine, the English court, the Pope and the Emperor Charles were all kept in the dark about this clandestine ritual. Wolsey hoped to use his powers as papal legate to hustle through an annulment and quietly to negotiate the Pope's agreement. But on June 1, 1527, came news that the Emperor's troops had run riot and sacked Rome. They had acted in defiance of Charles' orders, but the result of their mutiny was that the Pope had become Charles' prisoner.

The sack of Rome effectively spelled the end of Cardinal Wolsey's usefulness as Henry VIII's chief minister. While the Pope was in the hands of Catherine's nephew, there was little that a mere cardinal could achieve. In 1528 the Pope agreed to send another legate, Cardinal Campeggio, to England to listen to both parties in the divorce case. But Campeggio's secret orders were to delay and obstruct proceedings for as long as possible. In July, 1529, having listened for months to the arguments presented by Henry and Catherine, he announced, as his secret instructions required, that the whole matter must again be referred to Rome for the Pope's personal adjudication. Within two days of Campeggio's departure for Rome, Cardinal Wolsey was deprived of his seals as Lord Chancellor of England. It was time for new personalities to guide the King in new directions.

The most important single influence on Henry through the early years of the Reformation was Anne Boleyn, the raven-haired sister of one of his former mistresses, Mary. Henry wooed Anne for five long years (1527–32) and her particular attraction lay in her refusal to surrender to him until the very end of that time. He had had mistresses before—by one

List of signatories on a declaration by English clergy against papal supremacy: one example of the way in which Henry put pressure on the Pope to fall in with his wishes.

Henry's surcoat and the trappings of his horse embroidered with Catherine of Aragon's initials. Henry's lack of a male heir caused him to repudiate Catherine after twenty years of marriage. In earlier and happier days, to celebrate the birth of their son Henry, who lived less than two months, Henry had jousted before Catherine.

of them, Bessie Blount, he had a son, Henry Fitzroy, whom he had made Duke of Richmond and whom he contemplated legitimizing as his heir—but Anne was different. She wanted to be a queen, not a mistress, and her single-minded pursuit of that ambition—resisting the frustrated Henry for as long as necessary—was a major factor in prompting the King to break completely with Catherine and promise Anne marriage, rather than simply legitimizing the baby Duke of Richmond or any bastard son he might have with Anne.

Thomas Cromwell, the other main influence upon Henry in the late 1520s and early 1530s, was the key figure in the process that was to turn the King's matrimonial problems from a passing event into a milestone of English—and world—history. A stocky, hard-working administrator of middle-class background, Cromwell rose through the entourage of Wolsey to become the Cardinal's right hand man and business manager. After his master's fall, he was given increased responsibility. By Christmas, 1531, he had become one of the inner ring of trusted royal advisers, and at the time of Anne's pregnancy he was undoubtedly Henry's chief minister. Less ostentatious and greedy than Wolsey, Cromwell was more subtle, thorough and successful. With Cromwell's rise the English Reformation took on a different and carefully planned character. There would be no more disputations over contradictory biblical texts, nor fanciful ecclesiastical intrigues, but a resolute, logical plan of campaign.

Henry had summoned Parliament in 1529, sensing that the popular anti-clericalism it would express might help him in his quarrel with the Pope. But it was Cromwell who showed the King how to use this assembly as an instrument of royal will. The Parliament, to be known as the Reformation Parliament, sat for seven years. Soon after it began, Cromwell gathered all the grievances that ordinary people felt against the Church into one great list, the Supplication against the Ordinaries. He then proposed that the King be given the power to investigate and reform these abuses. As he foresaw, the move was generally popular, but clerical members of Parliament were obliged to oppose it. The motion provided Henry with an ideal opportunity to force these clerics to state whether their loyalty lay with their King or with Rome: "We thought that the clergy of our realm had been our subjects wholly, but now we have well perceived that they be but half our subjects, yea, and scarce our subjects."

Cromwell then turned the screw tighter by preparing a bill that would cut off the annates (fees) that newly elected bishops paid to Rome. It would also set up machinery to appoint new bishops without consulting the papacy. The measure was to be delayed for twelve months, giving Rome time to reconsider its attitude toward Henry's divorce. The blackmail was obvious, but effective in an unforeseen way, for Cromwell's move coincided with Anne's surrender to the King's advances. Her resulting pregnancy brought matters swiftly to a head. On January 25, 1533, Henry contracted a secret marriage with Anne in a turret in Whitehall. (Catherine of Aragon had for some time been banished to the country, effectively living under house arrest.) The old Archbishop of Canterbury had died the previous summer and by threatening to terminate the papacy's annates, Henry had secured papal blessing to appoint as primate of England an obscure cleric named Thomas Cranmer.

Cranmer was Henry's servant—and Cromwell's. Within weeks of his appointment he was asking Henry to explain why, for over twenty years, he had been living in sin with his brother's widow, and on May 23, 1533, he declared that the King's marriage to Catherine was void and that to Anne valid. Just over a week later, on June 1, 1533, Anne was crowned Queen of England, and Cromwell enshrined the legality of his coup with a great statute, the Act of Appeals. This not only made it illegal to appeal Archbishop Cranmer's decision to any authority outside England, but also set out a new doctrine of royal authority: "This realm of England, is an empire . . . governed by one Supreme Head and King." The King of England was, in other words, a totally independent sovereign in every respect, free from all foreign authority. When the annates act was made effective in July, 1533, the Pope had been deprived of all power in England.

It was a momentous step with far-reaching effects. A series of statutes drafted by Cromwell permanently altered the beliefs and religious practices of the entire nation. There were no more Church courts and services were increasingly said in English. Men like Thomas More and John Fisher, who refused to acknowledge the spiritual authority of the King or his new Church of England, were executed. The King became the owner of all the Church's land and wealth, and when, starting in 1536, he chose to sell much of it and to dissolve the monasteries, a new bureaucratic machine was set up by Cromwell to administer this great upheaval and all the income that flowed from it. Henry not only laid claim to great power, his servants created for him the machine that made sure he could use it.

Thus, 1533 was the key year in a revolution in England's government, Church and society. But the event that should have been a joyous and triumphant finale brought Henry disappointment and frustration and marked the beginning of fifteen more years of struggle and four more wives in the search for the prize that continued to elude him—a healthy and strong male heir. On the afternoon of Sunday, September 7, 1533, in Greenwich Palace, Anne Boleyn was delivered of a bouncing, delightful baby girl.

The following Wednesday the Lord Mayor and aldermen of the City of London came down river in their ermine robes and chains to attend the service in which the little girl, destined to be England's greatest queen, was christened Elizabeth. It was an impressive and dignified ceremony. But the King was not present.

ROBERT LACEY

Above Supported by Cromwell and Cranmer, Henry VIII presides as Head of the Established Church of England. Under Henry's feet lies Pope Clement VII, tended by Bishop Fisher.

Thomas Cromwell, after Holbein. Cromwell set up the machinery that was to enable Henry to exercise the new powers which he had acquired.

1533–1543 The Reformation creates new divisions in

William Tyndale, translator of the Bible into English, who was burned for heresy in 1536.

Henry VIII, although in favor of an authoritative English translation of the Scriptures, was only gradually persuaded by Cranmer and Cromwell that Miles Coverdale's translation—the first complete Bible in the English tongue—contained no heresies despite the fact that it had been prepared on the Continent and printed in Zurich. "If there be no heresies," announced the monarch, "in God's name let it go abroad among our people."

But another translator William Tyndale was burned as a heretic in Antwerp in 1536. His tract, *Obedience of a Christian Man*, had prophetically outlined the cardinal principles of the English Reformation: the supremacy of the ruler and the authority of the Scriptures. Tyndale had found it dangerous to continue his work of translating the Bible while living in his native England, and in 1526 he emigrated to Worms, where his English New Testament was printed. Many copies of Tyndale's New Testament were smuggled into England and some of those were seized and burned by the common hangman. Archbishop Warham even sent agents to Europe to buy and destroy copies of Tyndale's work. Ironically, his New Testament, coupled with Coverdale's version of both Testaments, formed the basis of the official "Great Bible" that was prepared under Cranmer's guidance in 1539.

As a result of the labors of Coverdale and Tyndale, the English became known as "The People of the Book." Later English-language versions of the Bible embodied many of their cadences.

Calvin at Geneva

While England was tottering undecided on the brink of the Reformation, Geneva plunged energetically into a form of Protestantism more extreme than that of Luther. The leader of the Reformation in Geneva, John Calvin, was a Frenchman who fled to Switzerland in 1535. He had feared imprisonment if he remained in France, because his "sudden conversion" (as he called it) had made him a vociferous champion of the Protestant cause in Paris.

Calvin's *Institutes of the Christian Religion*, published when he was twenty-seven, was intended to be a justification of the principles of the Reformation. Over the years between 1536 and 1559 the work was expanded by its author from six to eighty chapters. Calvin's *Institutes* was to have as profound an influence on the Reformation as Luther's Bible. His style was incisive and his familiarity with the work of the early fathers was complete. Like Luther, Calvin believed in the primacy of Scripture, but perhaps even more than Luther he believed in predestination. He gave a new twist to the doctrine of predestination that St. Augustine had enunciated, by arguing that a strict moral code was the basis for Christian life. In Calvinist theology, discipline was fundamental. Calvin was determined to avoid the danger of the complete collapse of ecclesiastical authority that was presaged by the rise of Anabaptism and of Antinomianism. The *Institutes* was intended as a justification of properly constituted religious and secular authority, which Calvin saw as virtually identical.

John Calvin, father of Presbyterianism.

After various difficulties, Calvin was appointed city preacher at Geneva in 1536. Here he was able to put into practice his plans for completely reorganizing religious life. All the inhabitants of the city were forced to accept formally a Calvinist profession of faith. This caused great anger and as a result Calvin was expelled from the city in 1539. Two years later, however, he was allowed to return, and under his theocratic government the town became "the most perfect school of Christ." The state was restructured to establish the supremacy of the Christian Church and became intolerant of religious disagreement. In 1553, the anti-Trinitarian heretic, Michael Servetus, was burned because he refused to retract his views.

The Anabaptists

Lutherans and Roman Catholics alike found a common enemy in the Anabaptists, the extreme left wing of the Reformation movement. Protestantism's radical left was composed of a variety of sects that were collectively dubbed "Anabaptists" by their detractors because they all rejected infant baptism. The Anabaptists believed that baptism was a personal, adult act of repentance. (Indeed, the mass baptisms performed in Amsterdam in the early 1500s astounded Luther and Pope Clement as much as they did the Anabaptists.) Such novel doctrines threatened the foundations of authoritarian religion, and those who believed in them were mercilessly persecuted

The Anabaptist Dovecote, the title-page of a contemporary work ridiculing their beliefs.

Calvin was the most distinguished biblical scholar of his generation and his views spread rapidly. An attraction perhaps even greater than Calvin's learning was the authoritarian nature of his views. As a result, Calvin's ideas were adopted by the reformed Churches of Holland and Scotland and were influential in Germany (where Calvinism established itself in Prussia and on the Rhineland). To a lesser extent, Calvinism took root in England and among Protestants in France and Poland. Calvinists found any distinction between Church and State unreal, and in Calvinism the medieval idea of a Christian commonwealth at last found reality.

both by Roman Catholics and Protestants.

To escape such treatment, a group of Anabaptists under John of Leyden settled in Münster in Westphalia. They gained control of the city in February, 1534, and established a "communist state," whose activities—admittedly grossly distorted in contemporary reports—were nonetheless remarkable. Because women outnumbered men four to one in Münster, John of Leyden made polygamy lawful—he personally took sixteen wives. Attempts to unseat John were repulsed with considerable bloodshed, but in the spring of 1535, a joint expedition of Roman Catholic and Lutheran princes forced Münster to surrender. The sect's leaders were executed and the Bishop of Münster was recalled.

Although the events at Münster lent Anabaptism an air of disreputability, it continued to have advocates throughout the sixteenth century. Almost all the countries of Europe were troubled to some extent by Anabaptist groups. But the only really influential and long-lasting Anabaptist Church was that of the Mennonites, who have continued to exist in the United States. The Mennonites were founded in about 1538 by Menno Simons (1496–1561), a Dutch ex-priest. During the seventeenth century many Mennonites, like the members of other persecuted religious minorities, emigrated to America.

The Schmalkaldic League

German politics were dominated by the religious question, which was in reality a new aspect of the old quarrel between the Emperor and the princes. Charles v seemed to be at the height of his power in 1530. Sultan Suleiman was forced to raise the siege of Vienna, and the Turkish threat seemed to be declining. The treaty between Charles v and Clement vii in 1529 led to Charles' coronation as Holy Roman Emperor—the last coronation of an emperor by a pope. The Archduke Ferdinand of Austria was elected King of the Romans, thus fulfilling the ambitions of Charles' grandfather, Maximilian, which were to establish the Hapsburgs securely as the imperial dynasty. Charles showed his determination to interfere energetically in papal affairs—Clement vii was forced to refuse Henry viii's request for an annulment of his marriage to Catherine of Aragon. Clement proved to be more determined in his refusal to summon a council. Their experience with the fifteenth-century conciliar movement had made the popes suspicious of general councils. It was almost as if Clement preferred to see the whole of the Church crumble away around him than to risk the danger of criticism by a council. If the imperial coronation increased Charles' influence on the Pope, it also increased Clement's influence on the Emperor. Clement was prepared to do almost anything—short of summoning a council—to overcome the Protestant challenge. Since he saw little chance of reaching an acceptable agreement by discussion with the Protestants, he began trying to persuade Charles to use force against them. The failure of the Diet of Augsburg to reach agreement strengthened Clement's call for the use of force.

The failure of Augsburg also persuaded the Protestants that their religious independence overrode their responsibilities to the Emperor. In 1531, six princes and ten cities formed the League of Schmalkalden. Most of the other Protestant cities and states joined the League during the following years, and it rapidly became the center of Protestant resistance to the claims of the Emperor and the Roman Catholic princes. During the years after 1530, Protestantism was able to spread rapidly. Many of the northern cities and several important principalities, including Württemburg, Brandenburg and Schleswig-Holstein, accepted Lutheran ideas and threw out bishops and priests who refused to accept the change.

Charles and Ferdinand found themselves almost completely unable to fight the spread of Protestantism. Their attentions were divided. The Turkish attacks on Hungary and Austria forced the Hapsburgs to devote much of their attention, as well as resources that they could ill afford, to defense. The Mediterranean, too, needed attention. The North African piracy, always a threat to shipping, was growing increasingly bold—partly as a result of French intrigues and encouragement. The main threat was the growing power of Barbarossa (c. 1480–1546), who had turned Algiers into the center of a flourishing pirate kingdom, which paid tribute to Suleiman of Turkey. Charles was deeply disturbed by these developments in North Africa and gave Malta to the Knights of St. John of Jerusalem as a replacement for the lost island of Rhodes. But the Hospitallers did not succeed in suppressing Barbarossa's activities and the pirate king was even able to raid Hapsburg possessions in southern Italy. In 1531, Barbarossa increased his territory by conquering Tunisia. Charles gathered together a fleet of over a hundred warships as well as several hundred transport and other smaller vessels and captured Tunis. But campaigns such as this distracted his attention from Germany and the Protestant problem. It became all the more necessary for Charles to avoid war with the Protestant princes, and he was forced to make temporary truce after temporary truce with them.

The decline of the Hanseatic League

The wars of the Reformation did not help the Hanseatic League, which had already been weakened by the rise of Antwerp and Amsterdam as the leading ports for northern Europe. In 1494, the Hanse had already been forced to close its yard at Novgorod, and throughout the sixteenth century, its trade was slipping away. It failed almost entirely to share in the trade boom caused by the settlement of the colonies in America. The effect of the revived power of Sweden was decisive in breaking its final claims to power in the Baltic itself. In 1535, the League was defeated by a joint Swedish and Danish fleet, and it never recovered from this blow. In England the privileges of the League lasted until the reign of Queen Elizabeth. Although the Hanse was not formally abandoned, it had ceased to have any international power and influence by about 1600. After that it was concerned only with German domestic trade, largely among its own member towns.

A ship of the Hanseatic League.

An attempt by Charles V's fleet to capture Algiers, the center of Barbarossa's pirate kingdom, in 1542.

1543 The Earth Dethroned

By September of 1543, it had become obvious to the citizens of Frauenburg, Poland, that their beloved physician, Nicholas Copernicus, would not live out the year. The good doctor's failing health was a matter of special concern to his brash young disciple, Georg Joachim, who had long urged his mentor—a noted amateur astronomer—to publish his observations on planetary motion. After months of pleading, Joachim had at last been given permission to deliver Copernicus' manuscript to a local printer—and a copy of the published text reached the doctor on his deathbed. That volume postulated the first really new theory of planetary motion in almost two thousand years. Copernicus' insistence that the sun—not the earth—was the center of the universe helped usher in an epoch of broad scientific inquiry that earned the modest astronomer the title "Father of the Scientific Revolution."

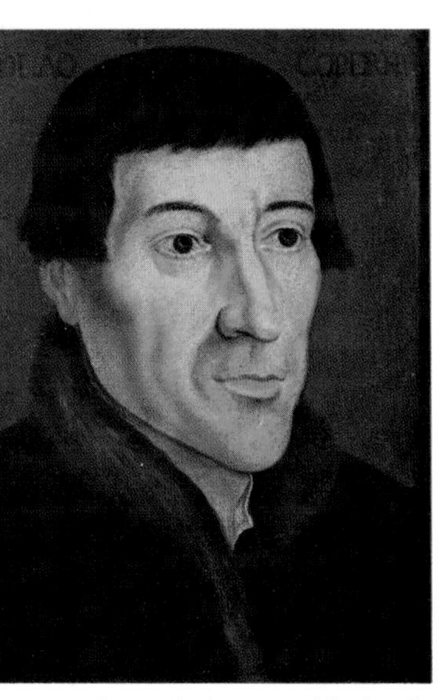

A copy by Lorman of Berlin of a contemporary portrait of Nicholas Copernicus.

Nicholas Copernicus, the Polish astronomer whose theory of planetary motion helped revolutionize scientific thought in the late sixteenth century, was born on February 19, 1473, at Torun, a Hanseatic community that had fallen under the protection of the King of Poland.

Little is known of Copernicus' childhood. His father died when he was only ten, and Nicholas, his brother Andrew and their two sisters were adopted by their maternal uncle, Lucas Watzelrode (or Waczenrode). A scholar and Roman Catholic priest, Watzelrode was consecrated Bishop of Ermland six years after he adopted the Koppernigk children. At that time, the See of Ermland was virtually an autonomous state, almost encircled by lands controlled by the Teutonic Knights. It owed nominal allegiance to Poland, but the Bishop served as both temporal ruler and spiritual head of the See. His palace was located at Heilsberg (about thirty-nine miles south of present-day Kalingrad, Russia) and his cathedral was located in the coastal city of Frauenberg, some forty miles to the northwest.

In 1491, when Nicholas was eighteen, he and his brother were sent to the university at Cracow, where young Copernicus pursued an interest in astronomy that he had first demonstrated while a schoolchild in Torun. The University of Cracow, one of the first institutions of higher learning in northern Europe to be influenced by the rediscovery of Greek science, was renowned for its high intellectual standards and was consequently attended by numerous foreign students. Copernicus studied mathematics and astronomy at the university.

While still a student, Copernicus began to assemble a collection of astronomical books that he was to keep by him for the rest of his life. The young student's interest in astronomy was looked upon with favor by the Church, which was at that time much concerned with the possible reform of the calendar. When Copernicus left Cracow, his uncle wanted to have him installed in a canonry in Frauenberg, but until a suitable vacancy occurred, the Bishop felt that his nephew might profitably seek a degree in ecclesiastical law. Accordingly, Nicholas departed for the famous law school at Bologna in 1496.

While in Bologna, Nicholas lodged at the home of Domenico Maria da Novara, a professor of astronomy. The two men observed the heavens together, and spent many hours discussing possible improvements that they felt could be made in the prevailing theory of planetary motion. Nicholas remained in Bologna for three and a half years and then journeyed to Rome for the celebrations attending the 1,500th anniversary of Christ's birth. He lingered in the city for a year, and during that time made some celestial observations, particularly of an eclipse of the moon, and gave informal lectures on astronomy and mathematics.

During the years that he was in law school, a canonry became vacant at Frauenberg and Nicholas was elected to fill it. On July 27, 1501, he was duly installed—and promptly was granted further leave of absence so that he might go to Padua to study medicine and complete his law studies. Nicholas chose, however, to graduate in ecclesiastical law at Ferrara, and in 1503 was made a Doctor of Canon Law there. He then returned to medical school at Padua.

In Italy, as elsewhere in sixteenth-century Europe, medical training was largely theoretical. The teaching of medicine was based on certain rules attributed to Hippocrates, a Greek physician who lived in the fifth century B.C. Those rules, coupled with the writings of the Roman surgeon Galen (circa A.D. 200) and those of the eleventh-century Arabian chemist and physician Avicenna, composed the bulk of contemporary medical lore. Practical treatment involved the study of astronomy, because the current belief was that the celestial bodies exerted an influence on the human body and on the herbal drugs that were prescribed as cures.

When Copernicus, by then in his early thirties,

Opposite A room in the house at Frauenberg that Copernicus inherited from his uncle, and where he carried out most of his astronomical work.

A picture from *The Travels of Sir John Mandeville*; astrologers as well as travelers found that the stars had their uses.

returned to Heilsberg in 1506, he was appointed medical attendant to his uncle (with whom Nicholas shared certain governmental duties). In March, 1512, Watzelrode died, and by June of that year Copernicus was installed at Frauenberg cathedral. Nicholas' gratitude for all that the old man had done on his behalf was expressed in a book that he published in 1509, three years before the Bishop's death. The work, a Latin translation of some Greek verses by Theophylactus, was dedicated to Lucas Watzelrode.

At Frauenberg, Copernicus carried out a number of ecclesiastical and temporal duties. He lived in the modest style expected of canons, possessing but two servants and three horses. He set up his own astronomical observatory. In 1514 he was invited to Rome to assist in the reform of the calendar but felt it necessary to refuse, believing that the proposals were premature and that more research was needed into the motion of the sun and moon. Two years later he moved about fifty miles from the cathedral in order better to administer several of its large estates. Copernicus was now forced to spend long periods away from his observatory, and his absences grew more frequent when war broke out between Poland and the Teutonic Knights in 1519.

When, at the end of the war, a new Bishop was appointed, Copernicus returned to Frauenberg. The astronomer's final years were spent tending not only the Bishop and his successors, but also the town's poor, who grew to love him. Indeed, in Copernicus' own lifetime, it was for his medical skill and not his astronomical theory that he was noted.

Copernicus carried out his astronomical work whenever he was freed of his other duties. Initially, he had become dissatisfied, as many astronomers of his day were, with the generally accepted theory of the universe. That concept, based on the teachings of Greek philosophers, placed the Earth, fixed and immovable, at the center of the universe. Around it, in order, orbited the moon, Mercury, Venus, the sun, Mars, Jupiter and Saturn. Beyond Saturn lay the sphere of the fixed stars, which supposedly rotated once every twenty-four hours. Heaven lay beyond this starry sphere.

The problem with this theory—one that still troubled astronomers in the sixteenth century—was how to account accurately for the movements of the sun, moon and planets. To resolve this dilemma, ancient astronomers had evolved three basic provisos: first, that motion took place about the Earth; second, that such motion was uniform in speed; and third, that movement must be in a circle. The great difficulty was that the sun, moon and planets did not move across the sky evenly; they moved faster at some times than at others, and, worst of all, the planets appeared to perform loops in the sky as they wandered across the background of the stars.

Throughout antiquity solutions designed to explain some or all of these observed effects had been proposed, and in the second century A.D. the Alexandrian astronomer Ptolemy had worked out a comprehensive scheme of planetary motion that was still in use in Copernicus' day. Ptolemy explained planetary motion by using a collection of circular motions devised in the fourth century B.C. by Apollonios of Perga. Basically, each planet was conceived of as orbiting in a small circle, known as an "epicycle." The epicycle, in turn, moved at a regular rate around the circumference of a larger circle, known as a "deferent," at whose center lay the Earth. Ptolemy ingeniously modified this system not only to account for the planet's orbital loops, but also to account for changes in the apparent distances of given planets from the Earth, and for unevenness in their motion. He did this by offsetting the deferents from the center of the Earth, by allowing the deferents and epicycles to rock, and by using more than one epicycle for each planet. It was a brilliant system, and it remained in use (in modified form) for nearly 1,400 years.

By Copernicus' time, Ptolemy's system had been interwoven with the ideas of Aristotle, who had conceived of the universe as composed of a series of concentric spheres, with the Earth at the center. Many sixteenth-century astronomers thought of Aristotle's spheres as real, although transparent, and made of the purest crystal. According to Aristotle's generally accepted laws of physics, celestial bodies were eternal and composed of a heavenly material—quite different from anything on Earth—whose natural place was the sky. Heavy bodies fell to the ground, Aristotle taught, because their natural place was the center of the universe (which was, of course, the center of the Earth). These laws were to have an important bearing on the acceptance of Copernicus' proposals.

While still a university student, Copernicus had had grown dissatisfied with the views of Ptolemy. He decided to read the Greek authors for himself to see whether he could find a clue to any other explanation of planetary motion. To seek new ideas from ancient writings was not unusual: for one thing, it was commonly held that the Greek philosophers had special knowledge of scientific matters; and for another, appeals to ancient authority—to the Scriptures, the teachings of the Church or some other early source—were customary. In his reading of Greek authors, Copernicus discovered that several did not accept the geocentric view of the universe. At least one bold thinker had even gone so far as to suggest that the Earth and planets orbit the sun—and it was this view that Copernicus eventually revived.

The resurrection of some unusual and unfamiliar Greek speculations would not have been enough—by itself—to make Copernicus famous, had he not spent years perfecting the mathematics of his new view, computing future planetary positions and making observations to provide additional evidence. He prepared a carefully reasoned argument in support of his theory, using arguments somewhat similar to those adopted 1,800 years before by Aristotle, but reaching a different conclusion. In 1530, while Copernicus was at work on his theory but before he was ready to set down his views in detail, the astronomer issued a manuscript that contained the essential facts. The manuscript was called *Commentariolus (The Litttle Commentary)*, and although it boasted no diagrams or detailed descriptions, it aroused considerable interest. Indeed, in 1533 John Widmanstad, the Papal Secretary, lectured to the Pope and some of his cardinals on the views it contained. At this time, such religious opposition as there was to Copernicus' theory of a moving Earth came from the Protestants, who believed it to be contrary to a literal interpretation of the Scriptures.

Copernicus was urged to publish his theory in full, but claimed that he was not ready. Indeed, he might never have agreed that his facts and figures were sufficiently complete had it not been for the efforts of Georg Joachim, a young Protestant scholar who came to see him in the spring of 1539. Better known by his Latinized name Rheticus, Joachim remained with Copernicus for almost three years, and it says much for the characters of both men—and for the stimulation that their scientific study provided—that in an age torn by religious dissension, the two men worked harmoniously together.

In 1540 Rheticus persuaded his host to publish a summary of his views, which was subsequently printed in Nuremberg under the title *Narratio Prima (A First Narrative)*. Not content with this, Rheticus continued to urge Copernicus to draw up his theory in detail. In the end he prevailed, and in 1543 a complete manuscript was delivered to Johann Petrejus, the Nürnberg publisher who had printed the *Narratio Prima*. Unfortunately, Rheticus moved to the University of Leipzig soon after delivering the manuscript, and he was forced to leave the technical details to his old tutor, Johannes Schoner, and a Lutheran divine, Andreas Osiander.

Osiander, worried about religious opposition to Copernicus' work, gave the publication a title without consulting Copernicus. (Copernicus had left his manuscript untitled, and was therefore partly to blame.) The book appeared as *De Revolutionibus Orbium Coelestium (On the Revolutions of the Celestial Spheres)*, although it is clear that Copernicus himself did not believe in the reality of Aristotle's spheres. More significant, however, was the fact that Osiander inserted an unsigned preface, disclaiming any physical reality to the movement of the Earth and explaining that Copernicus' theory was no more than an ingenious way of computing future planetary positions. The book appeared in 1543, and tradition has it that a copy reached Copernicus on his deathbed in October of that year.

Copernicus' theory as set out in *De Revolutionibus* places the sun firmly at the center of the universe, with the planets orbiting around it. The Earth is dethroned from its privileged position in the midst of all creation and is relegated to the role of mere satellite, orbiting the sun and rotating once on its axis every twenty-four hours. (It still acts as the body

The Lutheran divine, Andreas Osiander, who gave Copernicus' book its misleading title, and explained away many of his ideas in order to reduce opposition to Copernicus' theories.

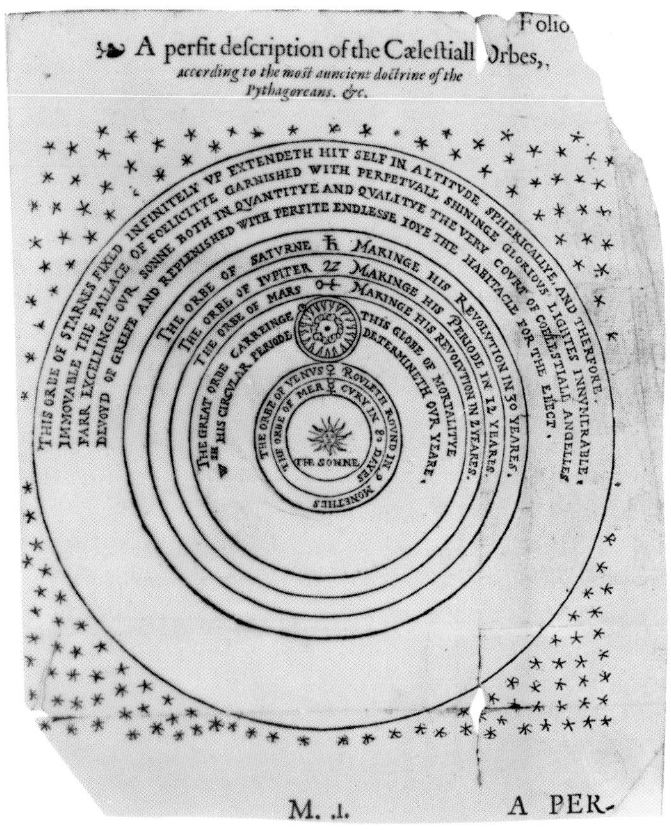

M. i.   A PER-

The Copernican solar system as depicted by Thomas Digges in the 1576 edition of his father's *Prognostication Everlasting*.

Sixteenth-century astrolabe used to tell the altitude of stars and planets.

about which the moon performs its monthly orbit, however.) The epicycles and deferents of Ptolemic astronomy are retained, and no changes are made in Aristotelian physics. Copernicus could not free himself from the ancient Greek beliefs that the heavens were incorruptible and that celestial movements must be circular and regular. Yet his system did possess regular motion centered on the sun, instead of off-centered motion about the Earth, which Ptolemy had advocated.

To Copernicus, this new scheme seemed virtually a moral victory, for it kept the true spirit of the Greek belief in circular motion. Moreover, his system was more elegant mathematically—as contemporary mathematicians were quick to realize—and it appeared to give more accurate results when used for computing the future positions of the planets. The tables in *De Revolutionibus* were used by the mathematician Erasmus Reinhold to prepare, under the patronage of Duke Albert of Prussia, a new set of tables of future planetary positions. These *Prussian Tables*, as they were called, were more precise than any previously published.

In England, the new theory received considerable support, particularly from Thomas Digges, a distinguished Elizabethan mathematician. Digges followed up a new consequence of the Copernican theory, which he realized affected all commonly held assumptions about the extent of the universe. Aristotle and other Greek philosophers had argued that since the sphere of the stars rotated once every twenty-four hours, that sphere must be finite in size—for if it was infinite, it would have to rotate at an infinite speed to complete a revolution in the same period. Digges appreciated that in a heliocentric universe, where the Earth turned on its axis while orbiting round the sun, this argument was no longer valid. In an astronomical handbook published in 1576 and titled *Prognostication Everlasting*, Digges proposed an infinite universe of stars, each similar to our sun; his proposition completely refuted the idea of a spherical universe.

But if the Copernican theory met with support in England and much of Germany, it also faced some opposition. That opposition was of two types—scientific and religious. The former was based on arguments founded on Aristotle's physics: how could so heavy a body as the Earth be thought to move? Why, if it moved, should bodies still fall to the ground and the moon remain with it in space? How could it rotate once a day without setting up tidal waves and hurricanes as it rushed around in the surrounding air? Another significant scientific argument was based on observation: if the Earth orbited the sun, then at one time of year it would necessarily be nearer to some stars than to others, and as it moved, the nearer stars would be replaced by others. Some change in star positions ought, then, to be observable, but the most careful examinations of the sky showed no change at all. Copernicus, who had foreseen this argument, countered it by saying that the stars were too far away for any change to be observed. This deduction was perfectly correct, as we now know, but in the sixteenth century, it seemed insane to assert that God had made a universe with an immense gap between the planetary orbits and the stars. Only telescopic observations made from 1600 onwards, coupled with the gradual rejection of Aristotle's physics, removed these objections.

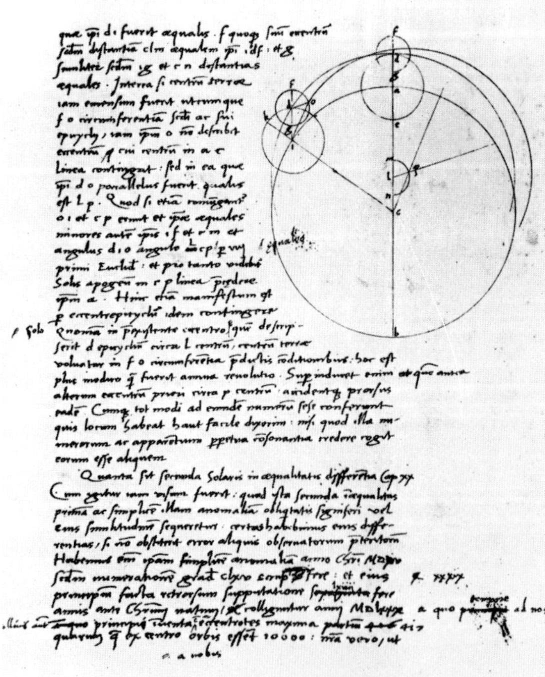

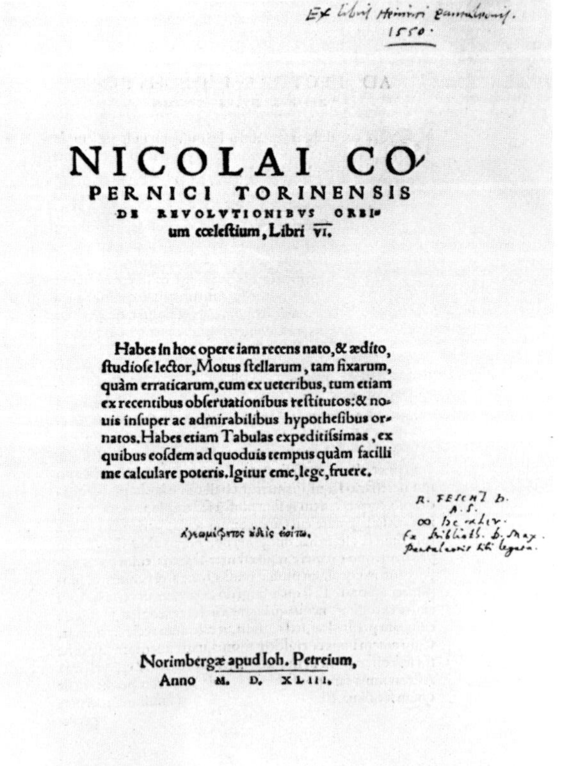

NICOLAI CO-
PERNICI TORINENSIS
DE REVOLVTIONIBVS ORBI-
um cœlestium, Libri VI.

Habes in hoc opere iam recens nato, & ædito, studiose lector, Motus stellarum, tam fixarum, quàm erraticarum, cum ex ueteribus, tum etiam ex recentibus obseruationibus restitutos: & nouis insuper ac admirabilibus hypothesibus ornatos. Habes etiam Tabulas expeditissimas, ex quibus eosdem ad quoduis tempus quàm facillime calculare poteris. Igitur eme, lege, fruere.

Ἀγεωμέτρητος οὐδεὶς εἰσίτω.

Norimbergæ apud Ioh. Petreium,
Anno M. D. XLIII.

A page from the original manuscript of Copernicus' *De Revolutionibus*, and the title-page of the first edition.

A celestial globe of the mid-sixteenth century.

Some Protestants rejected the theory from a religious point of view, citing Biblical passages which asserted that the Earth stood still. There were others who were less committed to so literal an interpretation, however; Copernicus had dedicated *De Revolutionibus* to Pope Paul III, and the Roman Catholic Church had raised no objections to the theory. Copernican astronomy was strongly advocated by Giordano Bruno, who learned of it while on a visit to England in 1583. Bruno, a former Dominican, had found much to criticize in his Church and had published many contumacious books attacking it. In these books, which supported a magical form of anti-authoritarian government, Bruno extolled the Copernican view of a heliocentric universe (although not for scientific reasons) and it was this, more than anything else, that led to *De Revolutionibus Orbium Coelestium* being placed on the Index of Prohibited Books in 1616.

Although his detailed descriptions of planetary motion were to be superseded within the next 150 years, Copernicus' theory was nonetheless a profound break with scientific tradition—the first dramatically new view of the universe in almost two thousand years. Copernicus' work acted as a powerful stimulus to future scholars, encouraging them to rethink the principles underlying the behavior of the universe. The new laws of planetary motion described by Johannes Kepler between 1609 and 1621, and something of Galileo Galilei's mathematical physics published in 1638 and his earlier observations with a telescope, owe a debt to the spirit of *De Revolutionibus*. The publication of Newton's *Principia* in 1687 culminated an era of intense scientific inquiry of which Nicholas Copernicus had been one of the pioneers.

COLIN RONAN

Science and Art begin to break with the

It was not only in astronomy that scientific advances were being made. A consequence of the Renaissance was an increasing concentration on study for its own sake and a willingness to follow ideas wherever they led, regardless of the constraints of religious or scientific orthodoxies. This did not mean that ancient and medieval theories were at once abandoned; medieval ideas about "vital forces" were to remain common scientific currency until the middle of the nineteenth century.

A sixteenth-century design for mine ventilating machinery.

Nor did it mean that all established ideas were immediately reexamined; it was only very gradually that different ideas were subjected to the gaze of objective searchers after scientific truth. But it did mean that if premises appeared to be at variance with observation and experiment, it was no longer necessary to suppose that it was the observation and the experiment that were wrong. It was no longer necessary to go on indefinitely adding to the complexity of traditional ideas in order "to save the appearances." A doctrine of the medieval English philosopher William of Ockham, known as "Ockham's razor," suggested that it was most likely that the simplest possible explanation would be the correct one. The old ideas in general continued to be accepted until the burden of proving them right became too great, and it was only then that experiments were carried out in any consistent way.

Outside astronomy, the most notable scientific advances were in medical knowledge, particularly in anatomy and surgery. The father of modern surgery was Paracelsus (c. 1490–1541) who believed that academic education could teach nothing. "Whence have I all my secrets," he wrote, "out of what writers and authors? Ask rather how the beasts have learned their arts. If nature can instruct irrational beasts, can it not do much more for men?" The reaction of more orthodox medical practitioners forced Paracelsus to leave Basel, where he had taught in the university, in 1530. Despite the eccentricity of many of his ideas, he had a formative influence on surgical study through his works, the first of which was published in 1528.

More orthodox, more thoughtful, more scholarly and perhaps even more influential was the Flemish anatomist Andreas Vesalius (1514–64), whose *De Fabrica Corporis Humani* was published in the same year as Copernicus' *De Revolutionibus*. It was no less revolutionary; what Copernicus' work did to the authority of Ptolemy, Vesalius' did to that of Galen, the second-century physician whose ideas were accepted as the standard of medical orthodoxy throughout the Middle Ages. Although surgeons had on occasion dissected human corpses during the later Middle Ages, Vesalius was the first to put together a manual which showed the many errors in Galen. The significance of the *De Fabrica* did not escape contemporaries.

In mathematics, too, the frontiers of knowledge were being pushed rapidly back. Complex algebraic calculations appear to have given particular delight to sixteenth-century mathematicians.

Technological advance during the sixteenth century was hardly behind that of astronomy or medicine. The main fields were military technology, mining and navigational aids. The wheel-lock musket was invented in 1517, and several important books on weaponry were published later in the century: the Italian mathematician, Niccolò Tartaglia (1500–57) explained the trajectory of bullets in his *La Nuova Scienzia* (1537) and the *Della Pirotecnica* of Vannoccio Biringucci (1480–1539), which was posthumously published in 1540, discussed the manufacture of gunpowder. The growing importance of gold and silver mining in the Americas during the sixteenth century created an enormous interest in mining technology, which Georg Agricola (1490–1555) attempted to satisfy in his *De Re Metallica* (1556). Improvements in ships' rigging, which made possible the great voyages of discovery of the late fifteenth and early sixteenth centuries, were only one aspect of the development of navigational aids. Cartography advanced quickly. In 1541, the Flemish geographer Gerard Mercator (1512–94) produced a reasonably accurate terrestrial globe, and in 1569, his map of the world was published. The projection he used, which came to be known as Mercator's projection, soon became the most frequently used. The study of latitude and longitude was pushed forward by the Louvain astronomer, Gemma Frisius, who was one of the few energetic advocates of Copernican ideas. The standard navigational treatise from the time of its publication in 1556 was Martin Cortes' *Arte De Navigar*, which was quickly translated into the main European languages.

Detail from *Bacchus and Ariadne* by Titian.

The influence of printing on the future of scientific developments was very great. Printed books made it possible for the learned community throughout Europe to be quickly aware of, and sensitive to, ideas that would previously have taken decades to spread. Even more important was the improvement in the quality of printed books, as it became possible to publish work accurately in diagramatic form. Part of Vesalius' influence was unquestionably due to the high quality of the diagrams in *De Fabrica*.

The growing importance of scientific ideas made it increasingly necessary as the sixteenth century wore on for an educated man to have a reasonable knowledge of science. As early as 1532, François Rabelais' bawdy masterpiece *Pantagruel* recommended an educational curriculum based on the study of the sciences. In practice, Rabelais' recommendation was ignored, and the educational ideal remained all-embracing rather than confined to a single discipline.

But if the knowledge of science was becoming gradually more widespread as it became part of a "gentleman's" education, there was some opposition to this. Science had not yet escaped from the confines of astrology or religion. The search for the philosopher's stone, which would turn base metals into gold, remained a formidable attraction. The desire to grasp an understanding of man from a study of the stars continued to lead men of considerable learning into far-fetched theories. Other forces were at work, too: elaborate pseudoreligions, such as Rosicrucianism, imposed a secrecy on their members; and fear of persecution by the authorities in science and religion gave an added reason for secrecy. Throughout the sixteenth and seventeenth centuries, when non-scientific books were increasingly being written in the vernacular, the major works of scientific authors continued to be in Latin. The scientific community might be unable to separate science from the rest of knowledge, but tried nevertheless to restrict the flow of scientific ideas to the *cognoscenti* by hiding behind an elaborate jargon and forbidding covers. It is too easy to see the scientific revolution, which can be said to have begun with Vesalius and Copernicus, as a modern movement. The whole era of the scientific revolution was still deeply involved in non-scientific thought.

models of antiquity

Titian

Titian (1490–1576), the greatest of all Venetian artists, is often considered the founder of modern painting. His contemporary fame was based on the *Bacchanals*, which he painted for the Duke of Ferrara, and on the outsize painting of *The Assumption* in the Frari Church in Venice. Titian eventually abandoned religious themes for those of classical mythology and for portraiture. The friend of kings and popes, he established what subsequent generations would come to regard as "the official portrait" concept. Titian's later style, with its disregard for contours, was in some respects "Impressionistic," and his technique was equally remarkable. The master constantly revised his canvases and, according to one of his pupils, if he "found something in a painting that displeased him, he went to work like a surgeon."

Art in the north

Despite the individual genius of Titian, the artistic achievement of the sixteenth century belonged to a great extent to northern Europe, just as the achievements of the fourteenth and fifteenth centuries were Italian. The decline in Italy's position in Europe during the sixteenth century was not merely political, but was cultural also. Italy's contribution to late sixteenth-century art was to be Mannerism; the art of the north was very much more realistic. The artistic tradition of north and south, which seemed to be converging in the late fifteenth century, drew apart again during the sixteenth century.

The art of the north was, however, to a great extent based on the Italian achievement of the previous century and a half. There were artists who escaped the impact of the Renaissance, but they were isolated individuals. The bizarre brilliance of Hieronymus Bosch (1415–1516), for example, owes almost nothing to Italian models. It is difficult to understand what his paintings, full of the most fantastic imaginings, mean, but they were enormously popular during the sixteenth century, and were mostly valued possessions of wealthy royal patrons, such as Queen Isabella of Spain. So popular were his paintings that forgers attempted to imitate his work—a rare tribute in an age before paintings came to be valued chiefly as investments rather than as works of art. Although Bosch's name has recently been linked by some scholars with an obscure heresy of the time in an attempt to explain the peculiarities of his pictures, there is no evidence to suggest that any explanation—apart from artistic imagination—is needed. Matthias Grünewald (1480–1528) was another artist on whom the influence of the Renaissance was relatively slight, but Grünewald used Renaissance techniques to help heighten an imagery that was little changed from that of the Burgundian court artists of the fifteenth century. His use of perspective and light is characteristic of the Italian Renaissance, while the feeling and subject matter of his paintings are more typical of fifteenth-century German art.

Man with Pigs by Albrecht Dürer.

More typical in his acceptance of Renaissance ideas was the highly influential Albrecht Dürer (1471–1528), who had traveled in Italy in order to learn the latest techniques. He was strongly influenced by Giovanni Bellini and by Leonardo da Vinci. He was appointed court painter to the Emperor Maximilian in 1516, and was reappointed by Charles v in 1520. Few of his paintings survive, as he was primarily a graphic artist and most of his work was in the form of engravings and woodcuts. His woodcuts achieved an enormously wide popularity, even in Italy.

The Garden of Earthly Delights by Hieronymous Bosch.

The Reformation had a profound impact on art in Germany as well as on individual artists. Grünewald, for example, gave up painting his tortured and diseased figures. Indeed he appears to have given up painting altogether in his later years and to have devoted himself with enthusiasm to the social and religious conflicts of the Lutheran revolt. Dürer, too, was influenced by Lutheranism, and the subject matter of his engravings changed during his later years. For example, he is known to have abandoned work on an altarpiece showing the Virgin and child and instead to have executed a painting of the four apostles.

The Reformation led to the destruction of much medieval devotional art; Karlstadt, for example, tore down church altarpieces in Wittenberg. But there was little to justify Erasmus' complaint that "wherever Lutheranism rules, learning is banned." Art flourished in the Reformation era. Lukas Cranach (1472–1553) was the leading artist of the Reformation. He portrayed Protestant princes and biblical stories, while his son took pleasure in drawing caricatures of popes and cardinals.

Other artists were less affected by the Reformation. Albrecht Altdorfer (1480–1538), under the influence of Dürer, brought the feeling of engraving to many of his pictures. The Reformation helped to isolate Italy and Germany culturally, and as a result artists such as Pieter Breughel (1525–69) were deprived of Italian influence and created an entirely native school although the influence of Dürer brought them into contact with Renaissance ideas at second hand.

Outside Germany the three most distinguished artists of the time were Jean Clouet (1485–1541) and the two Hans Holbeins, father (1465–1524) and son (1497–1543). Clouet worked in France, and the younger Holbein, driven out of Switzerland, spent his later years in England, where he portrayed many of the leading figures of the time.

The Council of Trent 1544

By calling the Council of Trent, Pope Paul III *set in motion the Counter-Reformation. Originally convened to unite Christendom, overhaul ecclesiastical administration and procedures and unify the Christian princes of Europe against the Turks, the council failed in its first and third aims. In the second, however, it was brilliantly successful. In addition, the Council established questions of faith and doctrine so authoritatively they still apply today.*

On November 19, 1544, Pope Paul III issued a bull *Laetare Jerusalem* summoning the Church's hierarchy to a general council, under Jesuit guidance, in northern Italy. The Pope set before the council three objectives: to heal the divisions within the Church; to draw up proposals for the reformation of ecclesiastical life and administration; and to establish peace among the European princes so that they might make common cause against the Turks. It was in the second of these objectives that the council achieved its major success.

There was much to reform. It was easy to find fault with the Church in the century or so before the council. Churchmen were deeply involved in political life. Perhaps that was unavoidable, but the abuse of their spiritual authority for political ends had become scandalous. Nepotism flourished—too many bishops put the interests of their relatives and friends before the good of their dioceses. Too many popes had been more concerned with the territorial integrity of the Papal States than with the spiritual welfare of the Church. Pluralism was rife—in pursuit of wealth the hierarchy collected benefice upon benefice, leaving the laity to the care of poverty-stricken, and often uneducated, local curates. Despite constantly repeated prohibitions clerical concubinage was widespread. And simony—the selling of church offices—was common.

But it would be inaccurate to paint too grim a picture. The movement for reform had begun long before the council. In the fourteenth century, Gerard Groote had founded the Brethren of the Common Life who were instrumental in spreading the *devotio moderna* which led to a revival of personal piety. Among those influenced by the Brethren was Thomas à Kempis, whose *Imitation of Christ* is still considered one of the most moving books of Christian spiritual literature. The hallmark of the *devotio moderna* was an intense personal commitment to the figure of Christ. Lives of Christ abounded. One of the most influential, by Ludolph the Carthusian of Saxony, played a large part in the conversion of Ignatius of Loyola, who founded the Society of Jesus in 1540. The Jesuits have since become the largest religious order in the Church, but at the time they were only one among several groups of "reformed priests." The Jesuits, the Theatines and the Barnabites were all evidence of the beginnings of reform in the Church in the half century before Trent. There were many other similar signs, from individual bishops concerned for the spiritual welfare of their dioceses to reforming synods.

Except in Spain, where new theological faculties had been started under Cardinal Cisneros, the standard of religious studies in universities was far from satisfactory. The Nominalist philosophy and theology taught to Martin Luther in the first decade of the sixteenth century led only too easily to a belief that God's action in the world was arbitrary. This being the case, reasoned Luther, the gap between man and God was unbridgeable. If man could do nothing to win God's favor, salvation must depend upon faith alone. Man remains always a sinner, but his faith would justify him before God. These ideas seem to have been in Luther's mind from 1514. He formulated them in a lecture given in the summer of 1517 on Paul's Epistle to the Romans. The following October he composed his *Ninety-Five Theses*. A preaching tour by the Dominican Johann Tetzel, selling indulgences to raise money for the rebuilding of St. Peter's in Rome, provided the occasion. Tetzel's tours were typical of ecclesiastical abuses, an example of the unhappy involvement of Church and high finance.

The theses caused great excitement. Archbishop Albrecht of Mainz, who had a financial interest in Tetzel's enterprise that amounted to simony, now saw this source of income threatened. In 1518 Albrecht sued Luther in Rome, but the Elector of Saxony arranged for the examination to be held in

Apotheosis of the Virgin by Domenichino, an example of the religious art inspired by the Council of Trent.

Opposite A painting of the Council of Trent by Titian. Called to reunite Christendom, the Council confirmed the breach, synthesizing Catholic doctrine and ushering in the Counter-Reformation.

Vasari's painting of Pope Clement VII and the Emperor Charles V. The sack of Rome by Charles' troops finally forced Clement to agree to a council.

Augsburg. Luther claimed that a general council of the Church should meet as soon as possible to decide the issue, and that the Pope should submit to its authority. In 1520 his *Address to the Christian Nobility of the German Nation* called upon the German princes to take reform into their own hands, if necessary by calling a council. Three years later, the Diet of Nuremberg proposed a free Christian council to be held in Germany. "Free" meant free of the Pope's interference; "Christian," the summoning of all Christian people whether Protestant or Catholic, clerical or lay. The council was to be held in Germany, far from the influence of Rome.

Luther had broken all the rules in appealing for a general council. Such an action was strictly forbidden by the papacy, which feared the revival of conciliarism, the movement that claimed that the pope could be overruled by a general council. Moreover, a meeting of both clerics and laity such as that proposed at Nuremberg would undermine the authority of the ecclesiastical hierarchy. Political motives, however, were the strongest reason for the refusal to call a council. The House of Hapsburg, headed by the Emperor Charles V, threatened the Papal States from north and south. A divided Germany suited both the Pope and the French King Francis I. In 1526 Clement and Francis formed an alliance, the League of Cognac, against Charles, but were swiftly defeated. On May 6, 1527, the Emperor's troops sacked the city of Rome and Clement VII was forced to agree to a council.

Paul III made several fruitless attempts to convoke a council. At last one was summoned to meet at Mantua, but when war broke out again between Charles and Francis, the Duke of Mantua laid down impossible conditions, and the venue had to be changed to Vicenza. Meanwhile Paul made some effort to reform the Church, and to heal the breach in Germany, without resorting to the ultimate weapon of a general council. A powerful commission of cardinals met in Rome, recommending sweeping changes in the papal curia, the central administration of the Church. At the same time there were attempts to reconcile Catholics and Protestants in Germany. Possibly the most successful was the Colloquy of Regensburg (1541), at which both sides managed to agree on a formula on the central issue of justification by faith alone. But they failed to reach a compromise on the Eucharist and both Rome and Luther rejected the agreed statement on justification.

The Pope by now had no alternative but to call

Above Pope Julius III. He opened the Council's second phase which was reluctantly attended by the Protestants. The religious rift was steadily widening.

Left A contemporary engraving of the princes of the Schmalkaldic League. Leaders of the Protestant opposition in Germany, their hostility to the Council disrupted its working.

a council. There was a danger that Charles would support a national German synod, which would meet away from papal influence and which, in the cause of German unity, would be likely to tolerate theological views that Rome could never accept. There was also the growing threat of Protestantism in the north of Italy, an area which had hitherto remained loyal to the Holy See. Paul summoned a council to meet at Trent. The site was significant. Trent was acceptable to the Germans because it was within their Empire, yet its relative proximity to Rome gave hope of papal influence. The council's opening was fixed for May 22, 1542, but once again it had to be postponed because of renewed fighting between Charles and Francis. This war did not last long. After the defeat of France, the terms of the Peace of Crépy (September, 1544) obliged Francis not only to agree to the council but to send representatives. A new date, March 15, 1545, was fixed. By this time, Charles promised, the Protestant princes—the Schmalkaldic League—would have been defeated and forced, along with the French, to attend. Charles' expectations proved premature. The council was delayed another nine months, and began on December 13, 1545, without the Protestants.

But the council's vicissitudes were far from over. An outbreak of typhus precipitated a move from Trent to Bologna, the second city of the Papal States. The imperial representatives protested, and remained behind. In January, 1548, Paul III had to agree to return to Trent, but prorogued the council the following year.

In 1551 Pope Julius III reconvened the bishops. This time the Protestants unwillingly attended, forced to do so by the Interim of Augsburg (1548), a truce between Charles and the Schmalkaldic League. They refused to deal directly with the papal legates, and demanded that the bishops' oath of fidelity to the Holy See be abolished. They also asserted, as successive popes had feared, the doctrine of conciliarism, and demanded that everything decided in their absence should be discussed anew. But this session of the council did not last long. In April, 1552, the advance of the troops of the Schmalkaldic League of German Protestant princes threatened Trent and German bishops had to hurry home to guard their dioceses. The council met for the last time under Pius IV to confront the challenge of Calvinism, which was threatening France. The final session lasted from January 1562 to December 1563. On December 3–4, 1563, two hundred and fifty-five fathers gathered in the cathedral of Santa Maria. They not only promulgated the decrees decided upon in the final session, but reaffirmed those enacted in earlier years. The Pope gave his approval in January, 1564.

The first of the objectives set for the council by Pope Paul III—the reconciliation within the Western Church—failed to materialize. By the time the council met it was too late to heal the rift. Instead the bishops at Trent produced an amazingly successful, or at least durable, synthesis of the Roman Catholic faith. Even Catholics could no longer tolerate the diversity of theological opinion so common in the Middle Ages. The papacy needed,

St. Ignatius Loyola kneeling before Pope Paul III. He founded the Jesuits which became the largest and most zealous of the new Counter-Reformation orders.

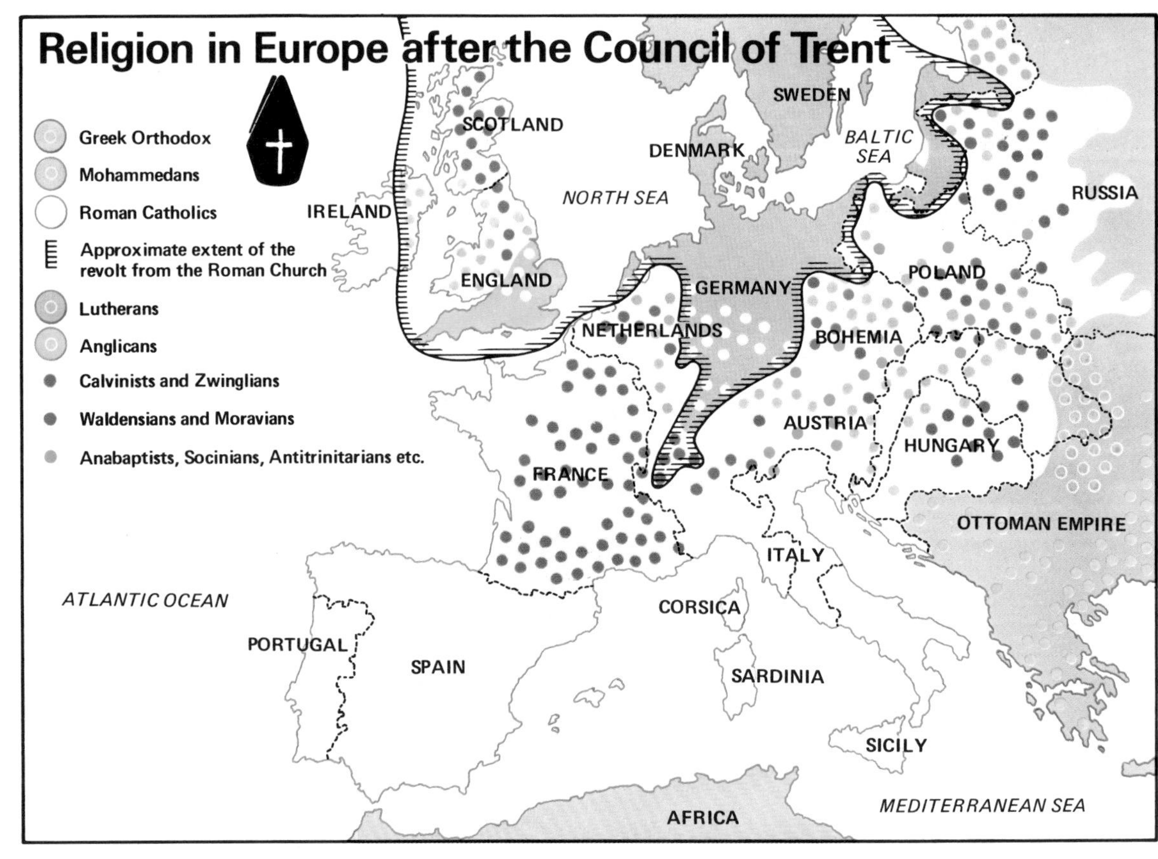

Paul III dreams of calling the Council of Trent. The achievements of the Council were to be very different to those he envisaged.

and was given, a clear-cut doctrine with which to confront Protestantism.

Some measure of freedom still remained, however. When Seripando, the head of the Augustinian Order to which Luther had once belonged, proposed a theory of double justification similar to that agreed at Regensburg, the council did not accept it. But neither did it declare it heretical. The decisive voice in rejecting Seripando's proposal was that of a Jesuit, Diego Laynez. He argued that the theory of double justification would undermine the sacramental system of the Church. The sacraments were one of the main areas of controversy between Catholicism and Protestantism, and were therefore a central issue at Trent. The council fathers asserted that there were seven sacraments, all of which were effective signs of grace. The performance of the rite itself conferred the grace *ex opere operato* (by the action itself). The faith and the state of soul of either minister or recipient were secondary. The sacrificial nature of the Mass was upheld, although how precisely it was a sacrifice was left an open question. It was declared that the presence of Christ in the Eucharist was suitably described by the word "transubstantiation," and that His presence did not depend upon the faith of the communicant. Luther's doctrine on the subject—"consubstantiation"—was rejected.

Each of the sacraments was debated in turn, and propositions agreed. But the reformers' protests had not been limited to theology. They had also complained of abuses in the Church's administration. At first the council could not decide whether doctrine or reform should have priority, but on January 22, 1546, it was decided that they should be discussed *pari passu* (together). It is difficult to say which of the two aspects of the council proved more important, but the bishops brought about administrative and disciplinary changes in the Catholic Church that have determined its shape to the present day.

Many of the reforms did not have an easy passage. One of the great evils of the Church had been pluralism, along with its attendant absenteeism. This was remedied by insisting that a bishop reside

Clothing the Naked by Giovanni della Robbia. One of the effects of the Council was a demand for the clergy to exercise greater practical charity.

in his diocese. There was a group at the council who wished to make the obligation of residence an obligation of divine law, others opposed this on the grounds that it would be an unwarranted limitation of the pope's authority. The eventual compromise insisted on residence, but avoided mentioning the nature of the obligation. Far too many benefices had fallen into the hands either of lay patrons or the curia. The council asserted a bishop's right to choose his own clergy. Only the local bishop could grant a licence to preach within the territorial limits of his diocese. The obligation of residence was imposed equally on the lower clergy. No priest could be absent from his living for an extended period without the permission of his bishop, and without finding a replacement. No one was to be ordained to the priesthood unless he had a living to go to. Clergy living in concubinage could either conform to the law of celibacy or abandon their benefice. Most important of all, seminaries—colleges for the training of clergy—were to be established, and the level of ecclesiastical education raised.

This is a bare summary of some of the most important reforms. They could not be implemented immediately. Indeed in some countries they were never officially accepted. A synod of the French clergy as late as 1615 approved the reforms proposed by Trent, but the King rejected them on the ground that they contradicted the ancient liberties of the Gallican Church. The decree *Tametsi*, which laid down the form of marriage service which the Roman Catholic Church would henceforth regard as valid, only came into force in England in the early years of the present century. Seminaries were established reasonably quickly in Spain and Italy, but progress in France was much slower. Trent had ordered the convocation of regular diocesan and provincial synods. As these depended upon the goodwill of local bishops, they met only spasmodically.

If local reforms depended upon the bishop, reform of the central administration in Rome depended upon the character of the pope. Some of the post-conciliar pontiffs continued to behave much as their rather less worthy Renaissance predecessors had done. Others were active in eradicating corruption and introducing changes. One of the first acts of the council had been to call for a new edition of the Bible. The Clementine Vulgate appeared in 1593. In the six years after the council a new missal, a new office-book for the clergy, and a Tridentine catechism were published. The *Catechismus Romanus*, a handbook for the clergy contained the new theological synthesis achieved by the council. To solve problems in interpreting the conciliar decrees the Congregation of the Council, a special committee of the cardinals, was instituted. The new-found vigor of the Church not only expressed itself by a renewed offensive against Protestantism—the Counter-Reformation—but also in widespread missionary activity. A Congregation for the Conversion of Unbelievers was established, better known by its later, and rather unhappy, name of Propaganda.

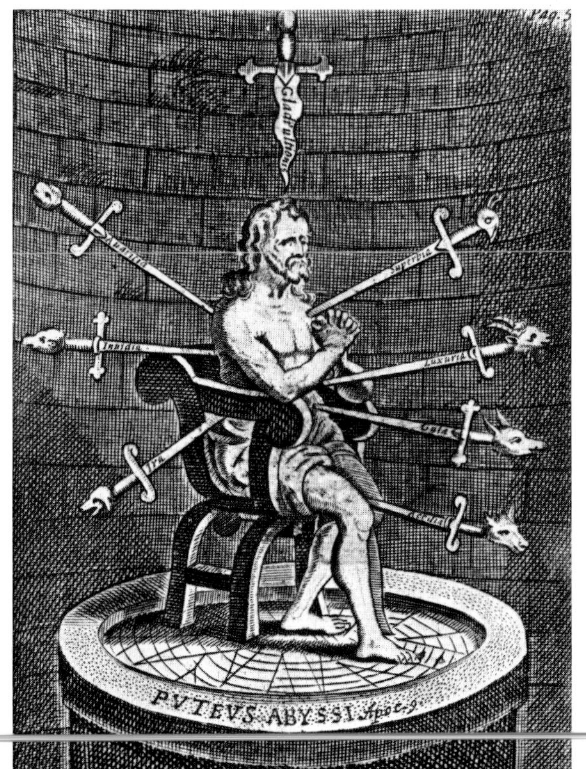

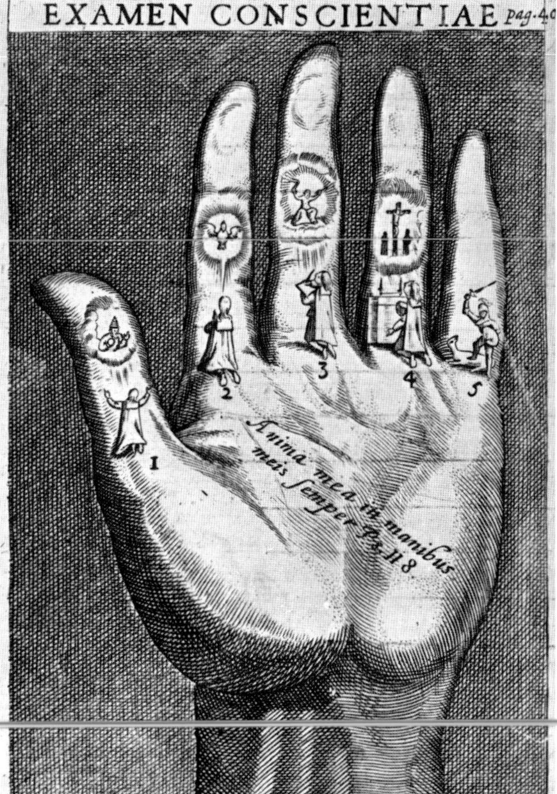

Another effect was the increased revival of personal piety, an example of which is St. Ignatius' *Spiritual Exercises*: The seven deadly sins (*left*); The examination of conscience (*right*).

It still exists with the less controversial title Congregation for the Evangelization of Peoples. A college for the training of missionaries was set up by Propaganda in 1627. Other colleges in Rome prepared priests to return to countries which had largely become Protestant. The central administration of the Roman Church was improved. Tighter links and better communications were established between the papal curia and local hierarchies. To preside over the central administration a real effort was made to appoint holier and more learned cardinals.

Almost the last act of the Council of Trent had been to promulgate a series of decrees on the nature of Purgatory, relics, the veneration of saints and images and indulgences. It was an act of defiance. It was a forceful reassertion of all that the Protestants abhorred. The Church's new self-confidence did not show itself only in theology. There followed a great flowering of Baroque architecture and music so offensive to Puritan sensibilities. After Trent there were no more talks of compromise: positions had been taken. They endured. The synthesis of the Catholic faith achieved between 1545 and 1563 survived centuries of bitter controversy. Until the Second Vatican Council met four hundred years later, it was hardly called into question. But there was one major subject which Trent left almost untouched: the nature of the Church. It was that problem to which Vatican II turned its attention.

MICHAEL J. WALSH

THE

NEVV TESTAMENT

OF IESVS CHRIST, TRANSLATED FAITHFVLLY INTO ENGLISH,

out of the authentical Latin, according to the beſt corrected copies of the ſame, diligently conferred vvith the Greeke and other editions in diuers languages: Vvith ARGVMENTS of bookes and chapters, ANNOTATIONS, and other neceſſarie helpes, for the better vnderſtanding of the text, and ſpecially for the diſcouerie of the CORRVPTIONS of diuers late tranſlations, and for cleering the CONTROVERSIES in religion, of theſe daies:

IN THE ENGLISH COLLEGE OF RHEMES.

Pſal. 118.

Da mihi intellectum, & ſcrutabor legem tuam, & cuſtodiam illam in toto corde meo.

That is,

Giue me vnderſtanding, and I vvil ſearche thy lavv, and vvil keepe it vvith my vvhole hart.

S. Aug. tract. 2. in Epiſt. Ioan.

Omnia quæ leguntur in Scripturis ſanctis, ad inſtructionem & ſalutem noſtram intentè oportet audire: maximè tamen memoriæ commendanda ſunt, quæ aduerſus Hæreticos valent plurimùm: quorum inſidiæ infirmiores quoſque & negligentiores circumuenire non ceſſant.

That is,

Al things that are readde in holy Scriptures, vve muſt heare vvith great attention, to our inſtruction and ſaluation: but thoſe things ſpecially muſt be commended to memorie, vvhich make moſt againſt Heretikes: vvhoſe deceites ceaſe not to circumuent and beguile al the vveaker ſort and the more negligent perſons.

PRINTED AT RHEMES,

by Iohn Fogny.

1582.

CVM PRIVILEGIO.

The spread of the Counter-Reformation was aided by the establishment of colleges to train priests returning to Protestant lands. The English Roman Catholic College at Reims translated the first English Roman Catholic New Testament (1582).

1544–1564 Fearing for her throne, Elizabeth imprisons

Henry VIII, Tudor despot.

The religious changes that took place during the latter part of Henry VIII's reign continued to be linked with his marital affairs, which were as rapidly changing as those of any self-respecting Hollywood movie-star. Anne Boleyn was beheaded in 1536, after she had been found guilty of adultery and of incest with her brother. Protestantism continued in the ascendant during Henry's next marriage, to Jane Seymour, which took place with indecent haste only ten days after Anne's execution. Jane died in the following year having at last borne Henry a male heir, the future Edward VI. Thomas Cromwell, in order to buttress his position, proposed that Henry should marry a Protestant princess, Anne, daughter of Duke William of Cleves. Henry was impressed by Holbein's portrait of Anne and by the description of her forwarded by Cromwell, and the marriage took place by proxy. But when she arrived in England, Anne proved to be extremely ugly—so much so that she was nicknamed "The Flanders Mare."

During these years the Reformation had continued. In 1536 most of the smaller monasteries in England were suppressed, and in 1539 they were followed by all the remaining religious houses (except for the colleges of Oxford and Cambridge and a few schools). This proved a valuable source of revenue to the crown, and at the same time a useful way of gaining the support of the gentry, to whom large grants or sales of land were made. In order to make it look as though the money was being used for religious purposes, six new bishoprics were set up and Trinity College, Cambridge, was founded. At the same time Wolsey's foundation of Cardinal College at Oxford was transformed into Christ Church. But the suppression was unpopular among the people, particularly in the north, and in 1536 there was a rising known as the Pilgrimage of Grace. In the same year the moderately Protestant Ten Articles were passed, although soon a much more conservative statement of faith was made in the Six Articles of 1539. In addition churches were ordered to display a copy of the English Bible.

Henry, willing as he was to confiscate monastic property, remained at heart a Catholic. His proudest boast was his title *Fidei Defensor*, given him by the Pope after he had attacked Luther. Henry annulled his marriage with Anne of Cleves almost as soon as it had taken place. As soon as Henry had shed Anne, the Duke of Norfolk, who had ousted Cromwell as chief minister to the King after the latter was executed on a charge of treason, cemented his position by marrying his niece Catherine Howard to the King. Catherine eventually trod the same path to Traitor's Gate that her cousin Anne Boleyn had walked, and Henry ended his matrimonial adventures in 1543 by marrying Catherine Parr, a widow of scholarly tastes—who managed to survive him. Henry's final marriage brought with it a more moderate religious policy, which satisfied neither Protestants nor Roman Catholics. The advocates both of reformation and of reaction were forced to wait for Henry's death.

Henry's unslakable thirst for military glory squandered his resources. The King's victory over the Scots at Solway Moss in November, 1542, was overshadowed by a disastrous campaign in France in 1544. Charles V came to terms with Francis I without consulting his English ally, and all Henry could salvage from his conquests was Boulogne. Yet for all his excesses, Henry VIII laid the foundations of a strong national state. To Europe's considerable astonishment, he had defied the pope and had brought both Church and State under his forceful rule in England and Wales.

Edward VI

Henry died in 1547 leaving the throne to his ten-year-old son. Defying the arrangements that had been made for Edward's minority, the prince's uncle, Edward Seymour, seized power as Lord Protector, took the title of Duke of Somerset, and unleashed a doctrinal reformation. The religious changes, instead of simply being ordered by the King as supreme head of the Church, were imposed by Act of Parliament. The small endowed religious foundations, known as chantries, were suppressed and some of the money was used to found grammar schools, although the bulk of the chantry land ended up in the hands of the gentry. The Act of Six Articles was repealed, and the clergy were allowed to marry. A prayer book compiled by Cranmer was forced upon the Church in 1549 by the Act of Uniformity, and the West Country rose to demand the restoration of the old liturgy. Before the rising was put down, Robert Kett led a revolt in Norfolk in protest at the enclosure movement. John Dudley (who was soon to become Earl of Northumberland) defeated Kett and conspired to replace Seymour. In October, 1549, Seymour was ousted and Northumberland assumed effective control of the government; he was to rule England for the remainder of Edward's reign. In 1552, a second, more radically Protestant, prayer book, with a virtually Zwinglian doctrine of the "Lord's Supper," was introduced, and the clergy were ordered to subscribe to forty-two articles which set out the essential basis of Anglicanism, many of them very Protestant in tone.

To remain in control of the government and to ensure the survival of a Protestant England after the sixteen-year-old King's death, Northumberland married his son Guildford Dudley to Lady Jane Grey, eldest claimant to the throne in the Suffolk line of the succession. He prevailed upon the dying King to bestow the crown on Lady Jane rather than on Princess Mary, the rightful heir. Against her will, Jane was proclaimed Queen in July, 1553, and she reigned for thirteen days. Meanwhile Mary's supporters rallied in East Anglia, and when an army sent to engage them deserted or disbanded, Northumberland surrendered and both he and Jane were executed.

Mary I's Spanish marriage

Queen Mary (1553–58) was a Roman Catholic both by conviction and by political necessity; if the annulment of Catherine of Aragon's marriage was valid, Mary was illegitimate and her claim to the throne void. Mary was determined to bring her country into the Roman Catholic fold, and Parliament was kept busy during her reign with repealing the Reformation legislation of Henry VIII and Edward VI. Archbishop Cranmer—whom Mary regarded as her chief enemy because of his part in the annulment of her parents' marriage—was burned as were three other bishops. The Latin Mass was reimposed. But despite all the efforts of Mary and of her chief religious advisers, Cardinal Reginald Pole (1500–58) and Bishop Stephen Gardiner (1493–1555), the old monastic lands could not be prised from the greedy grasp of the

A symbolic representation of Edward VI and the overthrow of the pope.

Mary Queen of Scots

Philip II of Spain with Mary Tudor.

gentry. The balance of power in England had been irrevocably shifted from Church to State; Parliament could now legislate on religious matters, and the Church's wealth, the main buttress of its power, had been drastically reduced.

Perhaps the Marian reaction would have succeeded if it had not been linked with an alliance with the Hapsburgs, who had rapidly been replacing the French as the national enemy in the popular imagination. In 1554, Mary married Philip of Spain, son of Charles v, but when Parliament opposed his plans to secure an English crown, Philip left the country. He returned only once, to ensure that England would join Spain in a war against France—a war in which England lost Calais, the last English foothold on the Continent. The seizure of Calais in 1588 ended Philip's hope of succeeding to the English throne.

Mary said that after her death the word "Calais" would be found engraved on her heart. By the time of her death later in the same year her failure was obvious to all. There was no chance of Philip adding England to the Hapsburg dominions. Henry VIII's younger daughter, Elizabeth, who was as firmly committed to the anti-papal cause as her sister had been to Roman Catholicism, and for similar reasons—her legitimacy depended on it—succeeded. With Mary's death it became obvious that the English Church would once again separate itself from Rome.

James V and Mary Queen of Scots

Buttressed by interlineal marriages, Scotland maintained the "Auld Alliance" with France until 1560. Within a year of the death of his first wife, Madeleine of France, James v married Mary of Guise. Continuing border strife with Henry VIII's troops culminated in the Scots' defeat at Solway Moss in 1542. James v, who was mortally wounded in the battle, left as his successor a six-day-old daughter, Mary Queen of Scots. She was betrothed to Edward Tudor under the peace treaty of Greenwich in July, 1543, but after Cardinal Beaton's bid for the regency, the treaty was repudiated by the Scottish Parliament. Protector Somerset invaded Scotland again in 1547 and captured Edinburgh in a vain effort to reimpose a marriage treaty that would unite the two kingdoms. The young Queen of Scots, who was already betrothed to the Dauphin, was whisked away to France leaving the rule of Scotland to her mother. The "Auld Alliance" had never appeared as menacing to England as it did in the years that Mary of Guise ruled a Scotland garrisoned with French troops while her brothers, the Duke of Guise and the Cardinal of Lorraine, dictated French policy.

The growth of Protestantism north of the border altered the entire situation. Enflamed by Cardinal Beaton's persecution of heretics, the Protestant party assassinated him in 1546, and in 1555 John Knox returned from Geneva to preach reform of the Scottish Church. The first Covenant was signed in 1557, and Knox urged the Protestant Lords of the Congregation to rebel. In 1559 they sacked religious houses, seized Edinburgh and deposed Mary of Guise. Elizabeth answered the Scottish lords'

Mary Stuart, Queen of Scots.

appeal to help by sending troops and ships north to drive the French from Scotland. The following summer she signed the Treaty of Edinburgh with the Protestant Council of Regents, thus ending the endemic strife between the two kingdoms that had persisted for centuries. The Parliament in Edinburgh abolished papal jurisdiction and approved a Calvinistic confession of faith, drawn up by Knox, that established the Presbyterian Church of Scotland.

Francis II, King of France.

The Dauphin, whom Mary Queen of Scots had married, succeeded his father as Francis II in 1559, but reigned for only eighteen months. Mary, who claimed the throne of England as the granddaughter of Henry VIII's elder sister Margaret, regarded Elizabeth as a usurper and never ratified the Treaty of Greenwich. After Francis' death she returned to Scotland. She longed for a meeting with Elizabeth and an assurance that she would inherit the throne of England, but her claims and her search for another husband exasperated Elizabeth. The beautiful, imperious and impulsive widow outraged her own subjects by her devotion to Catholicism, and the gaiety of her court at Holyrood House angered the Church elders, who soon questioned her fitness to rule.

Mary married the worthless Lord Darnley in 1565. Darnley was soon discredited for his complicity in the murder of David Rizzio, the Queen's Italian favorite. Darnley, in turn, was assassinated in Edinburgh in 1567 on the orders of James, Earl of Bothwell, who then seized Mary and married her. In a matter of weeks the Lords of the Congregation had routed Bothwell's supporters at Carberry Hill, placed Mary in Loch Leven Castle and forced her to abdicate in favor of her infant son James VI. Mary's step-brother the Earl of Moray, was named regent. In May, 1568, Mary escaped to England, where she expected to find support for her efforts to regain the Scottish throne. Elizabeth, who feared Mary's influence among English Catholics and was wary of her designs upon the kingdom, decided to keep her in captivity.

1564 "He Who Resists Power, Resists God"

Tsar Ivan IV *inherited from his father a firm belief in autocratic government together with a large and unruly aristocratic class—the boyars. Ivan adopted a policy of calculated terror, and by murder, banishment and execution for treason, decimated the ranks and power of the boyars and confiscated their land, which he conferred on his own loyal followers. In his successful bid to exercise all power, he earned for himself the sobriquet "the Terrible."*

Ivan IV "the Terrible," Tsar of Russia. By his policy of terror against the boyar aristocracy he imposed on Russia an autocratic rule which remained unchanged until the twentieth century.

Opposite The crown of the Tartar Kingdom of Kazan worn by Ivan IV. His conquest of Kazan and Astrakhan extended Russian control over the entire Volga and opened the way for expansion into Asia.

In December, 1564, Tsar Ivan IV ("the Terrible") suddenly left Moscow escorted by mounted guards and made for the small town of Aleksandrov sixty miles away. On January 3, 1565, he sent two public letters to the capital, explaining that he had been forced to abdicate by the "treachery" of certain members of the aristocratic boyar class. He had no quarrel with the townspeople of Moscow, but was thoroughly convinced that nothing could persuade the boyars to accept his concept of tsarist power. By February, Ivan had allowed himself to be persuaded to return—on two conditions. The first was that he retain the right to punish "traitors" as and when he saw fit; the second, that an independent state within Muscovy be created, known as the *oprichnina* (literally, "apart-land"), which would belong to the Tsar and be managed by him as landlord. This *oprichnina* zone would contain most of the estates belonging to the offending boyars. In effect, Ivan IV was threatening to abdicate unless he was given the power to redistribute boyar lands among his chosen *oprichniki*, who were to be recruited from among the families of the lesser, "service" nobility (on whose loyalty the Tsar could always rely). By getting his two conditions accepted, Ivan acquired both the right and the administrative machinery to purge an entire class.

Ivan's actions should be viewed in the wider context of the growth of Muscovite autocracy and the removal of traditional checks on the Russian sovereign's power. His predecessors, Ivan III (1462–1505) and Basil III (1505–33), had laid the foundations of tsarist absolutism so thoroughly that Baron Sigismund von Herberstein, the Austrian ambassador, could write of Basil III: "In the sway which he holds over his people, he surpasses all the monarchs of the whole world ... he holds unlimited control over the lives and property of *all* his subjects ..." When Ivan IV adopted the famous slogan, "He who resists power, resists God," he was simply expressing a logical, theoretical extension of his predecessors' policy of centralization. But at the beginning of Ivan the Terrible's reign there remained one potential check on the full development of Russian autocracy—the power of the boyars.

This class, whose forebears had been grand princes and appanage princes (known collectively as *kniazhata* or "Serving Princes of the Royal Blood"), were members of aristocratic clans that had contributed to the rise of the Muscovite dynasty, and of regional nobility that had gained status comparatively recently for services rendered to the tsars. Their numbers had rapidly increased with the growth of the Russian state. In the early fifteenth century, only forty boyar families served the Muscovite Grand Prince, but by the beginning of Ivan IV's reign, the number had increased to well over two hundred. The ancient princely families still found it difficult to accept the ascendancy of the Muscovite dynasty and, unlike the opportunistic "service" nobility, who could be depended upon to support any regime that gave them status, the hereditary boyars insisted that it was their traditional prerogative to choose the prince they wished to serve. Thus an open confrontation between autocracy and aristocracy could have occurred at almost any time between 1533 and 1565.

Tsar Basil III died in 1533, when Ivan was a child of three, and left the government of Russia to Ivan's mother, Helen Glinski, who was expected to rule in close consultation with the boyar council (or *duma*). Almost immediately, the *kniazhata* asserted their position. In 1537, for example, Ivan's uncle, Prince Andrei Staritsa, tried to persuade the boyars to ignore their rightful tsar and switch their allegiance to himself. This attempted palace revolution failed, but in 1538 (after the death, probably by poisoning, of Helen Glinski) two powerful boyar factions—the Shuiskis and the Belskis—tried to take advantage of Ivan's minority. For several years they squabbled

A sixteenth-century engraving of a Russian warrior. Ivan standardized the military obligations of the boyars on a feudal basis, setting each landowner a quota of armed men to be supplied for the Tsar's service.

over who was to take the important political decisions: the Shuiskis won the struggle in the end, and Ivan never forgot the way they treated him. Only on formal state occasions was he allowed to go through the motions of being lawful Tsar, and even then, he was not given the respect he thought his due.

On January 16, 1547, at a ceremony of his own devising, Ivan IV was crowned "Tsar, by the Will of God." By that time, Andrei Shuiski had been torn to pieces by a pack of Ivan's hounds, and his faction destroyed as a significant political force—this was the Tsar's way of celebrating his coming of age. The chroniclers expressed the hope that the boyars would, in the future, respect and fear their "awe-inspiring" (or "terrible") sovereign.

This hope was short-lived. Soon after the coronation, some of Ivan's courtiers began openly to express their annoyance at the Tsar's choice of a wife: Anastasia Romanova Iurieva was of non-royal boyar stock. It was felt that Ivan had degraded his *kniazhata* by choosing a bride whose family had no princely standing at all. Later in the same year, the boyars showed their disapproval of the Tsar's actions in a more effective manner. They took advantage of the chaos caused by the great fire of Moscow to overthrow the unpopular, but influential, pressure group headed by Yuri Glinski, Ivan's uncle and protector. The Glinskis were accused of starting the fire by black magic. For this "crime," Prince Yuri was clubbed to death (in church), and many of his supporters brutally murdered. At one stage, even the Tsar's life was in danger.

So it is not surprising that when Ivan convened the first full "Assembly of the Land" (or *Zemskii Sobor*) in Red Square on February 27, 1549, he decided publicly to denounce the boyars for persistently trying to harass his regime: they had, as he put it, caused "much blood to flow." The Tsar, however, was prepared to forget the past, and announced that in future he would work in closer consultation with his favorite advisers, Sylvester the Priest and Alexei Adashev, and with his informal, hand-picked "Chosen Council," in an attempt to create a more balanced relationship between autocracy and aristocracy.

For the next four years this arrangement worked well. A new code of law was promulgated, land inheritance was closely controlled, and locally elected "service" officials began to play a more significant role in regional government. Ivan increased the membership of the boyar council from twelve to thirty-two—thus cunningly reducing the influence of the most powerful princely families. This reform program culminated in the Tsar's attempt to standardize the military obligations of the boyars. A series of campaigns against the Mongol khanates of Kazan and the Crimea in the early 1550s had convinced him that the *kniazhata* were spending too much valuable time in petty squabbles about their seniority on the archaic "table of ranks" (*mestnichestvo*), instead of defending their country. In the future there was to be a clear-cut relationship between the size of the boyar's estate and the number of fully-armed, mounted warriors he had to supply for the autocrat's service. If the landlord was unable to supply the appropriate number, then his "surplus" land would be confiscated.

But Ivan's publicly expressed hope that the boyars would join with him in a new era of "Christian love" proved fanciful. Two events in particular convinced him that, if the Muscovite autocracy was to remain entirely secure, the boyars had to be destroyed as a significant pressure group. In retrospect, the Tsar was to see these events as major turning points in his reign.

At the beginning of March, 1553, a large and anxious crowd gathered in the Kremlin. They had heard rumors that Ivan the Terrible was dying of a fever. Some thought that the Tsar was already dead, and that God was punishing the Russian people for their sins. Others, who because of their social standing were allowed inside the palace, knew better. Ivan IV had been persuaded that his illness might prove fatal and, as a precaution, the last rites had been administered. But the key question was whether the nobility could be expected to swear allegiance to his son, the infant Tsarevich Dimitri, as sole heir and successor, or whether they would dare to support the other princes of Ivan's family—Yuri, his mentally retarded brother, and Vladimir Staritsa, his ambitious cousin, the son of Prince Andrei who had been executed for treason in 1538. Vladimir was clearly the most likely candidate.

Representatives of the boyar class were summoned to the Tsar's antechamber to pledge their fealty to Dimitri in the traditional Russian way, by kissing the cross. Suddenly the boyars in the antechamber, and even a few who were by the Tsar's bedside, began to argue furiously among themselves. Ivan was shattered to hear that many of them were refusing to take the oath. The excuse was that, since Dimitri was a mere child, his "succession" might lead to anarchy on a scale similar to that experienced by Ivan IV himself, during the years of *his* minority from 1533 until 1547. In fact, many of the boyars were simply asserting their traditional freedom to

Feast for a foreign embassy at Moscow. The English, reaching Moscow by way of the White Sea and Archangel in 1553, formed an important link in Russia's communications with the West.

choose the prince they would consent to serve. In a sense, they were testing the Tsar, to see if he was in a strong enough position to force his will upon them, for there was as yet no law of succession.

Eventually, Ivan managed to make himself heard above the general uproar: "Have you forgotten your oath to serve only me and my children? ... I will now hold the cross for you to kiss—I *command* you to serve my son, Dimitri!" But the arguments continued. One prince, Semeon Rostovski, even went up to the Tsar and shouted: "Why should we agree to serve the infant Tsar? We would do much better to serve the grown-up Prince Vladimir ..." In reply, Ivan denounced those boyars who refused to take the oath, and begged the troublemakers to have second thoughts about their gesture of defiance. It was not long before the majority had been persuaded by the Tsar's harangue, and finally Prince Vladimir, sensing that his chance had gone, reluctantly kissed the cross. The immediate danger had passed, but Ivan never forgot the occasion—for he could no longer trust his closest advisers.

As soon as he was fit enough, the Tsar's first action was to get away from Moscow, with his wife and son, as quickly as possible. At the Volokolamsk monastery he gave thanks to God for "miraculously" releasing him from his illness, and discussed with Vassian, an elderly monk, the implications of the melodramatic scene which had occurred at his sickbed. "How should I rule in future," he asked "if I am to keep my nobles obedient to me?" Vassian gave Ivan some "sound advice:" the Tsar should rule as an autocrat, accepting advice from his councils only when he felt like it, and he should never rely on the boyars for support. Prince Kurbskii, the powerful boyar spokesman, later claimed that the idea of "purging" the aristocracy was first suggested to Ivan IV during this conversation.

The coronation of the youthful Ivan IV. The first Russian ruler formally to assume the title "Tsar," Ivan established a chosen council of personally selected advisers to counterbalance the boyar council or *duma*.

Clearly, the time for appeasement was rapidly running out. The atmosphere at court was tense. In July, 1554, Prince Nikita Rostovski was caught planning to defect to the hostile Lithuanians. When interrogated, he admitted that he was not acting on his own initiative, but that his father, Prince Semeon Rostovski—the same boyar who had been so outspoken about Vladimir Staritsa in the Tsar's presence just over a year before—had arranged the defection as part of an intricately planned conspiracy by all the senior members of the Rostovski faction. They would show their independence of the Tsar by swearing allegiance to the Grand Duke of Lithuania. Prince Semeon had also been selling state secrets. He was condemned to death by the boyar council but, after appealing to the senior churchmen of Moscow, was sentenced instead to life imprisonment. Tsar Ivan accepted this leniency with outward calm.

Nevertheless, it was only a matter of time before Ivan could be expected to lose patience both with his close advisers and with the untrustworthy boyars. Sylvester the Priest and Adashev had interpreted the Tsar's policy after March, 1553, as a sign of weakness. Consequently, they made every effort to terrify Ivan into promoting the interests of their supporters. As Kurbskii subsequently admitted, their standard technique was to flatter the Tsar, then immediately afterward to "attack and abuse you with biting words, cutting as it were with a razor ..." This constant pressure had worked well enough during the early years of Ivan's reign, but by 1554 he was becoming noticeably more resilient. If he continued to have dealings with Sylvester and Adashev, this was only because he still needed their services to help implement his reform program.

In 1560, the Tsar turned on his two counsellors. On August 7 of that year, his young wife Anastasia had suddenly died. Convinced that Sylvester and

Adashev had poisoned her, Ivan proceeded to have them condemned by an extraordinary tribunal. Shortly after this, "the guilty ones" (everyone remotely connected with the "Chosen Council," as well as their wives and children) were exiled or executed without trial. Some leading boyars, such as Prince Kurbskii, were lucky enough to escape across the border into Lithuania; others were less fortunate. Prince Vladimir Staritsa was accused of "conspiring" to poison the entire royal family, and was ordered to drink poison himself. Those of Vladimir's supporters who had shown reluctance to kiss the cross in March, 1553, were rounded up and some were executed. Several others died under torture while they were being interrogated. The members of the Rostovski family who had been imprisoned in 1554 for plotting to swear allegiance to the Grand Duke of Lithuania were eventually murdered—thirteen years after the event took place.

Prince Kurbskii later wrote that the death of Anastasia had driven the Tsar mad, and that after 1560, Ivan lived in constant, irrational dread of "plots" against his life. Jerome Horsey, an English merchant who visited Russia in 1572, formed the same opinion: "He lived in great fear of treasons and being done away with." But when Ivan the Terrible himself reminisced about the events of the early 1560s, he made no mention of any sudden conspiracies. Rather, he listed those events which occurred in the earlier part of his reign, and which had convinced him by the mid-1550s that the boyars would never have any intention of supporting his regime. In particular, he laid emphasis on the anarchy of his minority, the aftermath of the great fire of Moscow and the plots of 1553–54. It seems likely that by 1560, Ivan had at last found the confidence to rule alone (as he had always hoped to do), and that he celebrated this discovery by punishing the "Chosen Council," the supporters of the Staritska, the Rostovski faction and any other boyar clans that had proved disloyal in the past. In January, 1565, when the Tsar threatened abdication and imposed his two conditions on the Muscovite people, he was negotiating from a position of strength. His autocracy had never been more secure.

The chroniclers describe the events of December, 1564, to February, 1565, in colorful terms. Ivan IV apparently left Moscow almost in triumph, with the fire of youth in his eyes; he returned, two and a half months later, looking like an old man. His right to punish "traitors" had been confirmed, and his weird *oprichnina* plan had been accepted, but he had still to ensure that the boyar class would never again pose a threat to the regime. The prospect was daunting, even to Ivan.

Between 1564 and 1572, the Tsar made full use of the right he had been granted, by extending the "terror" from individuals to entire towns; Novgorod, Klin and Torzhok were completely devastated, and their inhabitants exterminated. And the *oprichnina* zone was quickly set up. Originally intended to encompass most of the estates belonging to the *kniazhata*, it eventually covered half the Muscovite state. The original owners were either murdered or banished. The *oprichniki* (initially one thousand in number, but later at least six thousand) had to wear black uniforms, ride black horses and attach the Tsar's specially designed emblem—a dog's head and a broom—to their saddles. It was their job to terrorize not only the *kniazhata*, but any boyars who happened to live in their neighborhood. By the time that Ivan formally announced in 1572 that his insane creation no longer existed—and decreed that anyone who so much as mentioned its name in future should be executed—only a few of the *kniazhata* families had survived, and well over a thousand "traitors" had been despatched. A "solution" to the boyar problem had at last been found.

Two important collections of documents—both dating from Ivan the Terrible's reign—help us to view the purges in their historical perspective. The first, Ivan Peresvetov's *Story of Sultan Mehmet*, was compiled in 1549 in an attempt to persuade the Tsar that the boyars were becoming too powerful. Peresvetov was a Lithuanian immigrant who ran a small business supplying Russian troops with leather shields. Since he had no connections in court, Church or higher military circles, his *Story* can perhaps be taken to represent the opinions of the silent majority of Muscovite townspeople—traders, lesser gentry, small property owners, in fact, just those social groups which had recently been excluded from contributing to Ivan IV's first full "Assembly of the Land." In the *Story* Peresvetov criticizes recent developments in Muscovite politics, under the cover of describing life in Turkish society. He concludes, by analogy, that Ivan's powers are gradually being usurped by the "rich and indolent" boyars. The Tsar, like the Sultan, must beware of allowing himself to be dominated by the hereditary

Russian boyars. Members of the princely families that contributed to the rise of the Muscovite dynasty, the boyars considered it their prerogative to choose the prince they served.

Sixteenth-century map of Russia and Tartary with a depiction of Ivan IV in the top left corner. Despite some success in the south and east, Ivan's foreign policy was a failure; the foothold on the Baltic, gained briefly in the Livonian wars, was subsequently lost to the Swedes and Poles.

nobility; instead, he must create a new order of service nobility, based on military prowess and administrative talent. Peresvetov's *Story* provides a link between popular protest at boyar misrule in the 1540s and the willing acceptance of Ivan's two "conditions" by the Muscovite townspeople in 1565.

The second collection of documents—Prince Andrei Kurbskii's series of public letters, which he exchanged with the Tsar between 1564 and 1579—dates from a later time, when most of Peresvetov's specific suggestions had proved to be inadequate for Tsar Ivan's purposes.

Kurbskii's first epistle to Ivan explains in four pages why he decided to defect to the Lithuanians in April, 1564, and lists the wider socio-political repercussions that would inevitably result from Ivan's purges of the boyars. It elicited a furious, eighty-six page reply from the Tsar himself. Kurbskii claimed to be writing this open letter because of Ivan's violent displays of ingratitude toward a class that had always tried to defend Russia "with heroic bravery .... Thus have you rewarded us, your poor servants—destroying us by whole families. . . ." The Tsar's recent policies had caused an unprecedented disjunction in the state. By ignoring the advice of the boyar council, Ivan had shown that he was more interested in entrenching his own position than in stabilizing the government of Muscovy.

The Tsar's immediate reply—which was evidently written in a violent fit of anger—accused Prince Kurbskii of acting in a "self-willed" and "treacherous" manner. In common with so many members of his class, Kurbskii would have preferred the new Muscovite nation to be established on oligarchic—not autocratic—principles. Nations which are not "under one authority," wrote Ivan, soon destroy themselves. "Did God, having led Israel out of captivity, appoint a priest or numerous governors to command over men? No, he made Moses alone lord over them, like a Tsar." Ever since the beginning of the reign, "our boyars, those traitors whom you call martyrs," had been plotting to make the Tsar "sovereign only in word." They had refused to accept on any terms those policies which aimed to unite Muscovite lands under the centralized administration of the lawful autocrat—that alone justified the purges.

Peresvetov, Kurbskii and Ivan IV analyzed the relationship between autocracy and aristocracy in sixteenth-century Russia with rare insight—each with a highly individual (and partisan) purpose in mind. In their three different ways, they show why boyar opposition to the Tsar's concept of sovereignty was of such crucial importance in the development of the Russian nation.

Perhaps Ivan did overestimate the influence of the boyars and act in a psychotic, tyrannical manner during the second part of his reign, as Kurbskii suggests. Perhaps the only salvation for the Muscovite state was a policy of terror directed against the "rich and indolent" aristocrats, as Peresvetov suggests. In either case, the Tsar's own account reveals that *he* thought that every possible chance had been given to the hereditary nobles. Whether the "plots" were real or imaginary, there is little doubt that by 1560, the twin concepts of "Tsar, by the will of God," and "Autocrat" had been so fully developed, that they could not exist side by side with the traditional boyar belief in a "balanced" state.

CHRISTOPHER FRAYLING

1564–1566 The Empire is split following Charles V's

An allegorical portrayal of the abdication of Charles V.

After the capture of Tunis in 1535, Charles was again free to devote his attention to his huge empire. In 1538, the leading Roman Catholic princes of Germany formed a league at Nuremberg to oppose the Schmalkaldic League. The leading members of the new League were Charles, Ferdinand of Austria, the Duke of Bavaria and the Archbishop of Mainz. At the same time Charles opened negotiations with his old enemy and rival, Francis I of France. This led to the Treaty of Nice in 1538, which promised a ten-year truce—although in fact war broke out again within five years. The fresh outbreak of war made it impossible for Ferdinand to defend Hungary, and as a result much of that country fell into Turkish hands. But the war in the west was more successful for Charles, and in 1544, by the Treaty of Crépy, Francis was forced finally to renounce French claims to Naples, the southern Netherlands and Savoy.

In 1546, open war between the Schmalkaldic and Nuremberg leagues broke out. At first the Roman Catholics seemed sure of victory, but from 1552, when Henry II of France—himself a Roman Catholic—allied himself with the Schmalkaldic League, the position changed. As a result the Protestant princes were able to fight Charles to a standstill in 1553, while the French gained the bishoprics of Metz, Toul and Verdun in Lorraine, which had long been in dispute. By the peace at Augsburg in 1555 the religious question in Germany was more or less settled for a generation. The principle of *cuius regio, eius religio* (whose rule, his faith) gave princes the right to enforce their own religion within their territories, a major concession to the Protestants.

As early as 1535, Charles had begun to think about abdicating. In 1555 and 1556 he finally surrendered all his many crowns, having been the dominant figure in European politics for almost forty years. During his reign he had seen the Hapsburg territories strengthened, developed and enlarged; members of the family now held the Empire, the Kingdom of Bohemia and part of that of Hungary, the Kingdom of Spain, most of the Netherlands, the Archduchy of Austria with its extensions in Silesia and the Tyrol and Franche Comté. Half of Italy—the kingdoms of Naples, Sicily and Sardinia and the Duchy of Milan—were also in Hapsburg hands. In addition it seemed likely that England, whose queen, Mary, had married Charles' son Philip, Portugal and Poland might become Hapsburg possessions.

But, despite the appearance of a Christian Europe fast falling into Hapsburg hands, the reality was a good deal less favorable. The huge size of the Empire made it ungovernable as a whole. Separate regions were in practice largely independent of each other, and the Empire was in effect a group of nation states with their own separate ambitions. The inflation caused by Spain's enormous imports of gold and silver from her New World colonies was already apparent, although its cause was not. Territorialization in Germany made central government impossible, and although the Holy Roman Empire was firmly in Hapsburg hands there were family rivalries. Charles' brother, Ferdinand of Austria, wanted to succeed to the Empire, while Charles, wanting to keep the Hapsburg possessions united, was eager that his son Philip, heir to Spain and Burgundy, should succeed. In 1552 agreement had been reached that Ferdinand would succeed Charles as Emperor, but that Philip would become King of the Romans, which would give him the right of succession to Ferdinand. This was upset in 1555 by the Diet of Augsburg when the princes allied themselves with Ferdinand of Austria to force Philip to renounce his claims in favor of Ferdinand's son, Maximilian. Meanwhile Charles retired in 1555 and spent his last few years living in a monastery in Spain. Philip became King of Spain and the widespread Spanish possessions, while Ferdinand, who already held the Austrian domain, became Emperor in 1556. The final humiliation was that Pope Paul IV refused to crown Ferdinand because it was suspected that his son Maximilian was a Protestant.

The succession in Austria

Despite all his efforts, Charles had failed to create a unified Hapsburg state that would dominate Europe—his main aim. Ferdinand lacked the Spanish resources that had been available to his brother. He was forced to use his military power to hold back the constant and dangerous Turkish threat. Within the Empire, the Emperor was now virtually powerless, as the Diet of Augsburg had made it impossible for him to discipline the Protestant princes—a majority among the nearly three hundred principalities of varying size that made up the Empire. Although the Roman Catholics had an inbuilt majority among the electors—four to three—this conferred no power on them as they were in practice limited in choice to a Hapsburg.

The monastery of Yuste near Cáceres to which Charles V retired.

Antwerp

During the sixteenth century, the Netherlands—like the other countries on Europe's western seaboard—developed rapidly and grew in importance. The port of Antwerp in particular benefited from the decline in the position of the towns of the Hanseatic League and the shift of interest from the Mediterranean to the northwest as a result of the discovery of the New World.

The Antwerp bourse; an engraving from Ludovico Guicciardini's description of the Low Countries, 1531.

Antwerp had rapidly become the continental center for England's main export, cloth. The Emperor Maximilian I had favored the town because it was one of the few places on whose support he was consistently able to rely. The opening up of the Portuguese spice trade with the Far East also benefited Antwerp, and in addition it became a major financial center. The population of the city grew rapidly during the first half of the sixteenth century—probably from around 40,000 to 100,000, making it the third largest city in northern Europe.

Antwerp reached the high point of its prosperity at about the time of Charles V's abdication. The Venetian ambassador to Antwerp in the 1560s, Ludovico Guicciardini, was amazed by the city's prosperity, which he thought greater even than Venice's. Around seventy per cent of Dutch and Flemish trade passed through Antwerp, and Antwerp alone handled more outgoing and incoming traffic than all the ports of England combined. English cloth was the largest single item in Antwerp's trade and accounted for nearly one-third of its imports; probably well over half the cloth exported from England was sent to Antwerp. Both English and the finer Italian cloth were finished in Antwerp and then reexported as manufactured garments. But this was only a small part of Antwerp's trade. Many other industries—in particular, the sale of armaments made in Germany—were important. By 1560, Antwerp had become the largest port, not merely in northern Europe but in the whole continent. It was with only slight exaggeration Guicciardini wrote that Antwerp handled as much trade in three weeks as Venice did in a whole year.

But, if the rise of Antwerp's trade was caused largely by the expansion of Europe's trade overseas, so too was its decline. A massive superstructure of international finance was built on top of the trading community. As is often the case with large-scale finance, this depended almost entirely on international confidence. But, as a result of the huge influx of gold and silver from Spain's American colonies, Europe was caught in a dangerous inflationary spiral, of which the first sign was the bankruptcy of the kingdoms of Spain, Portugal and France between 1557 and 1560. All three governments had borrowed heavily from the bankers of Antwerp, who now found themselves in turn virtually bankrupt. The magnificent town hall of Antwerp, designed by Cornelius Floris, was begun in 1561, just as Antwerp's prosperity was beginning to fade. The city's decline was rapid. The bankruptcy of Spain was merely the first of a series of blows to hit Antwerp.

The war between Spain, France and the Dutch was to destroy Antwerp's position in the space of a few years. The Spanish blockaded the city, which had become a center of Calvinism and of opposition to Spanish rule. Because of the reduced trading possibilities caused by the blockade, the English Merchant Adventurers Company ceased their operations in Antwerp in 1564. The city was sacked by the Spanish in 1576, by the French in 1583, and again by the Spanish under the Duke of Parma two years later.

During the rest of the sixteenth and seventeenth centuries the focal point of economic activity in the Netherlands moved northward. Despite the troubles that were to affect the United Provinces no less than they did Antwerp, the north grew increasingly powerful economically. Amsterdam never came to hold a position of dominance equal to that which Antwerp held at the middle of the sixteenth century, but it showed itself better able to survive political, military and economic upsets.

Origins of the revolt in the Netherlands

The dangers implicit in the huge Hapsburg successes of the previous eighty years quickly became clear after the abdication of Charles V. Unlike his father, Philip II was insensitive to the rights of the nobility and the States General of the Netherlands, where representatives of the seventeen provinces met. But religious differences were even more important than constitutional disputes. The new religious ideas of the sixteenth century—Calvinism, Lutheranism and Mennonitism—all found a ready audience in the Netherlands. Charles V, although personally orthodox, had done little to prevent the spread of heresy in the Low Countries; to him heresy had been only a minor problem. Philip, more conscious of the responsibilities that went with his title "the most Catholic king," took a much more energetic line. He strengthened the ecclesiastical organization; the sees of Utrecht and Malines were raised to archbishoprics in 1560, and were made independent of Cologne and Reims. Fourteen new bishoprics, subject to Utrecht and Malines, were set up. This move was unpopular, and it was rumored that Philip was about to introduce the Spanish Inquisition. Particularly in the south, discontent began to boil over into rebellion.

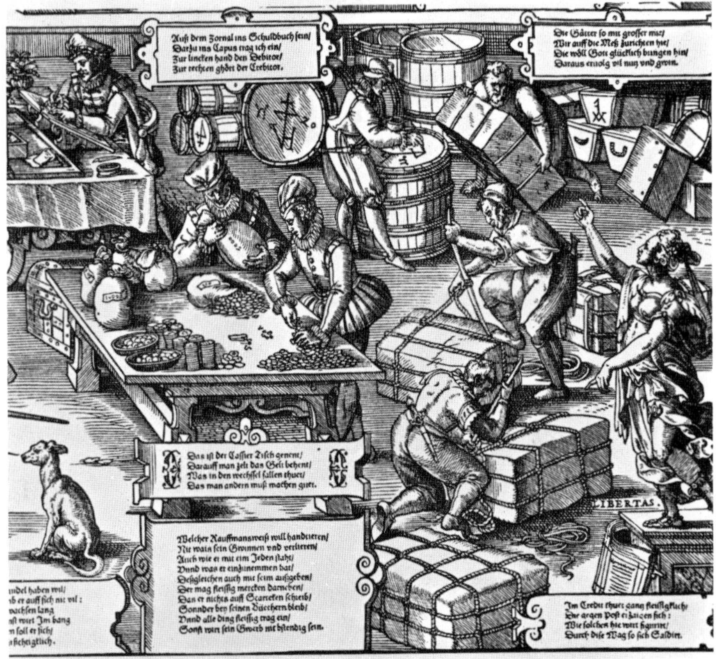

Commerce in the sixteenth century; detail from an allegorical engraving by Jost Amman.

HAERLEM.

The Revolt of the Beggars

1566

The accession of Philip II *caused grave problems among the strong-willed, largely Protestant nobility of the Low Countries. When a group of them presented a "Request" for more lenient treatment, they were described by one Spanish counsellor as "Beggars," a name they immediately adopted. The activities pursued in the name of the Beggars were mostly desecration of churches and looting. Nonetheless, these activities touched off a war that eventually led to the independence of the Netherlands.*

In Brussels on April 5, 1566, Margaret of Parma, half-sister of Philip II of Spain and his governor of the Netherlands, gave audience to a body of "petitioners." Their spokesman, Count Brederode, read and then handed over a "Request" subscribed to by hundreds of minor nobles and burghers of the seventeen provinces that then comprised the Low Countries. In loyal and respectful terms, they asked Margaret to get Philip's agreement to annul the decrees curbing the activities of Protestants in the Netherlands and an assurance that the Spanish Inquisition would not be established there. They claimed that the decrees imposed the Council of Trent's condemnation of divorce, ecclesiastical pluralism and other irregularities on the provinces, and renewed the old laws against heresy which Philip had earlier relaxed. They argued that they were thus laid open to accusations of rebellion, trial for treason and execution or the confiscation of their property. The decrees, they maintained, had already created an atmosphere in which civil commotion was imminent and in such a situation their houses and lands were exposed to pillage and destruction.

Margaret's council of state considered the "Request." Her advisers included William, Prince of Orange, whom Philip II's father, the Emperor Charles V, had raised from obscurity to prominence. William argued against the majority in the council who considered the petitioners "seditious rebels" out to better their fortunes. He insisted that they were "most loyal men of noble lineage." There were in fact among them some highly respectable, albeit militant, Protestants, including the Savoyard Philip de Marnix, Lord of Sainte Aldegonde, and William's younger brother Louis. But most were soldiers of fortune who had been unemployed since the wars terminated by Charles' Peace of Augsburg of 1555 and Philip's Treaty of Cateau-Cambrésis of 1559. Brederode was notorious for his debauchery when not on a field of battle and he was irredeemably in debt: concern for good government came curiously from his lips. Count Berlaymont, president of the finance council of the Netherlands as well as a member of Margaret's council of state, had no use for him or the men he represented. "Ma'am," he said, "is your Highness to be intimidated by *ces gueux*—these beggars?"

Despite the advice of the majority that she reject the "Request," Margaret handed Brederode a written reply in which she stated that she would consult her brother and in the meantime order moderation in action against the Protestants.

On Monday, April 8, there was a further meeting between Margaret and the petitioners. Brederode expressed modified satisfaction with her answer, and promised that he and his confederates would not force matters to a crisis. Margaret agreed to the official publication of the "Request," but when one of the confederates asked her for a written statement that they had done nothing inconsistent with their duty and a perfect respect for the King, she replied that she could not be the judge of their actions: only time and their future behavior could prove the sincerity of their words.

From the council chamber Brederode and his confederates went back to their headquarters, the Culemberg mansion, one of the many palatial residences of Brussels. Three hundred guests sat down to a banquet served on gold and silver plate. Toast after toast was drunk. The company, with the exception of Louis of Orange, was notoriously hard-drinking. They drank to their future as a confederacy. They discussed what they should call themselves. Brederode related to them Berlaymont's remark in council. Ordering a page to bring him a leather sack and money bowl, such as was carried by the professional beggar of the time, he put the thong of the sack round his neck, filled the bowl with wine, drank it at a draught and cried "*Vivent*

William of Nassau, Prince of Orange (also known as "the Silent"). Leader of the Netherlands revolt, he became first Stadholder or chief magistrate of the Dutch Republic.

Opposite Spanish soldiers executing Dutch rebels in Haarlem, from *de Leone Belgica* by Francis Hogenberg, 1585.

William of Orange pacifying Calvinist rioters, 1567. Attacks against Catholic clergy and churches in Flanders forced William, himself a Lutheran and a moderate, to show his hand and openly declare his opposition to the Hapsburgs.

les Gueux"—"Long live the Beggars." The sack and bowl were then passed to his neighbor who did as he had done, and so in turn did the whole assembly. This done, the instruments of the ritual were hung from a pillar. Each man put a pinch of salt into his goblet and swore:

> *Par le sel, par le pain, par le besache*
> *Les gueux ne changeront pas qu'on sefache*
> By this salt and bread and sack
> The Beggars shall stand firm
> Whatever trouble may result therefrom

The confederates went on to adopt a badge, a hair style and a uniform—gray doublets, hose and capes. Then they dispersed, Brederode going to Antwerp.

Over the next four months the atmosphere was uneasy, especially in Antwerp and the Walloon provinces. Calvinists and Anabaptists preached openly to gatherings of men armed with pistols, pikes, swords and arquebuses. Brederode harangued crowds which he led in shouting the slogan "Long live the Beggars." In mid-July the confederates assembled at St. Trond, near Liège, with some fifteen hundred armed attendants, and after two weeks of argument and revelry decided to raise a mercenary force of Germans to fight against a Spanish army, which they chose to believe was about to be landed in Flanders. There was then no such army, and the implementation of the decision to hire a mercenary force required more money than they could raise. Then suddenly, first in St. Omer and then, in rapid succession, in Antwerp and other cities and towns in Flanders, there were attacks on Catholic clergy and churches. In a fortnight four hundred were sacked—everything of value was taken, images were smashed, paintings slashed and manuscripts burned, to the cry of "Long live the Beggars."

Execution of the rebel lords Egmont and Hoorne in Brussels by the Duke of Alva. Alva's repression of "the Beggars" served only to fan growing Dutch national sentiment.

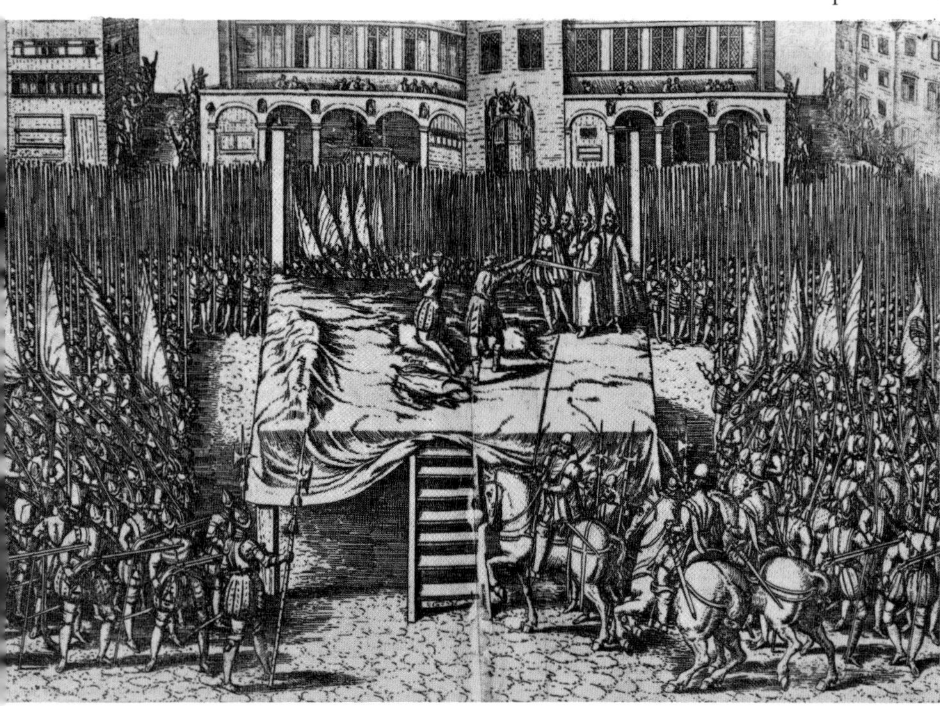

This iconoclasm was presented as a spontaneous revolt of the people, but the evidence of reports to foreign courts is otherwise. Richard Clough, assistant to Elizabeth's agent in Antwerp, Sir Thomas Gresham, asserted that it was all the work of small bands of "boys and rascals," aided and abetted by the women of the streets, drunkards and layabouts. Philip received similar intelligence; but the question of who had organized the bands remained. If Brederode and his Beggars, were they acting on their own account, or were they a front for people of greater importance? William of Orange, as Burgrave of Antwerp, ordered the execution of some of the rioters, but his fidelity to the Hapsburgs had been suspect for some time. Long before, the Duke of Alva had regarded him and his fellow members of the council, the Counts of Egmont and Hoorne and the Baron de Montigny, as conspirators who sought to acquire the Netherlands for themselves.

The key to these events, which eventually led to the establishment of the Dutch Republic, can be found on an occasion back in October, 1555, when, at a solemn ceremony in Brussels in the presence of Egmont and Hoorne, among others, and with William of Orange as his personal attendant, Charles v transferred his overlordship of the seventeen provinces to his son Philip. Charles had been born in Ghent. His accession to the throne of Spain had widened his cultural horizons, but his Flemish vassals still looked upon him as one of them. Philip unable to address them other than in Spanish, had a cast of thought wholly alien to them. When he had left for Spain in 1559, his appointment of Margaret, his half-sister, as governor of the Netherlands had been a sore disappointment to William, who had expected the post to fall to him. His was a disappointment shared by other Flemish nobles. The fruits of office under Margaret could be expected to be smaller than under another less closely linked with Philip. True, William and other nobles were given office in Margaret's council of state, but this was a body with limited powers. The *Consulta*, or inner council, was what mattered—a triumvirate in which there was only one of their number, Berlaymont, and he an honest and unambitious man. The other two members were an affront to them. Viglius, a scholar of no lineage, and Antoine Perrenot de Granvelle, son of Nicholas Perrenot, the "upstart" Burgundian chancellor of Charles' dynastic empire. Philip did not learn from the experience of his father, whose appointment to office in Spain of Flemish and Burgundian officials had irritated Spanish grandees into rebellion with popular support a generation earlier. He had thus created a grave threat to his inheritance—a discontented upper class.

Philip had been left a cause for much wider discontent—an army of 4,000 men. The Treaty of Cateau-Cambrésis bringing the war against France to an end had made this force redundant, but he had no money with which to pay it off. He had inherited a prodigious debt to the money-lenders of Europe which the gold, silver and other imports from the New World could barely service. While the troops waited for their pay, they had scant respect for the property of those among whom they were billeted. By 1561, they had been moved away from the Netherlands, but not before the specter of a "Spanish" army (Spanish in pay rather than composition) could be used as a bogey in stirring up opposition to Philip. The poverty of the mass of the people of the Low Countries could be attributed more truthfully to the depredations of their own nobles—the House of Orange was extremely wealthy—but immediate experience naturally had more force than the more remote.

Philip had also inherited a religious problem. Lutheranism had gained a foothold in the Low Countries as early as 1518, and Charles, seeing it there as well as in Germany as a challenge to his political authority, had contained it by savage edicts. Lutheranism had appealed to few outside the nobility, and the enforcement of the edicts by the city councils had not been difficult. But two other religious movements had gained more than a foothold before his abdication: Anabaptism, spiritually akin to the anarchism of a later age, especially attractive to the proletariat and impossible to suppress without the widespread use of armed force; and Calvinism, whose appeal extended to the men of middle wealth, prominent in the city councils. Charles' prescription of death as the sole penalty for all religious offences had been an irritant rather than a deterrent to the followers of these movements.

Philip II has long been regarded by both Catholics and Protestants as the champion of Catholicism. The assessment of his contemporary, Pope Sixtus v, was different, and in the light of the evidence must

A portrait of the Duke of Alva by Titian. Philip's military governor of the Low Countries, Alva ruthlessly suppressed all opposition and, setting up a tribunal more severe than the Spanish Inquisition, established for a while a semblance of order.

General view of Antwerp, in about 1540. Although the city was the world's largest commercial center in the mid-sixteenth century, Spain obtained little benefit from its riches.

be judged more accurate: "The King of Spain, as a temporal sovereign is anxious above all to safeguard and increase his dominions. ... The preservation of the Catholic religion is only a pretext for his Majesty whose principal aim is the security and aggrandizement of his dominions."

The possession of the Netherlands was seen by Philip and his advisers as vital to Spain's economy and security in a hostile world. The Netherlands were a market for Spain's considerable wool surpluses, Antwerp in particular, where in the year 1560 there were three hundred resident Spanish merchants. All trade to and from England and the Baltic passed through Antwerp. The Antwerp Bourse was the very hub of European commerce. From the Netherlands, Spain obtained textiles, mercury for use in her peninsular and American silver mines, weapons and other metal and metallurgical products and naval stores. Through the Netherlands came the cereals of which Spain was endemically short.

In Spain, the Netherlands were seen also as the ideal base for military operations against France, England or Germany, should the need arise. The obvious weaknesses were underestimated—the fact that they lay at the end of a thousand miles of often tempestuous seas, or a similar distance from Philip's Italian lands through Savoy and Lorraine, lines of communication which could easily be cut by squadrons based on French ports or regiments positioned on mountain passes. For that matter, the value to Spain of the Netherlands trade was more apparent than real. Spain, nominally the imperial power, was allowing herself to be exploited by the dependency. It was Spain that was exporting the raw materials for the very manufactured goods it was importing. Moreover the Antwerp moneylenders were demanding an interest rate of forty per cent on Philip's debt to them. A contemporary economist, Luis Ortiz, pointed out that the value of Spain's exports was no more than an eighth to a tenth that of her imports, but no one in authority took notice of him. It was axiomatic that the Netherlands had to be held. The question was how.

France had ceased to contend for the Netherlands after being defeated at the Battle of St. Quentin (1557). Elizabeth of England was in no position to act in Europe on her own account. The Holy Roman Empire and the Hapsburg lands were ruled by a member of Philip's own family. So the one remaining threat was from within, from the discontented nobles. As Philip saw it, two things were necessary. One was

The Dream of Philip II by El Greco. The kneeling figures represent the King, the Pope and the Doge of Venice. Philip's dream of a universal and centralized Spanish Empire inevitably led him to clamp down on discontent in the Low Countries.

to centralize the government. The autonomy enjoyed by the various "kingdoms" of the Iberian Peninsula was bad enough, but in the Low Countries there were not only seventeen provinces, each with its own political peculiarity (four duchies, six counties and two margravates), but within the provinces were numerous, virtually autonomous, cities. The other was to curb "heresy," since heresy was in itself a revolt against authority, and had frequently proved conducive to the destruction of political authority. Charles' edicts had been counter-productive in the Netherlands. His use of armed force in Germany could hardly be called successful in the light of the Peace of Augsburg and the right which this had granted princes to determine the religion of their subjects. The Council of Trent had pointed the way to the maintenance of orthodoxy, particularly by its establishment of a well-informed and moral clergy under good bishops. But nonetheless Protestantism—especially Calvinism—was on

The "Pacification of Ghent," redrawn from a contemporary print. By this treaty all the provinces united, regardless of religion, to drive out the Spaniards. The enclosure, symbolizing the Pacification, is guarded by the Belgian lion.

the rise. The success of the Calvinists could be attributed to the excellence of their preachers, especially at the local level, for whom the ill-instructed Catholic priests of Flanders were no match. Furthermore, there were but four bishoprics in the whole region, dependent for guidance on archbishops across the borders in Cologne and Rheims. The solution appeared simple. One of Philip's earliest acts, therefore, as overlord of the Netherlands was to lessen the severity of his father's decrees on religion. He also sought permission from the Pope to reorganize the Church there into three archbishoprics and fifteen dioceses. This was granted in 1559.

Here was a measure calculated on the one hand to improve the standards of the clergy and on the other, since Philip reserved for himself the choice of men for the new sees, to strengthen his authority. The new Archbishop of Malines and quasi-Primate was to be the most important member of Margaret's inner council, Granvelle, elevated to Cardinal in 1561.

The measure, however, gave rise to widespread discontent. The Flemish nobles feared, not without reason, that the new bishops would overshadow them socially and politically. To the provincial and city councils the measure appeared as a major step toward the centralization of government to the prejudice of their own authority. Popular agitation and rioting against it were stirred up by presenting it as an attack on local monasteries, since the revenues of those that had outlived their usefulness had indeed been appropriated to provide funds for the new sees. Not every bishop was able to take over his see.

The nobles went further. They represented the reorganization of the Church as the first step toward the establishment in the Netherlands of the Spanish Inquisition. Above all they worked for the downfall of Granvelle. They wrote and sent embassies to Philip who, in 1564, recalled the Cardinal from the Netherlands.

This concession merely encouraged the nobility to challenge every decision from Madrid. By 1565 it was clear that nothing short of full power would satisfy them. Brederode and his Beggars, however, were an embarrassment. The leaders were by no means ready to challenge Philip openly, and yet they could not allow the lesser nobles to appear more enthusiastic than themselves. William certainly, and Hoorne, Egmont and Montigny possibly, knew about the "Request" before it was read out in the council, but it is unlikely that they had a hand in organizing the bands that wrecked the churches in August. For one thing, the only Protestant among

The "Sea Beggars" taking Brill. Using this as their base, the rebels soon gained control over the entire Scheldt estuary and the approaches to Antwerp and kept alive the revolt against Spain.

The Milch Cow; Flemish school. A satirical painting of the situation in the Low Countries, with Philip attempting to get the Flanders cow to move while Elizabeth of England gives it much needed aid and William of Orange attempts to milk it.

them was William, and he a Lutheran, no less opposed to Anabaptists and even Calvinists than the Catholics were. For another, Montigny was then in Spain, having conveyed there the news of Margaret's meeting with the confederates and their "Request." What Philip's reaction would be to the sacking of churches was predictable, and they were not yet ready to pursue their aims, as now they would have to, in war.

Philip duly despatched from Italy an army of 8,800 infantry and 1,000 horse under the Duke of Alva. After his arrival in 1567, Alva established a semblance of order and a tribunal, more severe than any Spanish Inquisition, which in that and subsequent years condemned to death at least 1,700 "rebels." Egmont and Hoorne were executed in Brussels, Montigny in Spain. Now there followed eighty years of war in which the consciousness grew in seven of the seventeen provinces that they constituted a nation and should be a separate state, the Dutch Republic.

In that war the "Beggars" as such played no part. Brederode died of his debaucheries in Germany in 1568, but the name "Beggars" was subsequently assumed by rebel sea captains. Issued with letters of marque by William of Orange, these "Sea Beggars" formed an alliance of sorts with the Huguenots of La Rochelle and English pirates. Together they raided the ships carrying merchandise between Spain and the Netherlands. It was not they, however, but William Cecil of England who most embarrassed Alva at the crucial moment of the struggle to restore Philip's authority in the Low Countries. In December, 1568, Spanish ships carrying the money to pay Alva's forces took refuge in English ports. Elizabeth ordered that the money be escorted overland to Dover and across the Channel to Alva. Contrary to her orders Cecil had the money seized. Spain's German and Flemish mercenaries therefore took what they lacked from the people. Alva was constrained to impose a sales, or value added, tax, which infuriated the merchant class—and the cause of William of Orange and his Sea Beggars prospered. In April, 1572, they obtained a base of their own, Brill, and within a few weeks Flushing, all Zeeland and part of Holland were theirs. From Brill the "Sea Beggars" continued to harass Spanish sea communications for the rest of the century.

GEORGE HILLS

Under Suleiman the Magnificent, Ottoman

At much the same period as the emergence of the European nation-states and the rise of Mogul power in India, Japan was changing enormously. The civil wars between warlords competing for power, which had been a continuous feature of Japanese history for almost two and a half centuries, gradually gave way during the second half of the sixteenth century to a more ordered and peaceful society. Three great generals, Oda Nobunaga (1534–82), Toyotomi Hideyoshi (1536–98) and Tokugawa Ieyasu (1543–1616) were largely responsible for this change. Although they differed in approach and were often political rivals, all three had a vision of a unified Japan and sought to realize it.

A Japanese portrayal of resident Portuguese traders.

The arrival of Portuguese ships in 1542 brought Japan into contact with the West for the first time, and in 1549 St. Francis Xavier and two companions landed at Satsuma and set about converting the inhabitants. The princes of Japan were more interested in muskets than in missals, however—and it seemed likely for a time that the importation of more sophisticated methods of warfare would lead to unprecedented carnage. The Japanese found some guns in a wrecked Portuguese ship and began to manufacture "iron rods" themselves—perhaps the earliest example of the Japanese ability to take advantage of the technological advances of other countries. From 1571, the port of Nagasaki became the center of a flourishing two-way trade that was chiefly in the hands of the Portuguese.

From 1560, Nobunaga's power grew steadily and from being a minor warlord he gained control of Kyōtō and of the last of the Ashikaga shoguns, Yoshiaki. He removed Yoshiaki in 1573 and abolished the shogunate. Nobunaga's power was based on force (including the use of firearms), rather than on any office. Control of the Emperor—as much a puppet as ever—was sufficient justification for his rule. The centers of opposition to Nobunaga's power were the Buddhist monasteries, and perhaps as a result he favored the newly arrived Jesuit missionaries and permitted them to preach unhindered. His close links with the missionaries benefited both Nobunaga and the Jesuits.

Although the Jesuits were at first successful in Japan, both Nobunga's successors, Hideyoshi and Ieyasu, became deeply suspicious of their influence. As a result there was fairly frequent persecution of Christians, although it was usually only spasmodic and half-hearted.

China

In China, as in Japan, the advent of the West could not be ignored, although it made itself felt in a different way, largely by the introduction of crops such as corn. Christianity, too, was introduced,

Kumamoto Castle, a Japanese fortress of the late sixteenth century.

largely through the influence of the Italian Jesuit Matteo Ricci (1552–1610).

Politically, the era of peace that the Ming had introduced came to an end in the reign of Shih-tsung (1521–66). This was largely due to the apathy of the Emperor, who neither took much interest in the government of his country nor found an able minister to do it for him. Japan was becoming an increasingly troublesome neighbor, and disputes at court did nothing to help the situation. The emperors grew more and more remote from the affairs of government as the century wore on. The burden of rule was left increasingly in the hands of court eunuchs, but provincial governors were reluctant to accept their authority, and as a result the central administration was often unable to make its authority felt outside the capital.

The Turks after 1520

In the years after the death of Sultan Selim I, the advance of the Ottoman Empire was not halted. His son, Suleiman the Magnificent (1520–66) showed himself an able and ambitious general. Throughout his reign the boundaries of Ottoman power were pushed forward. He conquered Rhodes in 1522, advanced further into the Balkans and into the Kingdom of Hungary, most of which he conquered in 1541 after the death of John Zápolya, although a small strip of land running down to the Croatian coast of the Adriatic

A state procession of the Ming Emperor.

power reaches its zenith

remained in the hands of Ferdinand of Austria, and Transylvania continued to be held by Zápolya's son, Sigismund. The Prince of Transylvania was not, however, an independent ruler, but was in practice a subject of the Sultan, to whom he had to pay tribute. Parts of the small strip of coastline along the eastern shore of the Adriatic that had remained independent also came under indirect Ottoman control. Further east Suleiman annexed southern Bessarabia—the region where the Danube emerged into the Black Sea. The few remaining small Venetian colonies in Greece were also conquered, leaving the whole of the Greek mainland in Turkish hands. The remaining Venetian and Genoese colonies in the Aegean Sea were conquered too, although they posed no threat to Constantinople and had some trading value to the Turks.

Suleiman the Magnificent and his army.

On the Ottoman Empire's eastern borders the quarrel with Persia continued. Shah Ismael's successor, Tahmasp, was no match for Suleiman. Knowing that he could not defeat the Ottoman army, he refused to commit his forces to battle. While this prevented any disastrous loss, it laid open the western regions of Persia, which had long been in dispute with the Turks, to Turkish invasion. Suleiman was able to conquer Armenia and much of modern Iran without serious difficulty as a result of Tahmasp's delaying tactics. Suleiman even carried his warring into the Persian Gulf, where he built a fleet which was sent to harass the Portuguese in the Arabian Sea.

But Suleiman's greatest achievements lay neither to the north nor to the east but to the west. He was determined to wipe out the gains of Charles v in North Africa. With North Africa in his hands, or at any rate paying him tribute, the whole of wealthy and relatively ill-protected southern Europe would be open to attack. Neither Charles v nor Philip II was unconscious of the danger that resulted from the close alliance between Suleiman and the pirate Barbarossa. The Hapsburgs made a series of attacks on North Africa, but after 1535 none were successful, while the Turks in turn raided the Mediterranean coast of Europe, attacking towns in southern Italy and briefly capturing Nice in 1543. Charles v had given Malta to the seafaring Knights of St. John and they captured Tripoli in an attempt to make it impossible for the Turks to move into the western Mediterranean. In 1551, however, the Moslem admiral Dragut led a fierce attack on Malta, which forced the Knights to protect themselves. Before they had fully recovered from this, Dragut made a sudden attack on Tripoli, which fell fairly easily, a severe blow to the Knights' strategic planning.

The great siege of Malta and the fall of Cyprus

The conquest of Tripoli enabled Suleiman to attack shipping in the western Mediterranean. Philip II grew steadily more alarmed. In 1560, he gathered a large fleet to try to recapture Tripoli, but an

Naval battle between ships manned by the Knights Hospitaller and the Ottoman fleet.

Ottoman fleet caught the Christian ships unprepared, sinking many and forcing the remainder to retreat in disorder.

As a result the Hospitallers were isolated on Malta, while the Turks were able to bring larger forces to bear as they attacked the Spanish outposts in North Africa as far as Oran. The importance of Malta made it an obvious point for the Turkish forces to attack, as the fall of the island would have given them effective control of the Mediterranean. The Hospitallers, thrown into disorder by the loss of Tripoli, made strenuous efforts, under the leadership of their able grandmaster, Jean de la Valette (after whom Valetta, the Maltese capital was to be renamed), to strengthen the defenses of the island. In 1565 the expected attack came. A huge Turkish fleet brought an army of over 30,000 men from Constantinople. For five months the Turks besieged the island's main harbor, but—largely due to conflicts and divisions within the Turkish leadership—the Knights were able to withstand the attacks.

Despite the threat that the fall of Malta would have presented to Spain's Italian possessions—and, perhaps, even to Spain itself—the Spanish governor of Sicily took more than four months to gather an effective relief force, and by the time it arrived, the Turks had already raised the siege as they had almost exhausted their food and ammunition.

After his defeat at Malta, Suleiman again turned his attention to the Austrian Hapsburgs in Hungary. But by now he was old and tired. He was also beset by problems with his family. His two sons Selim and Bayazid had fought a civil war over the succession in 1559. Suleiman had eventually thrown his weight behind Selim, and Bayazid was executed. Suleiman did not long survive his Maltese defeat; he died in 1566 and was succeeded by Selim. At his death the Ottoman Empire had reached the height of its power. For a year after his death it showed little sign of decline, but it was increasingly subject to internal pressure. The new Sultan, Selim II (1566–74) was also known as "the Sot," being intelligent but indolent and much given to drink. He showed little of Suleiman's ability but managed to defend the frontiers of his empire, both in North Africa, where Tunis was recaptured, and in the eastern Mediterranean.

Although one of Selim's first actions on becoming Sultan had been to renew Suleiman's peace treaty with Venice, quarrels quickly developed on a number of issues. In 1520 the Turks demanded that Venice should hand over Cyprus. The Venetians prepared to defend the island, while the Pope, Pius v (1566–72), attempted to persuade Spain to help the embattled republic. But the Turkish armies were in a better position to attack the island than were the Venetians or the Spanish to defend it, and by the summer of 1571, the whole of Cyprus had fallen to the Turks. But the threat to Cyprus had at last alerted Philip II of Spain to the need for cooperation with Venice. It was no coincidence that the fall of Cyprus was followed only months later by the Battle of Lepanto; the Christian fleet that beat the Turks at Lepanto had been gathered to defend Cyprus.

1571 Cutting the Sultan's Beard

On September 16, 1571, a mammoth fleet composed of some three hundred ships weighed anchor in the Sicilian port of Messina and sailed for the Levant. Pope Pius V, *who had summoned that navy and blessed its undertaking, hoped that the combined might of his Holy League fleet could strike a crippling blow against the Ottoman Empire. The Turks' increasing boldness on both land and sea threatened not only Venetian trading rights in the eastern Mediterranean but the Pope's none-too-secure empire as well. Pius himself chose Don Juan, natural brother of Philip* II *of Spain, to lead the Holy League against the Infidel—and he chose well. In an epic sea battle that pitted the Christian fleet against the combined navies of Ottoman Emperor Selim* II *and his Near Eastern allies, Don Juan captured or sunk more than two hundred Turkish vessels and inflicted some* 25,000 *casualties. His stunning victory ended the Turkish naval threat into Europe for decades.*

The victor of Lepanto, Don Juan of Austria, bastard son of Charles V, from a portrait by Alonso Sánchez Coello.

Opposite Bruno del Priore's picture celebrating the victory at Lepanto. The figures in the lower left-hand corner represent Philip II of Spain, Pius V and the Republic of Venice, while on the right, Death stands over a kneeling Turk.

The first of July, 1571, was a day of rejoicing in Barcelona, Spain's principal seaport. On that scorchingly hot morning, a fleet of forty-seven war galleys lay at anchor in the harbor, and the city rippled with gaiety and excitement. Don Juan of Austria, half-brother of Philip II, the King of Spain, had just gone aboard the *Reale*, the flagship of the fleet, to introduce himself to its crew. The *Reale*, built in the shipyards of Barcelona, was painted red and gold—Don Juan's colors—and was bedecked with elaborate carved emblems. Multicolored pennants hung from the ship's rigging, and rose-colored velvet was draped over the planking.

Curiously, this day of triumph was to end with a humiliating rebuff for Don Juan. Upon returning to his quarters in the viceroy's palace, the young prince found a letter waiting for him from his half-brother, Philip II. The letter curtly ordered him to refrain from calling himself by the title of Highness and to confine himself to the title of Excellence, as befitted his station. Philip's note was a blunt reminder that Don Juan was illegitimate; he was the natural son of Charles V and a Flemish washerwoman, Barbara de Blomberg—and he was, therefore, a bastard. Don Juan began his proud reply to the King with the words: "God has made me the brother of Your Majesty. . . ."

In the eyes of history, Don Juan of Austria was the triumphant victor at Lepanto, but he was not the only actor in the drama by any means. Other personalities were to play equally important parts before, during and after the battle.

At the time of the Battle of Lepanto, Philip II was at his most powerful, and Spain was at the height of her glory. The Spanish regent had not inherited the great European hegemony that his father, Charles V, had conquered and subsequently relinquished. Nevertheless, Philip reigned over a completely independent Spain, which was no longer just another province of the Holy Roman Emperor. In addition, he controlled the Netherlands and Spain's profitable New World possessions, Mexico and Peru. As the ruler of Milan, Naples and Sicily, Philip also controlled nearly the whole of Italy—with the notable exception of Venice, which had maintained its independence ever since the ninth century, experiencing both prosperous and difficult times during that period.

The history of Venice has the rich, colorful texture of silk about it, and the flavor of Oriental spices. The Venetian merchants, creators of the sturdy *galeazze di mercanzia*, the huge trading vessels that were to prove their worth at Lepanto, were expert in the art of importing and exporting. For centuries they had been the custodians of the great international markets, and the principal suppliers of merchandise from the Orient to the Western countries. And from time to time the Venetians had found it necessary to defend their flourishing trade by force of arms. In the fifteenth century, Venice—which already ruled a Mediterranean empire that stretched from Istria and the Dalmatian coast to the Ionian islands and Crete—adopted a policy of territorial as well as maritime expansion. The Sultan of Turkey granted the Venetians exclusive trading rights within the Ottoman Empire, and in 1489, Venice annexed the island of Cyprus.

In Turkey, Selim II had succeeded his father, Suleiman the Magnificent, to the Ottoman throne. The new Sultan was very concerned about the annexation of Cyprus by Venice, for it hindered the free passage of Turkish ships across the waters lying within the vast Ottoman Empire. He determined that the Venetians had to be driven off Cyprus; if they refused to cede the island of their own free will, the Turkish fleet would have to intervene. Needless to say, the Venetians found the demands of the Sultan totally unacceptable, and when the Doge of Venice presented Selim's proposals to the Senate, they were angrily rejected as being contrary to the

GRÆ
CI
A

Philip II of Spain, who regarded Lepanto as a minor victory; he was more interested in stamping out heresy and crushing the Berbers. He was also jealous of the reputation of his half-brother, Don Juan.

The palace of the Escorial, the center of Philip II's vast empire.

peace treaty signed some years earlier with the Sublime Porte (the Ottoman government in Constantinople).

While the Venetians were trying to preserve their territorial possessions in the Mediterranean, Philip II of Spain was organizing an expedition to conquer the coastal strip of North Africa. Consequently, although there was little love lost between Spain and Venice, events combined to make a military alliance between the two states mutually beneficial. This community of interests needed only a moral justification, pronounced by some supreme and undisputed authority, to transform it into a true pact. The logical person to serve as this authority was Pope Pius V, and it was he who fashioned the Venetians' war of reprisal against the Turks into a religious crusade against the Infidel. Pius' creation, the Holy League, was ably supported by the fanatical Catholicism of Philip II.

The Holy League was confirmed by a treaty drawn up between Venice and Spain and approved and promulgated by the Pope, who was also one of the signatories. It consisted of a common declaration of war against the Turks and the Moors in Algeria, Tunis and Tripoli. It laid down the terms and conditions of intervention by the respective parties, and detailed the military contributions and the division of expenses between the two states and the Papacy. It was agreed that the conduct of the war should be under the leadership of three commanders: a Venetian, a Spaniard and a representative of the Papacy. However, in accordance with the wishes of the Holy Father, one paragraph of the treaty stipulated that Don Juan of Austria should become commander-in-chief of the joint forces.

The Holy League treaty was drawn up and signed in Rome on May 20, 1571. Two months later, on July 11, a convoy of eleven galleys, a protective vanguard for the main Spanish fleet, raised anchor and set sail from Barcelona. Nine days later, a second convoy, consisting of thirty-seven ships and led by the *Reale*, weighed anchor. It too was bound for Genoa. Don Juan stopped only briefly at this Italian port before pressing on to the Sicilian port of Messina, the assembly point for the allied squadrons.

The *Reale* reached her destination on the evening of August 23. By that time more than three hundred ships, thirty thousand soldiers, and fifty thousand rowers and sailors were gathered in Messina. Galleys and troops from Venice, Genoa, Naples, Sicily and the Papacy had joined Don Juan's fleet. Savoy and the Knights of Malta sent their contributions.

Don Juan carried out a lengthy, careful inspection of the force under his command. On board the *Reale*, he held meetings with his chief officers: the Genoese Andrea Doria, the Venetians Sebastiano Venier and Agostino Barbarigo, the Pope's delegate Marco Antonio Colonna, the Spaniards Santa Cruz and Requesens, and Alexander Farnese, Don Juan's childhood companion. The ships' captains received precise and secret instructions as to the order of battle and their own special duties.

The Turks, meanwhile, had left a trail of blood and fire behind them in Cyprus, where they occupied the main town of Famagusta, and in Corfu, which they destroyed. The city was in ruins when Don Juan stopped there on September 28. Two days later, he gave orders for his fleet to set sail for the Bay of Gomenitza, on the Albanian coast, for Don Juan had discovered that the enemy fleet was lying not far from the Turkish base of Lepanto, at the mouth of the Gulf of Patras in western Greece. The enemy fleet was composed of two hundred and eight fighting galleys, sixty-six galliots, or small galleys, and eighty-eight thousand men, twenty-five thousand of whom were soldiers.

On October 3, the Christian fleet left Gomenitza, and sailed south past the island of Corfu. Three days later, it passed the fortress of Preveza on the eastern shores of the Ionian Sea. During the night of October 6, the fleet moved south toward the island of Cephalonia, and anchored off Lepanto, north of the Gulf of Patras and close to the Cape of Actium (where Octavius and Marc Antony had fought their famous battle for control of the Roman Empire). At dawn on Sunday, October 7, Don Juan of Austria carried out a final inspection of his fleet. Everything seemed to be in order, and the prince felt confident, particularly when a light westerly breeze sprang up, giving the Christian fleet the advantage. At 11:45 A.M., Don Juan gave the order for the white banner of the Holy League to be hoisted on the mast of the *Reale*. The guns were fired, and the battle was on.

The Christian fleet, which consisted of two hundred and eight fighting galleons, six large galleys, and one hundred and two smaller craft carrying twelve to seventeen oars, formed a rectilinear front. Barbarigo was in command of the left flank of the fleet, and Doria of the right flank; the *Reale* lay in the center, surrounded by the galleys of Colonna and Venier. A relief galley, belonging to Requesens, lay next to the flagship, so close that the two were almost touching. Behind them, a fourth division, under the command of Santa Cruz, was waiting in reserve. The six huge Venetian *galeasses*, each weighing six hundred tons and each armed with 180 guns, were lined up in front of the main fleet. These enormous ships which were so ponderous that they had to be towed into position by galleys, were manned by a crew of one thousand men and four hundred and fifty rowers, eight men to each oar.

The Ottoman ships were spread out in a crescent-shaped formation facing the battle fleet of the Holy League. Scirocco, Pasha of Alexandria, and Ulüch Ali, Dey of Algiers, were in command of the right and left extremities of this curve, while the center of the formation was occupied by Pertev and Ali Pasha, whose flagship, the *Sultana*, lay opposite the *Reale*.

The two fleets joined battle, attacking each other with great violence. The Christian and Ottoman commanders-in-chief eyed each other warily from the two opposing flagships, separated by a distance of not more than five yards. Ali Pasha was wearing a caftan made of white brocade embroidered with precious stones, and on his head was a turban, wound around a steel helmet. He was surrounded by three hundred janissaries and a hundred archers. The two flagships collided with a tremendous crash. Drums were beating; bugles were blowing. The bright sun lit up the vivid yellows, greens and reds of the Moslem flags and glittered on the helmets of the Christian soldiers. Don Juan, standing on the forecastle of his galley, raised his sword high into the air, made the sign of the cross and plunged into the attack. Four hundred leather-booted Spaniards followed close behind, brandishing their halberds.

The battle lasted for five hours, and until the very end the outcome remained uncertain. Both the *Reale* and the *Sultana*, symbolic prizes in the contest, were invaded by the opposing side and then almost immediately abandoned. Turks and Christians alike displayed extraordinary valor; Alexander Farnese single-handedly captured the galley in which the treasure of the Turkish fleet was stored. A party led by Ulüch Ali, taking advantage of a breach in Doria's division, plunged forward to attack the galleys of the Knights of Malta, strangled the thirty knights, and captured the black flag of their Order. It looked as though the battle would go in favor of the Turks until the Holy League's reserve division, under the command of Santa Cruz, intervened.

Late in the afternoon, Don Juan himself managed to set foot on the deck of the *Sultana*. Just as he was about to capture Ali Pasha, the Turkish commander was struck in the head by a shot from an harquebus and fell dead. A Spaniard cut off the fallen leader's head and offered it to Don Juan. It was then stuck on the end of a pike and displayed to all the combatants. The air was filled with cries of joy from the Christians and cries of despair from the Turks at the sight. From that moment, the Holy League was assured of victory. Colonna succeeded in disengaging the *Reale* from the Turkish galleys that were hemming it in, and the battle deteriorated into a massacre. The Turkish galleys, inexorably blasted by the guns of the Christian ships, were set on fire, sunk or captured. The strength of the Christians, combined with the superiority of their armaments, was too much for the Moslems, despite the fact that the latter were more skilled at maneuvering their ships. By five o'clock in the afternoon it was all over; at the masthead of the Turkish flagship, the *Sultana*, the crucifix had replaced the flag of the Prophet.

A total of twenty-five thousand Turks were killed and five thousand taken prisoner—a total loss of thirty thousand men. Twelve thousand Christian slaves were freed from the captured galleys.

Not surprisingly, the whole of Christendom was filled with joy at the news of the victory at Lepanto. The Turks had suffered a spectacular and decisive defeat, at least when judged solely from the number of casualties sustained and ships lost. The Turkish fleet had not been wholly destroyed, however; the Algerian Ulüch Ali had managed to escape with forty ships. According to Pertev, the comrade-in-arms of Ali Pasha, the Christians' victory "had only

Andrea Doria of Genoa, who, acting on secret orders from Philip II, refused to fight. This unsuccessful attempt to reduce the effect of Don Juan's victory was part of Philip's campaign to subjugate the Republic of Venice.

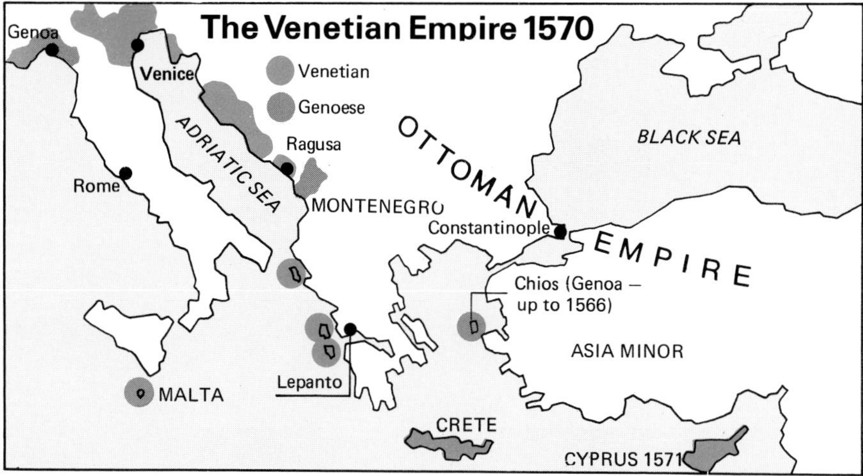

Alexander Farnese, a childhood companion of Don Juan, who was one of the leaders of the expedition.

A coin struck by Pope Pius V to celebrate Lepanto. The motto reads "O Lord, Thy right hand destroyed the enemy."

cut off the beard of the Sultan." His taunt implied that the beard would grow back again.

Nevertheless, the Republic of Venice had been saved for the time being from the danger of further attacks by the Ottomans, who had been menacing its frontiers, laying waste to its possessions and massacring its subjects. But for this setback, the Sultan might well have conquered Venice itself. All the same, Venice had lost the flower of its young nobility and a substantial portion of its fleet. Moreover, it had managed to maintain its political independence, but it was gradually losing its commercial supremacy. During the years that followed the Battle of Lepanto, Venetian galleys, driven out of the Levant, found that they no longer had any call to sail to northern ports. The English, unable to obtain the merchandise from the Mediterranean that they had grown to expect, decided to get it for themselves. They sailed through the Straits of Gibraltar, and soon established commercial relations with the Christian trading stations located in the eastern Mediterranean. They then went a step further, and opened trade negotiations with the Sultan, who badly needed tin for his guns. Thus, only ten years after Lepanto an English fleet of merchant ships flying the flag of the Levant Company was plying the Mediterranean. They sold English metals and manufactured articles to the Ottoman Empire and, in exchange, bought silks and spices from the Turks. These English traders were soon joined by Dutch merchants, who established commercial relations with the Sultan.

In this way, Venice was deprived of both its suppliers and its clients at the same time—to the benefit of the Turks. For the first time in history, northerners were trading in the Mediterranean, a sea that until then had been reserved for Mediterranean peoples. Venice, which suffered a great loss of economic prestige, grew apprehensive, for it still feared the possibility of a Turkish attack. To rectify this situation, Venice concluded a separate peace treaty with the Ottoman Empire several months after the Battle of Lepanto. The terms of the treaty were relatively honorable, but Cyprus became a Turkish possession once again.

The breaking of the pact of the Holy League by the Venetians, through their separate treaty with the Turks, did not anger Spain, as might have been expected. It had quite the contrary effect, for this move served Spain's interest admirably. And those interest were synonymous with the interests of Philip II, who had complete political control over the country. The personal policy he adopted in regard to the Lepanto expedition was so riddled with secret, subtle intentions that it often seemed to run counter to the national interests. For instance, when the Genoese Andrea Doria, who was in command of the right flank of the Christian fleet, abandoned his position and withdrew his forces—thus allowing the Algerian Ulüch Ali to penetrate the League's formation—this move was not in fact a miscalculation, but a positive decision not to fight. Nor was this refusal to fight a voluntary action on the part of

The Battle of Lepanto, by an unknown artist.

Doria—it was carried out on the secret orders of the King of Spain himself, without the knowledge of Don Juan of Austria. Philip II wanted a victory over the Turks, but he did not want this victory to be too spectacular. He wanted to save Venice only so that he could later annex it.

Although Philip II had seen to it that he did not become too deeply involved in the Lepanto expedition, he was prepared to pay the larger part of the expenses. The Spanish treasury had not merely run dry, but was also heavily mortgaged by costly loans contracted with the bankers of Genoa. However, the King of Spain refused to permit financial worries to divert him from his main objectives: crushing the Berbers and stamping out heresy. He expelled the Moriscos and Marranos from Spain—the Moslem and Jewish inhabitants who had been converted to Christianity—because he doubted the sincerity of their conversion and feared especially that the Moriscos might be the vanguard of an eventual Islamic invasion of Spain. Philip had good reason to fear the Moslems; less than a century had elapsed since Ferdinand and Isabella, Philip's great-grandparents, had succeeded in driving the Moors from Iberia. The King's religious zeal concealed a more practical motive, however. By confiscating the possessions of the Moriscos and Marranos, he was able to replenish the empty coffers of Spain.

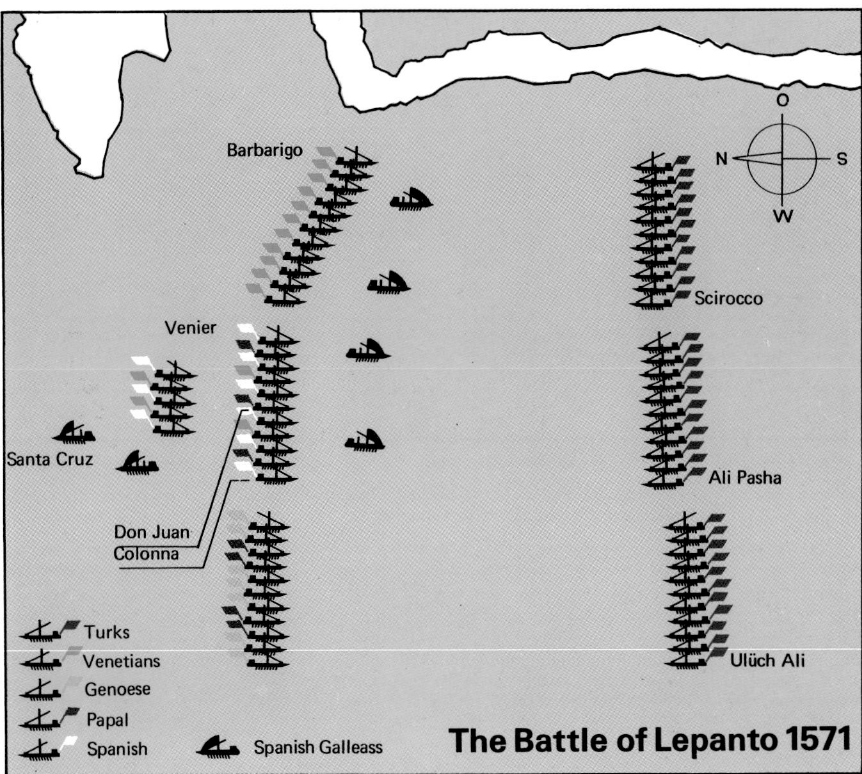

Taking advantage of the psychological effect of Don Juan's victory over the Turks, Philip II sent him off forthwith to conquer Tunis, in an effort to regain the Protectorate, which had been under Arab rule for many years. Within a month, Don Juan had captured Tunis; he begged leave of Philip II to be proclaimed king of it, but his request was refused. In any case, Don Juan's victory was only temporary: a year later, Ulüch Ali retook Tunis and the fort of La Goletta and exterminated the eight thousand Spaniards living there. Thus, Spain's military gains as a result of the Battle of Lepanto were negligible. Nevertheless, since he was at last safe from the menace of a Turkish attack, Philip II was able to turn his attention and energies to England and the Netherlands.

In short, the real victory of the Battle of Lepanto was gained by Christendom. The powerful Ottoman Empire suffered a decisive defeat in the waters of the Ionian Sea, a defeat that was to put an end to its territorial expansion. If there had been no Battle of Lepanto, the whole of Europe might have fallen into the hands of the Turks. Italy might have suffered the same fate as that of Greece, and Western Europe might have disintegrated in much the same way as the Roman Empire did during the fifth century. Moreover, the psychological and moral effects of Lepanto were profound, for this victory destroyed once and for all the myth of the invincible Turk.

JEAN DESCOLA

A mid-sixteenth-century Turkish quiver and arrows.

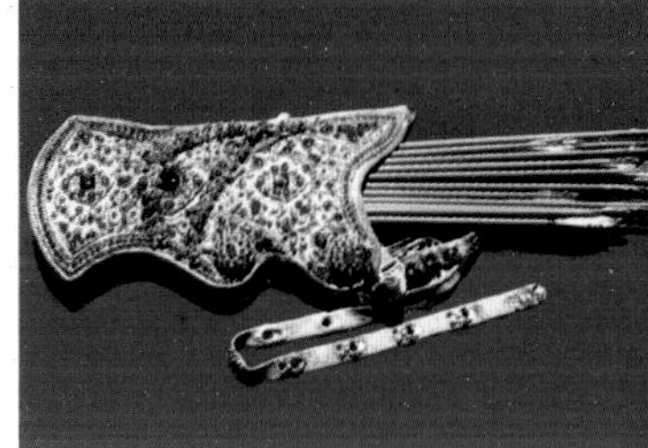

1571–1572 France is racked by wars of religion

Francis I, King of France, by Clouet; after his victory at Marignano the defeat at Pavia shattered Francis' Italian hopes.

Under Francis I the Church in France managed to avoid many of the difficulties that affected the Churches in England and Germany. This was largely because of the very close alliance that existed between the Church and the monarchy. A concordat made in 1516 between France and the papacy after the Battle of Marignano gave the King effective power to appoint to vacant bishoprics, and neither the pope nor the cathedral chapters were able to interfere. In practice, if not always in theory, the clergy were seen as ordinary citizens rather than as a separate estate, and the King was able to tax them without much difficulty. In addition the rights of clerical immunity from civil trial had been gradually eroded. Because the Church's temporal possessions were effectively under royal control, there was no danger of the widespread secularization that took place in England under Henry VIII and Edward VI. Henry VIII's Reformation was aimed at making the Anglican Church as subordinate to the King of England as was the Gallican Church to the King of France.

Because of the close control he exercised over the Church, and because of the identity of royal interests with those of the Church, Francis I was unsympathetic toward the Reformation. Lutheranism was not a serious danger in France, but Calvinism soon became popular. Francis pursued an energetic but unsuccessful policy of repression during the latter part of his reign. This repression of the religious minority was solely a domestic policy. Abroad, Francis continued to be dominated by his hatred of the Hapsburgs. He showed himself willing to make alliances with German Lutherans and Calvinists, and even with the Ottoman Empire. This combination of illiberalism at home and permissiveness abroad was to be taken up during the Thirty Years War by Cardinal Richelieu. The failure of Francis' attempts to destroy Calvinism and of his wild and romantic Italian ambitions was minor compared with his success in reducing the power of the aristocracy. He achieved the ambitions of the fifteenth-century King Louis XI by creating a centralized and highly autocratic monarchy—the pattern of the absolutism that was to flower so brilliantly under Louis XIV at the end of the seventeenth century.

But the road from the monarchy of Francis I to that of Louis XIV was to be long and bloody. Francis' Italian policy was expensive—France lacked the vast transatlantic wealth of the Hapsburgs—while the repression of heresy caused social discontent.

The tournament in which Henry II of France was fatally wounded by Montmorency.

Under Henry II (1547–59) and Francis II (1559–60) the internal troubles were for a time delayed. Henry was more successful in foreign politics than his father had been: the Lorraine bishoprics of Metz, Toul and Verdun were regained from the Hapsburgs by diplomacy; Piedmont was won from Hapsburg allies; Boulogne was bought, and Calais conquered from the English, who had held it for over two centuries.

Henry's aggressive policy was taken at the advice of the Guise family, which in the course of a few years came to have immense influence on French policy. The Guises, who were descended from the dukes of Lorraine, personified the paradox of France's aggressive policy toward its hereditary enemy the Hapsburgs—who were the champions of the Counter-Reformation—and toward the French Protestants (who were known as Huguenots). Henry's policy of persecution of the Huguenots was due largely to the influence of the Guises, who saw themselves as the upholders of religious orthodoxy in France. During the lifetime of Henry, the power of the Guises was built largely on the military successes of France's second Duke of Guise (1519–63); Henry himself was strong enough to control the family, but in 1559 the King was killed in a tournament, and the situation changed

Francis II, Charles IX and Henry III

The new King, Francis II, was only fifteen and a half, but by French law the king came of age at fourteen. This allowed the Guise family to take over effective power in France. Francis of Guise and his brother, the Cardinal of Lorraine, used their niece, Mary Queen of Scots, who was Francis II's wife, as their instrument. The Protestant nobility—which included many of the most distinguished men in France, such as Antoine, King of Navarre, the Prince of Condé and Gaspard de Coligny, Admiral of France—were quickly excluded from the royal councils. A group of discontented Protestants, disturbed by the increase in persecution, decided on a rising at Amboise in 1560. The plot, however, was betrayed to the Cardinal of Lorraine and was put down as soon as it began. Calvin wrote of the plot "Never was an enterprise so badly conceived or so stupidly executed." But the energetic revenge of the Guise family on their Protestant

Claude of Lorraine, Duke of Guise.

enemies, and a crude attempt to link the Bourbon family—which included Antoine of Navarre and Condé among its members—with the rising, gave the Protestants a unity that they had previously lacked. Condé was arrested and imprisoned, but, before the Guises could take any effective action, the King died.

Francis was succeeded by his ten-year-old brother, Charles IX (1560–74), whose reign was to be one of bloodshed and anarchy. Because of his youth, his mother, the strong-willed and able Catherine de' Medici, was made regent. She did not attack the Guises, but she released Condé from prison, returned Navarre and Coligny to favor and gave the Huguenots liberty of worship. Her policy of toleration and conciliation, which was favored by the Chancellor, Michel de L'Hopital, led to a slight improvement in the situation. The polarization between Roman Catholics and Protestants began to break down, and a third party (of moderate Roman Catholics) known as the *Politiques* appeared. But despite the calm at court, there was vigorous religious dispute throughout the country, as the Protestants illegally seized churches and the Roman Catholics fought to recover them. Civil war became more and more likely. It was the hot-headed Duke of Guise who eventually started it. He attacked a Protestant religious meeting and massacred twenty-three members of the congregation. Condé gathered a Protestant army together, while

Roman Catholics flocked to Guise. A battle at Dreux (1562) showed that the two sides were evenly matched—both Condé and the most effective of the Roman Catholics leaders, the Constable of France, Montmorency, were taken prisoner. The assassination of the Duke of Guise, whose army was encamped outside Orleans, and the incarceration of Condé, who was little less volatile, allowed both sides to negotiate for peace. The Edict of Amboise, which allowed Protestants to worship in public except in Paris, ended the first war of religion. It did not, however, end the religious disputes, and neither party regarded it as more than a temporary truce.

The regent was soon negotiating with the Spanish governor of the Netherlands, the Duke of Alva, on how to solve their common problem, the spread of Protestantism. Between 1567 and 1598, civil war was to become almost continuous. The Spanish aided the Roman Catholic party, while Queen Elizabeth of England and the Elector Palatine supported the Protestants. The crown, owing to the succession of a series of minors and weaklings, was too weak to dominate the country; Henry III, the brother of

Henry III, last Valois King of France.

Francis II and Charles IX, was no more able to rule than his brothers, although he lacked their excuse of youthful inexperience, as he succeeded to the throne in 1574 at twenty-three.

By the end of the third religious war in 1570, the Protestants were able to insist on substantial concessions. In addition to liberty of opinion and worship, Catherine was forced to allow them control of four well-defended towns, of which the most important was the large port of La Rochelle. King Charles now appeared to favor the Protestant party, and his sister married the new Protestant leader

Catherine de'Medici, mother of three kings.

Henry, King of Navarre. It was in order to regain control of the situation that Catherine agreed to the massacre of St. Bartholomew's Eve.

Jean Bodin

The wars of religion in France raised many serious political and constitutional issues. The struggle was by no means exclusively religious. To some extent it was political. Royal power over the country as a whole was threatened by Protestantism. Many of the great nobles sought to increase their power locally by demanding a solution similar to the *cuius regio, eius religio* agreement that had done so much to weaken the Emperor's constitutional power in Germany. In addition the wars were social. The educated professional classes, teachers, doctors and lawyers, as well as many leading merchants, tended to be Protestants.

More theoretical problems over the use of royal power and of the use of authority generally were raised also. Many sought to solve the problems, but the answers of Jean Bodin (1530–96) best expressed the mood of the time. Bodin, a former Carmelite friar who had become a lawyer, published his *Six Books on the Republic* in 1576. This was an attempt to explain that anarchy could be overcome only by the recognition of the state's sovereignty, which he saw as the sole absolute certainty that man had amid the shifting quicksands of life. He believed that the state's primary justification was to preserve peace and order. In order to do this, the state needed absolute power, a need paralleled by the duty of absolute obedience that is owed by the subjects to the state. Bodin did much to remove the state's dependence on religious justification.

Montaigne

The distinction of French philosophy and writing during the seventeenth century were due in large measure to the influence of Michel Eyquem, lord of Montaigne (1533–92). His influence was exerted through his three books of essays, which were only published in 1580 and 1588, although they had been written over many years. Amid the fury of religious persecution and civil war, Montaigne's quiet voice appealed for tolerance and toleration. His tolerance was partly due to his skepticism; he distrusted religious enthusiasm and perhaps religion itself, although he regarded religious values as being socially useful. His belief in man's basic moral qualities became a feature of French thought during the next half century, and was similar to the basic attitude of the party of the *Politiques*. It was to find its most developed expression in *De la Sagesse* (1601) by Pierre Charron, who was a lawyer and a theologian as well as a moralist.

But if Montaigne's ideas were influential, so too was the essay form, which he virtually created. His *Essais* were literally "attempts," made in an effort to test his mind. Their brevity, wit and argument made them immensely popular both in French and in English (into which they were translated in 1603). The great English lawyer Francis Bacon took up the form, although he refined and polished his essays far more than did Montaigne.

The massacre of St. Bartholomew's Eve.

The original "ivory tower": Montaigne's château.

The Massacre of St. Bartholomew's Eve

1572

The French wars of religion came to a climax on August 24, 1572, the eve of St. Bartholomew's Day. Catholics, under the leadership of the Guise family, rose up and attempted to massacre all of the Protestants—known as Huguenots—in Paris and the provinces. Although at least 5,000 people lost their lives, the atrocity helped unite the Huguenots and gave them increased determination to fight for their cause.

At about 2 A.M. on the night of August 24, 1572, the great bell of St. Germain l'Auxerrois in Paris began to sound an unexpected tocsin. It was the signal for one of the most notorious events in European history—the massacre of St. Bartholomew's Eve. The Catholic population of the city, headed by its leaders of the Guise party, fell murderously upon the unsuspecting Protestants—the Huguenots. The holocaust was intended to be silent, sudden and complete. How did it come about in a country as civilized as France, even in that age, that such a crime could even be thought of?

One of the most remarkable discoveries of the modern world is that people of different religion, and no religion, can live together harmoniously within the borders of the same country. Like that of the wheel, once the discovery is made it seems obvious enough, and one may wonder how men or nations ever managed to survive without it. The idea of mutual tolerance in religious matters, however, was by no means obvious in 1572 and is still not totally accepted today. Indeed present ideas on this subject in the West were the end product of a long struggle for supremacy between rival forms of Christianity. Eventually, it was realized that no supremacy was possible. The alternatives were mutual acceptance or mutual extinction. Wisely, civilization chose the former. However, in 1572 Catholics, generally speaking, envisaged the idea of living peaceably side by side with the devotees of other religions no more than did Protestants. Where the dissident religious minority was militant, as in France, the situation easily boiled over into civil war.

The French wars of religion began in 1562, when a number of Huguenots were killed while at service in their church at Wassy on Sunday, March 1. This event seemingly was no part of the original intention of the Catholic leader, Duke Francis of Guise. But not for the first time in history, an explosive situation was sparked by chance rather than intention.

Immediately before the first war broke out, Protestants and Catholics both tried to kidnap the young King Charles IX, so that under the cover of royal authority they could do what they wanted with a semblance of right. During the war, the Catholics, led by the Guises appealed to the Pope and to Philip II of Spain, while the Huguenots, led by the Prince of Condé, brought in German mercenaries, and signed a treaty with Elizabeth I of England. It is probable that the war would have ended with a resounding Huguenot defeat had it not been for another murder, this time of the Catholic leader, Francis of Guise. Guise was killed by a Huguenot in February, 1563, and the principal Huguenot leader, Gaspard de Coligny, was felt by many to be implicated in the killing, or at least to have done too little to prevent it. This untimely death of their leader obliged the Catholics to accept a peace in March, 1563.

Peace also met the desires of that remarkable woman, Catherine de' Medici. Wife of a king, Henry II, and mother of three more, Francis II, who died in 1560, Charles IX then reigning, and Henry III to follow, Catherine had learned to wait and calculate. She was the perfect Renaissance princess according to the Machiavellian ideal: not gratuitously cruel, but ruthless when occasion seemed to demand it. Her own attitude to religion was ambiguous, but she well realized its importance to others, and to herself as a factor in temporal politics. Recognizing the force of each, her main intention was to hold Catholicism and Protestantism in balance, however precarious. Convinced that she alone understood the real needs of France, she made every effort to keep Charles IX a puppet in her own hands. This balancing act was threatened with disaster when Protestant and Catholic alike took to settling their differences by force of arms and the assassin's dagger.

Catherine de'Medici by François Clouet. Formerly Queen-Regent in her own right and mother of three kings, Catherine wielded great power in the state, prevailing upon the King to sanction the massacre of French Protestant (Huguenot) leaders.

Opposite The massacre of St. Bartholomew's Eve, by François Dubois. The three-day slaughter of French Protestants was as useless as it was savage, confirming them in their conviction and stiffening their resolve to fight back.

Right A massacre of Huguenots at Cahors in 1561; from a contemporary engraving. Persecution compelled the Huguenots to take up arms and form a political party. The ensuing wars of religion thus formed part of a political and civil struggle for control of the government.

Opposite Henry of Lorraine, Duke of Guise and determined leader of the Catholic party. He directed the manhunt on St. Bartholomew's Eve.

Proscription of Huguenots in Paris. The St. Bartholomew's massacre was only the most notorious incident in the spiralling sectarian violence in France of the 1560s.

It is generally accepted that civil wars are more ruthlessly fought than others. The whole of France became in the 1560s an arena for a competition in beastliness. The starkest part of the tragedy lay in the irony that both sides fought for what was ostensibly a religion of love. Certainly, each side felt it was fighting for survival. The strife dragged on to the Peace of St. Germain in 1570. But this left the Protestants with what seemed to their opponents an altogether unfair advantage. Not only were they guaranteed in the possession of four places of refuge, but the highest state offices were opened to them. Their leader, Admiral Coligny, became a member of the King's Privy Council. What the Catholics—still the vast majority in France—feared was that this was not a step to coexistence but to a point of vantage from which the Huguenots would destroy them without pity. By this time, King Charles had accepted his mother's policy of coexistence with the Huguenots, as many thought, only too well. Indeed, he now preferred Huguenot friends and advisers to any others. Catherine herself began to be excluded, and this exclusion began to weigh on her increasingly. Young Charles' leanings to the Huguenots were not surprising. Their leaders, especially Coligny, were men of courage, charm and resource. Coligny, originally chosen by Catherine herself as the young King's mentor, now bid fair to displace her. This meant, as she saw it, ruin not only for herself but for France, since the necessary balance of beliefs and forces would be upset.

Catherine and the Catholics now grouped themselves around young Henry, third Duke of Guise, nephew of the murdered Francis. Duke Henry and King Charles might have been friends; they were roughly the same age. But the King was sickly and ailing while Henry was robust, physically attractive and already experienced in war. Charles could only envy the other for all the things he could not be himself and Henry had envious eyes on the crown. Meanwhile, in 1572, the Huguenot Admiral of France was a man some fifty-three years old; too old to be a rival, but old enough for the young King to call "Father," and respect him as such.

All boded ill for the Catholics. What the Huguenots could not gain by war, it seemed they would now gain by diplomacy and royal favor, despite the general wishes of France, and above all Paris. The 210,000 inhabitants of Paris were seething. Student-power is not an exclusively modern phenomenon. London had apprentices' riots and Paris had its violent demonstrations led by students of the University. There were also some 7,000 professional thieves, and another 8,000 tramps and beggars. And to swell the crowd-scene were the household retinues of all the notables visiting Paris for the wedding of Catherine's daughter, Margaret, to Henry of Navarre. The forces of order themselves were quite liable to turn their hand against social groups they disliked. Already they had looted and burned some of the Huguenot churches in the city in revenge for Huguenot outrages elsewhere. In-

Huguenot rioters looting a Catholic church and destroying sacred images. No more tolerant of other creeds than France's Catholic majority, the militant Huguenots were responsible for a series of outrages.

Opposite Admiral Coligny wounded; a painting by Giorgio Vasari. Catherine de'Medici sponsored the assassination attempt of August 22, 1572. Although this miscarried, de Coligny was personally executed by the Duke of Guise on St. Bartholomew's Eve.

evitably the priests were on the side of offended orthodoxy and vehemently attacked Huguenots in their sermons. But a war of words was not enough for many who felt better able to express themselves by blows.

Nevertheless, one cannot blame the St. Bartholomew demonstration simply on the mob. The pressure on the Catholic cause seemed to many to have reached desperation point on August 18, 1572, when Margaret of Valois, Catherine's daughter and a Catholic, married Henry of Bourbon, King of Navarre. This was the future Henry IV who was to become a convert to Catholicism—but on the day of his wedding and for many years afterward was a Protestant. It meant that one day the throne of France itself might be occupied by a Protestant; and if the Catholics cherished any illusion as to what that might mean for themselves, they had only to look to other kingdoms, including England, that had already changed their religion. Moreover, since their good fortune in winning the King's favor, many of the Huguenots had waxed arrogant. Coligny himself made no attempt to conceal the promised extent of the King's future favor. True, immediately after his own marriage to Elizabeth of Hapsburg, King Charles put off discussing the religious question with Coligny, but with the assurance: "Father, give me leave to amuse myself for four or five days, and after that, I promise on my royal word that I will make you happy: you and everyone else of your religion!"

Furthermore, Coligny in spite of adverse decisions in the council meetings of August 6 and 9, was still pushing for war with Spain. It was with reference to this that he was reported as saying to Catherine: "Madame, the King is avoiding a war which promises to bring him great advantages. God grant he does not involve himself in another which he cannot avoid!" This might have been taken to refer to the war in the Low Countries. In the event, a nervous Catherine decided that it referred to yet another civil war which Coligny and his Huguenot friends were quite capable of beginning at that moment. If this happened, and if this time the Huguenots won a decisive victory, the way to endless bloodshed might be opened.

Not the first in history to do so, Catherine succumbed to that most terrible of temptations for a ruler; the shedding of a little blood in order to prevent the shedding of much more. The Queen Dowager of France decided that Coligny must be removed by assassination. This decision does not make her uniquely wicked. In all times and ages down to our own, assassination has sometimes seemed the only way, or paradoxically, the least bloody way, out of a political impasse. Few people on the Allied side during World War II felt any disapproval of the German officers' attempt to assassinate Adolf Hitler. By Catherine's time the principle was well established.

Charles de Louviers, Lord of Maurevert, according to the Duke of Anjou, cheerfully accepted the commission of Catherine and her friends to make a bloody end of Gaspar de Coligny. It was Coligny's sheer good fortune that saved him. He made an unconscious avoiding movement at the very moment the assassin pressed the trigger on the morning of August 22 and Coligny escaped from the two bullets with a wounded hand and arm. The effect on his cause was inevitable. The Huguenots, now more united than ever, were ready to rise at a moment's notice. Indeed the Venetian envoy Michele reported their threat that the Admiral's arm would cost the arms of 40,000 men.

As the historian Ludwig von Pastor aptly cited in his *History of the Popes*: "This is the curse of an evil act, that it must needs go on producing evil." Catherine felt impelled by the failure of her first choice to push on relentlessly to an even more ghastly deed to ward off total failure. The solution now was to kill not only Coligny, but the other Huguenot leaders as well, and indeed, as many of their followers as possible.

The evidence for the events of August 22 to 24 is confused and contradictory. As usually happens when sources contradict themselves, historians commonly believe the evidence that agrees best with their own convictions and prejudices. At least it now seems certain that the massacre in the small hours of August 24 was an *ad hoc* expedient and not a crime long premeditated. Emotion still surrounds the scene like a strong magnetic field deflecting every effort to pierce the heart of the mystery. Nevertheless, the main lines and the principal responsibility for the carnage seem clear. Catherine, the Duke of Guise and the King himself, who was somehow brought finally to consent to the slaughter of his erstwhile friends, must bear the main responsibility. The motion initiated in the court swept downward in an ever widening holocaust, and seized most of France in a passing frenzy.

A portrait of King Charles IX by Clouet. An ineffectual ruler, the unprepossessing Charles was wholly under his mother's sway, his veneration for de Coligny notwithstanding.

The massacre began in Paris. Every effort was made to preserve an element of surprise, and to avoid confusing friends and enemies. So the Catholics wore a white sleeve, and a white cross in their caps. But cruelty and injustice are indiscriminate and many an old and dubious score was settled. The Catholic philosopher Pierre Ramus was murdered by a discredited rival. At the same time, there were Protestants who were rescued by Catholics. But when the news of the events in Paris reached the provinces, similar nightmare scenes were enacted in many important towns and cities. An occasional candle shone out amid the gloom. "At Nimes" we are told, "where the rivers had run with the blood of murdered Catholics, the inhabitants had so great magnanimity as not to touch a hair of the heads of their mortal enemies. At Vienne the Archbishop, Gribaldi, saved the threatened heretics from death. . . . At Lisieux, where the Bishop, Jean Le Hennuyer, protected the Huguenots, they almost all returned to the Church." Nevertheless, in Paris something like two thousand Huguenots died, as did another three thousand in the provinces. This is the most conservative estimate. Justly enough, the Protestants were able to regard this terrible calamity as a sweeping moral victory for themselves.

As nearly always happens in such cases, the worst effects were carried over into the future. The Huguenots and their friends could afford to forget outrages committed by their side in the past. The Catholic backlash now swept away all memory of these earlier horrors.

The massacre was seized upon, not unreasonably, in Protestant countries to demonstrate to the world that there could be no understanding with Rome and the papists. Rumors long current that the Pope had been planning some such thing with the Catholic powers generally, now seemed entirely confirmed. Even Henry of Navarre's marriage was seen not as an attempt at reconciliation, but as another step in a long and carefully planned treachery. Some of the Catholics themselves, including Catherine and Charles of Guise and the Cardinal of Lorraine, encouraged this view in their attempt to justify what they had done or approved of. Cardinal Pellevé saw Catherine de' Medici as another Judith, and Coligny as Holofernes.

Catholic Christendom achieved a valuable breathing-space, if not an armistice, by the victory of Lepanto on October 7, 1571, over the Turkish enemy on its frontier. However, the enemy within, as far as France was concerned, was not only left undestroyed by the massacre of St. Bartholomew's Eve; it was endowed with new determination to resist and prevail. In the long run, the massacre probably strengthened the Huguenot cause. Any previous Huguenot misdeeds seemed to pale into insignificance against the backdrop of this appalling outrage. It is significant that no attempt was made, after this one bloody demonstration, to follow up with a consistent policy of repression, as was adopted in England against the papists in the last quarter of the sixteenth century. Nevertheless, the Huguenots could not foresee this and many emigrated, some to England, where they settled at Sandwich and Norwich, for example. The vast majority, remaining behind in France, refused to submit and the outbreak of the fourth war of religion followed inevitably as "irresistible force and immovable object" collided.

The Huguenots formed a close-knit, intelligent

The Coligny brothers. Gaspard de Coligny, Admiral of France and Huguenot leader, is in the center. His growing influence over the weak Charles IX had promised to gain for the Huguenots by diplomacy what they failed to achieve by war.

and resourceful community within the community. Mainly by sheer persistence and determination they wrung from their champion, Henry of Navarre, the Edict of Nantes which, in April 1598, gave them a privileged position in France. By this arrangement, extraordinary at the time, a religious minority received from the state, financial support to maintain its clergy, and even garrisons in towns fortified to defend it; the best known of these was La Rochelle. Freedom of worship was permitted in many places and in the houses of Huguenot nobles, while there was liberty everywhere to adhere to the religion, hold public office, attend colleges and academies, and even to arrange synods and political meetings. True, this all proceeded, for the most part, from expediency rather than principle, and in the teeth of opposition from the Catholic clergy as a whole. The situation was considerably modified by Richelieu's Edict of Alais after the fall of La Rochelle in 1628. Nevertheless, the system persisted in essentials until 1685, when Louis XIV revoked the Edict of Nantes.

FRANCIS EDWARDS

In England the question of religion is

Queen Elizabeth I realized that it was necessary to enforce religious conformity to achieve national unity—and by promoting a broad, national Church she hoped to end the religious uncertainties of the previous two decades. Elizabeth regarded herself as the instrument of "God's Providence," but she did not consider it part of her mission to introduce Calvinist theology or the Presbyterian system of Church government into England. She stressed the continuity of the Church of England with the medieval Church by emphasizing the similarity of their episcopal governments.

Like her predecessors, Elizabeth appointed as Archbishop of Canterbury a man who could be relied upon to carry out the royal wishes. The death of Cardinal Pole on the same day as Queen Mary left Elizabeth free to appoint the moderate reformer Matthew Parker (1504–75) at once. The new Archbishop was largely responsible for the Elizabethan Church Settlement. He supervised a new translation of the Bible in 1568, and the issue in 1571 of the Thirty-Nine Articles, which formed a basis for agreement on belief. Elizabeth was made "supreme governor" of the Church—a modification of her father's position as "supreme head"—and the acts of Uniformity and Supremacy were reimposed. The more Puritan Edmund Grindal (1519–83) succeeded Parker, but his refusal to deal firmly with the growing Puritan problem led to his suspension in 1577. More to Elizabeth's taste was the scholarly and able John Whitgift (1530–1604),

John Whitgift, Archbishop of Canterbury.

who was energetic in his attacks on Puritanism, which was becoming a serious problem toward the end of Elizabeth's reign. The attempt to impose Anglicanism by law was buttressed by a major theological justification, *Of the Laws of Ecclesiastical Polity* by Richard Hooker (1554–1600), Master of the Temple. Although the Elizabethan Church Settlement did not find anything like universal support, it came far nearer to doing so than the attempts to impose uniformity by force in France, Germany and the Netherlands.

The Settlement was relatively successful in other ways too; it kept the Church firmly subordinate to the Queen's rule, and allowed her to use the Church's property for her own benefit during the often-prolonged episcopal vacancies in bishoprics.

Elizabeth favored a policy of complete toleration in the early part of her reign. But Protestant pressure combined with fear of Roman Catholic plots made necessary increasingly severe fines for those who failed to attend services in their parish churches as her reign continued.

Elizabeth I of England

Initially, Elizabeth had fewer problems with those who opposed her Church Settlement than with those Puritans and Catholics in Parliament who pressed her to settle the succession and marry. But she steadily refused to name her successor, claiming that within a month of doing so, she would find herself in the Tower. The Queen knew from her experience during Mary's reign that an heir apparent inevitably became the focus of opposition. Proposals of marriage came from various princes, and Elizabeth embarked upon a series of lengthy courtships—first with the Archduke Charles and later with Francis, Duke of Alençon (and later Anjou). The latter genuinely fascinated Elizabeth, but the difficulties of selecting a Catholic husband proved insuperable. If Robert Dudley's wife, Amy Robsart, had not died under suspicious circumstances, Elizabeth might well have married Dudley. He remained her favorite although his position was successively challenged by Raleigh, Hatton and Essex.

For most of Elizabeth's reign,

A painting of dancing at court, traditionally said to represent Elizabeth dancing with Robert Dudley.

England was isolated in a hostile Europe. The Queen stretched her friendship with Catholic Spain as far as she dared, permitting her seamen to harry Spanish shipping. Those incidents did not provoke an outbreak of hostilities—but the seizure of three Spanish treasure ships that had taken refuge in Plymouth did. Spain severed all commercial relations with England for six years (1568–74), and in the spring of 1572, Elizabeth signed a defensive treaty with France. That treaty proved to be a durable one: it survived the St. Bartholomew's Massacre; Elizabeth's imprisonment of Mary Queen of Scots; and England's subsidies to the Huguenots—all events that exacerbated already tense Catholic-Protestant relations. In July, 1595, the Guises overturned the alliance, but its existence had postponed the day of reckoning with Spain for more than a decade.

The problem of a successor was heightened by Mary Queen of Scots' arrival in England in 1568, for despite her obvious disadvantages, Mary was fundamentally a more suitable successor than any representative of the Suffolk claimants. The Northern Rebellion, a last attempt to reverse the course of England's religious and political development, coupled with the Duke of Norfolk's treason in the Ridolfi plot, ensured Mary's continued captivity, while Pius V's 1570 bull (which deposed Elizabeth and absolved her subjects from their allegiance to her) brought a spate of penal legislation against the English Catholics. Catholic opposition to Elizabeth's regime grew increasingly desperate under these circumstances; they now conspired for nothing less than Mary's release, and Elizabeth's assassination.

Walsingham's discovery of the Babington Plot, which implicated Mary in plans for Elizabeth's murder, led to the Scottish Queen's trial in 1586. Mary was found guilty of

Sir William Cecil, Principal Secretary of State to Queen Elizabeth.

treason and duly sentenced, but Elizabeth—who had often saved Mary from the militant Puritans in Parliament—could not bring herself to sign the warrant for her execution until February, 1587. She ultimately accepted the argument that she could never feel safe while Mary—the center and soul of every plot against her—was alive and she sent Mary to her death.

In reality the danger posed by Mary Queen of Scots was very much exaggerated. Elizabeth's hold on the throne was secure. In part, Elizabeth's success as a ruler was due to her ability to give way

settled by Queen Elizabeth

gracefully when it was politic to do so. Her choice of advisers also helped. Men such as William Cecil (1520–98), Lord Burghley, his son Robert (1563–1612), Earl of Salisbury, and Sir Francis Walsingham (c. 1530–90), who rose to high office in the state, were all of outstanding ability. Elizabeth's soldiers and sailors were little less capable, as was to be shown so brilliantly during the attempted invasion by the Spanish Armada.

Renaissance music

The polyphonic music that was developed during the fifteenth century by composers such as Dunstable, Dufay and Des Près continued to be the main feature of musical development during the sixteenth century. In the same way that the elaboration of Mannerist art contrasted with the simplicity of the art of the early Renaissance, the music of the sixteenth century differed from that of the fifteenth. The increasing elaboration of harmony, which reduced the audibility of the words, made the Church authorities very suspicious of musical development—as they had been during the fifteenth century. The Council of Trent banned "music in which anything impious or lascivious finds a part" from use in churches, and Pius IV set up a commission to examine the problem of elaborate harmony. There were even proposals that for church music each word should be given not more than one note. This proposal, which would have made it much easier for congregations to follow the words of the liturgy, would also have deprived the world of some of the greatest music ever written, for the late sixteenth century produced a group of outstanding and original composers. A similar movement toward simplicity was apparent in the Protestant churches where it was more successful.

But despite the papacy's suspicion of church musicians, the patronage of Church and State remained important. Lassus was raised to the nobility by the Emperor Maximilian II and knighted by Pope Gregory XIII. The greatest composer of the age, Giovanni Pierluigi da Palestrina (1525–94) was dependent on the patronage and favor of several popes. Palestrina broke the stranglehold that composers from the Netherlands had had on music in Italy when he was appointed as master of the music of one of the choirs of St. Peter's in 1553, and in 1555 he was made choirmaster of the Church of St. John Lateran. In 1571, Palestrina became choirmaster of St. Peter's. During these years he poured forth books of Masses and of other church music and also headed a commission set up to "purify" the Gregorian plainchant. He avoided the problem of inaudibility in most of his Masses, including the *Missa Papae Marcelli*, which many critics regard as his greatest, by giving each clause of the Mass to a soloist to sing before the whole choir developed it polyphonically.

Other leading Italian composers were the Neapolitan Carlo Gesualdo (1560–1613), Prince of Venosa, who played an important part in the development of the madrigal or part-song, although he gained far greater fame at the time by the murder of his wife, and Andrea (1510–86) and Giovanni Gabrielli (1557–1612), an uncle and nephew who played a key role in the development of Venice as a musical center over the following century.

Musical innovation was not confined to Italy, but was spread widely throughout Europe. Spain under Charles V and Philip II, largely because of its possessions in the Netherlands, was brought far more closely into the European musical tradition. The leading name connected with the Spanish school was Tomás Luis de Victoria (1549–1611), who was, like Palestrina, a prolific composer of church music. His deeply mystical approach to music found its greatest expression in the composition of Requiem Masses, such as that for his patroness, the Empress Maria. Vittoria's somewhat emotional approach to music contrasts sharply with the highly intellectual approach of Orlando Lassus (1532–94), whose tendency to replace inspiration by thought led an eighteenth-century critic to describe him as "a dwarf on stilts," a somewhat unfair judgement, as, at his best, Lassus was one of the finest composers of his day.

William Byrd, English composer.

In England, too, there were substantial developments, both in vocal and, toward the end of the century in particular, in instrumental music. The translation of the Mass into English made a new version of the old plainchant melodies necessary, as they only fitted the Latin words. So, just as Palestrina revised the plainchant of the Roman Church, John Merbecke (1510–85), in his *Booke of Common Praier Noted*, published in 1550, set the English liturgy to music. Others connected with the Chapels Royal such as Thomas Tallis (1505–85) and Thomas Morley (1555–1603) also composed music for use in the English Church. The outstanding English composer of the sixteenth century was one of Tallis' pupils, William Byrd (1542–1623), who wrote music for both the English and the Latin services.

The development of printing was an important cause of the huge changes in music during the sixteenth century. In England, for example, the impact of Tallis and Byrd was increased by the virtual monopoly of music publishing given to them by Queen Elizabeth. Although noted music was published from about 1500, it was only after about 1540, when Pierre Attaignant in Paris and Tylman Susato in Antwerp began work, that it became widespread.

Palestrina presents his first book of masses to Pope Julius III in 1554.

A New Empire for India

1573

In February, 1573, following a protracted siege, the Afghan stronghold of Surat capitulated to the Mogul Emperor Akbar. The Indian monarch's victory added the textile-rich province of Gujarat and its busy ports on the Arabian Sea to Akbar's burgeoning Empire—and it effectively ended decades of internecine strife in northern India. A generation earlier, Akbar's father, Humayun, had captured and briefly held Gujarat before launching an impetuous and disastrous campaign in the east. Akbar's reconquest of the province consolidated his holdings and radically diminished both internal and external threats to the Mogul throne. From this secure power base, Akbar was able to quell further outbreaks, promote amicable Moslem-Hindu relations, promulgate a new religion and lay the groundwork for a truly pan-Indian nation.

In the traditional view of Indian historians, the Mogul Empire in India was established in 1526 when Baber, a descendant of Genghis Khan, defeated the Afghan prince Ibrahim Lodi in the First Battle of Panipat. After the great Sikandar Lodi's death in 1517, the old Delhi sultanate—which dated from the first Moslem conquest at the end of the twelfth century—had been split up among contending members of the Lodi family, each of whom was supported by a different Afghan tribe. Disputes over the succession had raged for nearly a decade when Baber intervened in 1526. His action was clearly prompted by hopes of personal gain and not out of any sympathy for the squabbling Afghans, for Baber had already extended the boundaries of his central Asian empire of Farghana into parts of Afghanistan, and he was eager to acquire the Punjab and Delhi itself. The deeper Baber advanced into India, the less secure his own northern possessions became and he was obliged to wage a continual struggle to convert his implicit sovereignty over the Lodi into actual domination.

By the time of his death in 1530, Baber had become master of Delhi and Agra, moved down the Ganges to establish himself in Jaunpur, secured his western frontiers against the martial princes of Rajasthan and extended his sway in the east down to the border of Bengal. The conqueror established little more than his sovereignty in those regions, however; Baber introduced no new cultural or administrative ideas, developed no Indian "policy" and built no distinguished public structures. From the natives' point of view, one foreign ruler had been replaced by another; the difference was only one of tenancy of the Delhi sultanate.

Baber's son, Humayun, was even less effectual as an emperor. He assigned the government of the Punjab, Kandahar and Kabul to a brother in order to be free to direct the continuing Indian campaigns. Those campaigns were numerous and sizable, for both the Hindu kings and the Moslem rulers of India opposed Humayun. The beleaguered monarch was also at odds with his kinsmen the Mirzas—descendants of the great conqueror Timur (Tamerlane)—a turbulent lot who were only too anxious to grab for themselves any convenient slices of the cake that Baber had carved out of India. The Mirzas' hostility was ironic, for Baber had deliberately brought them to India to strengthen his hold over northern India.

In the course of his campaigning, Humayun defeated Bahadur, the Sultan of Gujarat, drove him out of the province, and then abandoned the chase to launch a vigorous assault against an Afghan force in the east. That Afghan army was led by Sher Shah of the Sur tribe—a man who was one of India's ablest sovereigns. While Humayun was preoccupied with Bahadur, with the Mirza rebellion and with safeguarding his western lands against his ambitious brother, Sher had established a trained army in southern Bihar and had extended his personal control into Bengal by defeating its sultan in 1538. Alarmed by Sher's welling strength, Humayun marched into the Bengal capital—only to find the city empty. Sher had withdrawn—and his army was sitting astride Humayun's sole line of communication with Delhi. The outgeneraled Mogul ruler was hounded back to his capital, and in 1540 he was driven out of India. The Delhi sultanate had a new ruler.

Sher Shah's accession marks the first great turning point in sixteenth-century Indian history, for Sher did much more than simply assume sovereignty over Humayun's former possessions. He retook Malwa, which Humayun had given up, established his authority in Rajasthan, and—more than any other contemporary Indian ruler—inspired a nationalistic following.

The keystone of Sher's reforms was a new revenue system: he abolished the old hit-and-miss system of crop-sharing in favor of a system based on the crop-bearing potential of measured areas, and employed

A portrait of Akbar, Mogul Emperor.

Opposite Building the city of Fathpur Sikri as part of the celebrations for the birth of Akbar's son.

a well-drilled civil service to conduct the necessary surveys, collect the revenues and maintain the accounts. Chief administrative officers were appointed in each district to insure that the revenues were collected, to settle cases of injustice in the system and to make sure that the cultivators were not being subjected to any form of oppression. The civilian population was further relieved from anxiety by a rigorous campaign against organized brigandage and other crime. "An old woman with a basketful of gold," says a contemporary historian, "could sleep safe out doors at night without a guard."

Sher Shah's achievements were a source of embarrassment to later Mogul historians, who sought to credit their own rulers with the achievements of his reign. The administrative measures that he introduced were later attributed to Baber's grandson Akbar by his sycophant-biographer, Abu'l Fazl. It is true that in 1571 Akbar's revenue minister, Todar Mall, eliminated some abuses that had crept into the system, but the fundamental structure of the Mogul revenue system—devised by Sher Shah—remained unchanged throughout the whole Mogul period. Indeed, Sher's reforms put India on a stable economic footing that lasted long beyond his own short reign.

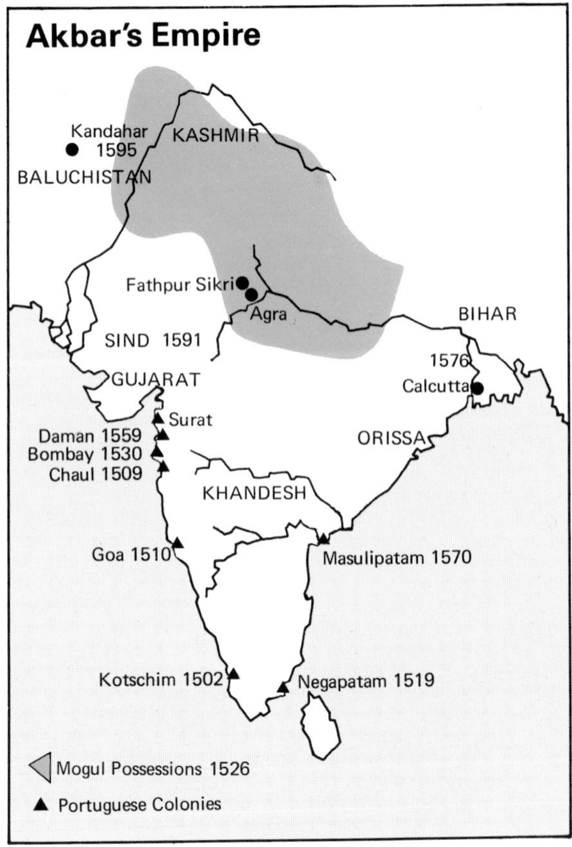

The central pillar of the Diwan-i Khassat at Fathpur Sikri, the city built by Akbar to celebrate the birth of his son.

After Sher Shah's death in 1545, political turmoil broke out afresh in northern India. Sher had left no one to succeed him, and Afghan tribal groups rallied to the support of a number of nobles of the Sur tribe. By 1554 the empire had been divided among three such nobles, each of whom was calling himself sultan. In the midst of the confusion Humayun—who had managed to recapture the Afghan capital of Kabul after fifteen years of wandering—marched on India to regain his lost kingdom. He defeated a Sur army at Sirhind in the Punjab in 1555 and went on to occupy Delhi without opposition. Within six months he died and his son Akbar—born during Humayun's exile and not yet fourteen years of age—succeeded to the somewhat precarious Mogul throne.

The affairs of Mogul government were initially well served by a council of regency, and the council in turn was blessed with competent generals. The three Sur pretenders to the throne were defeated, as was a former minister of one of the Sur "sultans." Hemur, a low-born man with a natural head for soldiering, was perhaps the most dangerous enemy of the Mogul state. He actually managed to occupy Delhi in 1556, but was killed in a clash between his followers and the Mogul forces at the Second Battle of Panipat. With these dangers removed, the Mogul generals soon recaptured Gwalior and Jaunpur.

In 1562, Akbar married the daughter of a Hindu

rajah. Such interfaith marriages were by no means unknown, but in Akbar's case there was one outstanding difference: by the Moslem ruler's decree, his wife's Hindu relatives were regarded as members of the royal family, were frequently appointed to high office and were permitted to practice their own religious rites. This policy, which earned Akbar the support of the Rajput princes, was continued by his successors during the heyday of the Mogul dynasty. It is noteworthy, however, that the rigid orthodoxy of Aurangzeb, Akbar's great-grandson, lost the Mogul Empire the support of its Hindu population and contributed to the Empire's decline. Akbar's decree was the first of many steps taken by the Mogul Emperor to make himself the ruler of all his people, Hindu as well as Moslem.

During the 1560s, the young ruler gradually rose to a position of strong personal power. Akbar's armies invaded Malwa and held the region despite some reverses; the Gond kingdom in east central India was annexed; Mogul armies captured Bihar, where there had been another attempt at Afghan resurgence; and military supremacy over the Rajputs was won. The Rana of Chitor, acknowledged head of the Rajput clans, had remained haughty and aloof during the early 1560s. He had spurned all contact with the Moguls, and had indicated his readiness to take up arms against them at any time. The successful campaign against Chitor, personally led by Akbar (who had already distinguished himself on the field against Malwa), was followed in 1569 by the fall of two other great Rajput strongholds. Akbar's paramountcy was assured, but he was still forced to contend with rebellious parties at home. In the middle of the decade there was a revolt by an Uzbek faction that tried to set up Akbar's cousin as the ruler. The cousin—and the Uzbek instigators of the rising—were suppressed, but rebellion persisted. The Mirzas, who had received small assignments of land during the Mogul restoration, invaded Malwa and made their way to Gujarat.

Below left Akbar's siege of a fort in Rajputam, 1568.

Below While watching an elephant fight, Akbar is told that his wife has had a baby.

Above Akbar receives a Western embassy.

Above right Rejoicing at the birth of Akbar's child.

At the time, Gujarat was in the midst of severe troubles. Sultan Bahadur had been assassinated through Portuguese treachery in 1537. His nephew, the ruler of the neighboring state of Khandesh, had died within weeks of receiving his summons to the Gujarat throne, and from that time the Gujarat sultanate had been held by a succession of minor sultans who were installed as puppet rulers. Suspicious nobles plotted against one another and against the best interests of the state, faction was rife and the ambitious Portuguese were a constant menace on the coasts.

The Portuguese, who had been established at Goa since 1510, were masters of the western seas. (Gujarati sailors were competent enough as coastal pirates, but naval warfare was scarcely known in India.) The foreigners sacked and burned more than one town on the Gujarat coast and—most disturbing of all to the Moslem powers of India—they were able to menace the peaceful pilgrim traffic to Mecca and the Hejaz.

The Gujarat state, which by the 1560s was little more than a polite fiction, was not strong enough to contain its own nobles, much less foreign aggressors. Gujarati nobles parceled out the land among themselves, and they were joined in their depredations by the Mirzas and by the local Habshis—a nominally Abyssinian group, which had been brought to India as slaves, soldiers and palace guards, but had risen to considerable local prominence. The nominal regent of Gujarat during this time of civil strife was I'timad Khan, a converted Hindu. Powerless and desperate, he invited Akbar's intervention.

Akbar had, in the meantime, grown disturbed by his failure to produce an heir. A visit to a Moslem mystic and recluse in the village of Sikri, twenty-three miles southwest of Agra, had given him hope, however, for the mystic, Shaykh Salim Chishti, had prophesied the birth of three sons. In 1569, Akbar's Hindu wife, sent to Sikri to live under the Shaykh's protection, gave birth to a son (who was later to succeed his father as the emperor Jahangir). In his delight, Akbar decided to build a vast mosque at Sikri in the Shaykh's honor, and to transfer his court to the city that he planned to build there. Construction began in 1571, and the spacious and varied structures bear witness to Akbar's taste. In general the styles owe more to Hindu tradition than to Moslem; only the mosque and the tombs show the influence of the builders and masons of Gujarat and Malwa. It was from Sikri in 1572 that Akbar set off in response to I'timad Khan's invitation.

The monarch's reception at Patan and Ahmadabad—where he received the submission of the Gujarati nobles—was more of a triumphal procession than a campaign. There was little resistance in the disheartened north, and what opposition there was came from the southern section of Gujarat, where the Mirzas and the rebellious Habshis formed a resistance party. They were defeated in battle by the Mogul forces at the end of 1572, and a protracted siege of the rebel stronghold at Surat ended in a Mogul victory in February, 1573. Akbar returned in triumph to Sikri, and Gujarat became a province of the Mogul power. In commemoration of the victory, the city of Sikri received the new name of Fathpur, "town of victory," and Akbar built a vast portal on the south wall of the mosque as a triumphal arch.

Moslem historians have probably attached too much importance to the "conquest" of Gujarat, for the victory over the province was by no means hard-fought. But although we can scarcely consider the conquest of Gujarat one of the decisive battles of history, the acquisition of the province did mark a new phase in Mogul affairs. Gujarat was a rich country, famous for its textiles and other valuable commodities such as indigo, saltpeter and salt.

Another province was soon added to Akbar's Empire: Bengal fell to the Moguls in 1576. By this time the Mogul ruler's attitude had outgrown the old concept of the Delhi sultanate, and had attained many of the qualities of an *imperium*. Akbar, who ruled a wider range of subjects than any of his forbears, soon set about organizing and unifying his Empire. He introduced a series of administrative reforms.

After his return from Gujarat, something happened that provoked Akbar's curious mind: a Moslem divine expressed the hope that Akbar might become his people's spiritual as well as their temporal ruler. Within seven years Akbar acted upon that suggestion. A document was issued that gave the ruler authority to pronounce on any question pertaining to the religion of Islam. In addition, Akbar initiated discussions on theological questions—and through those discussions it became increasingly obvious that the Emperor was entertaining doubts about the sufficiency of Islam. From 1579, representatives of faiths other than Islam were summoned to the debates, and a dispatch was sent to Goa asking that priests be sent to the court to satisfy Akbar's curiosity about the Christian faith. By the time that the two Jesuit missionaries arrived in Fathpur Sikri, Akbar's revisionist ideas had led him to forbid mention of the prophet Mohammed's name in public prayers. His partiality for the Jesuits, and for the Jains and Parsis that he invited to the court, alarmed his orthodox subjects and brought about the most serious crisis in his reign.

"Islam in danger" had more than once been a rallying cry in Moslem India, and it was invoked again in 1580. Aided by Akbar's half brother,

Baber, Humayun and Akbar, the first three Mogul emperors of India

A lion hunt.

A Mogul officer on horseback.

Opposite above A celebration; the costumes show the strong Western influence that Akbar encouraged.

Opposite below A late-sixteenth-century carpet from Lahore.

Mohammed Hakim, who advanced on the Punjab, discontented Afghan settlers in Bihar launched an open rebellion against Akbar's Christianized administration. A false step would have meant Akbar's ignominious disappearance from the Indian scene. He sent his most competent generals to deal with the rising and prepared an overwhelming force to counter his half brother's advance. The embattled Emperor's display of power terrified Mohammed Hakim, and Akbar soon subdued the traitor. The Emperor's generals dealt severely with the rebels in the east, and when Akbar returned to his capital at the end of 1581, he had overcome all obstacles.

In 1582 he renounced Islam and promulgated a rather naive syncretistic eclecticism, known as the *Din-i Ilahi*, or "Divine Faith," as the official religion of the Empire. Akbar became the supreme spiritual power in his realm, and the Jesuit mission withdrew. The Portuguese remained a threat in the west, but elsewhere his Empire continued to grow: Khandesh fell to the Moguls in 1577, Kashmir capitulated in 1586, and Sind, Oriss, Baluchistam and Qandahar succumbed within a decade. Repenting its earlier submission to Akbar, Khandesh resumed its independent status, only to be reoccupied in 1601, at the same time that the provinces of Ahmadnagar and Barar were added to Akbar's rapidly burgeoning Empire.

In relation to the world as a whole, the crucial years of Akbar's reign were those during which the sultanate expanded into an empire through acquisition of the wealth and commerce of Gujarat, the establishment of contacts with Europe through the Jesuit missions, and the painstaking reform of the administration. Essentially, those were Akbar's years at Fathpur Sikri—years in which Akbar first conceived of Moslem India in pan-Indian terms.

J. BURTON-PAGE

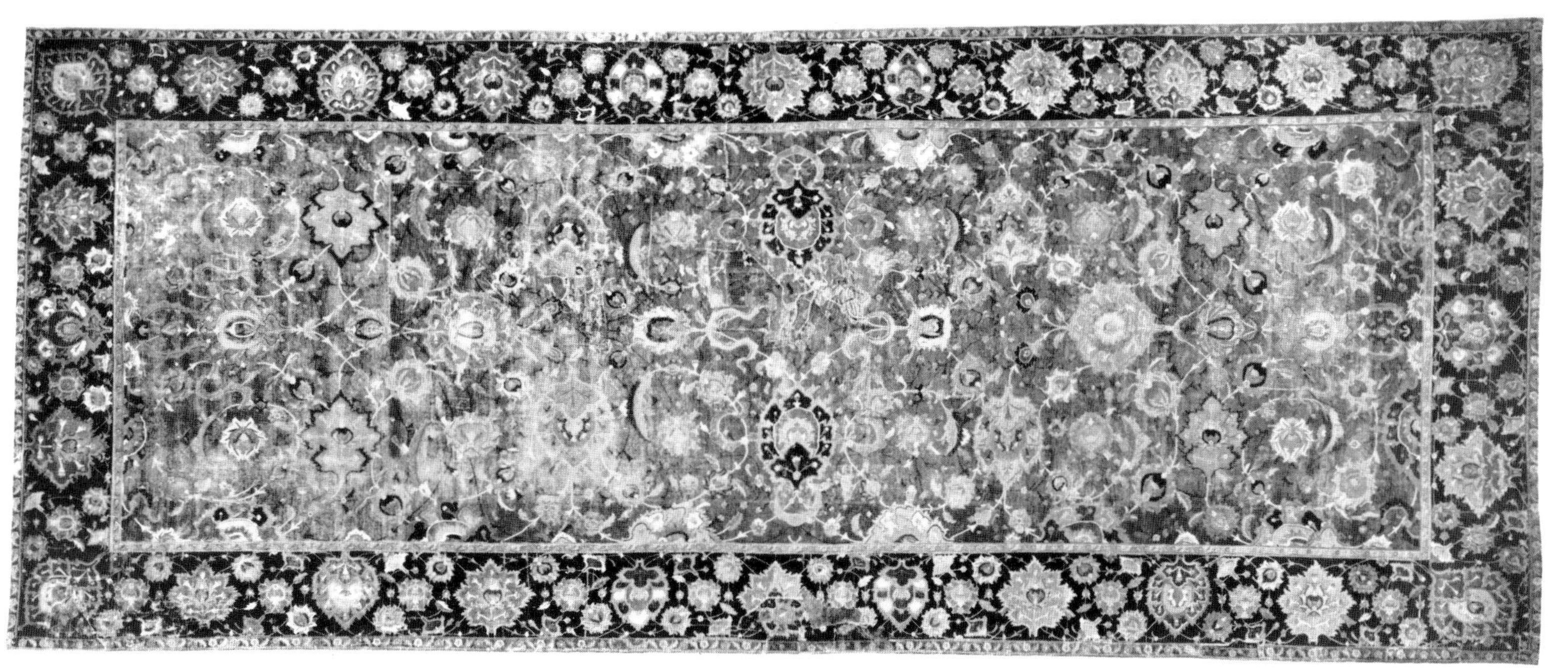

Spanish might is strained by the

William the Silent, Prince of Orange-Nassau.

In the years between the Battle of Lepanto and the defeat of the Spanish Armada, the center of gravity of European politics shifted from the Mediterranean to the Netherlands—and the sea power exemplified in those key naval actions was of fundamental importance in the Dutch struggle for independence from Spain. In 1572 William was elected Stadholder, or governor, by the provinces of Holland, Friesland and Zeeland. Promising to rid the Low Countries of Fernando Alva, Philip II's commander-in-chief, he led a Dutch army into the field. Although Haarlem fell to the Spanish, Alva failed to take Alkmaar. Finding his advances checked, the general asked Philip II to recall him. The Dutch rebels regained Zeeland in 1574, and saved Leyden by opening the dikes. A year later Don Luis Requesens, Alva's successor, cut communications between Holland and Zeeland, and a desperate William of Orange offered the sovereignty of the Netherlands to Elizabeth I, who refused his offer.

The Orangemen's war of independence was becoming an international affair: English adventurers were fighting in William's army while the Duke of Anjou, heir to the French throne, and John Casimir of the Palatinate both led mercenary forces against the Spanish. Philip II appointed his half brother, Don Juan of Austria, victor of Lepanto, as military governor of the Netherlands. Before Don Juan could reach his new command, the Spanish army—unpaid for many months as a result of financial crises in Spain—mutinied and sacked Antwerp. Before a month was out, representatives of all seventeen Dutch provinces had signed the Pacification of Ghent, a document which demanded that Philip recall his soldiers and grant religious toleration in the Netherlands (1576).

Differences between the Flemish southern provinces and the Dutch northern provinces had grown steadily as a result of conflicting religious allegiances, and in 1579 matters came to a head. By the Union of Utrecht, Holland, Zeeland and the five other "Dutch" provinces banded together to defend themselves against Spain. William of Orange was so dismayed that the Union excluded the southern provinces that he delayed adding his signature. The Union, ratified in 1581 by the Act of Abjuration (which renounced all allegiance to Philip II), was in effect the constitutional beginning of the Dutch Republic.

Don Juan of Austria died in 1578 and was succeeded by Alexander Farnese, the Duke of Parma. Greatest soldier of his day, Parma gradually made headway against William of Orange during this period. The French Duke of Anjou, abetted by Elizabeth I (to whom he was betrothed), fought episodic campaigns in the south, but was chiefly concerned with carving out a principality for himself. In 1583, his troops sacked Antwerp with such violence that their actions became known as the "French Fury." A year later Anjou died and Parma took Ypres and Ghent. On July 10 of that year William, the hero of the revolt, was assassinated at Philip II's instigation. Parma captured Antwerp in August, 1585.

The assassination of William of Orange at Delft in 1584.

Philip II

The revolt of the Netherlands came as a serious blow to Philip II of Spain, but it affected only a tiny part of his huge empire. His European possessions, large as they were, were merely a fraction of his domain, the source of whose wealth and decline lay buried in the silver-mines of central and south America. The Spanish Empire was not, however, a unified whole, but an amorphous agglomeration of countries with enormous constitutional and cultural differences. The unifying factors were loyalty to the King and rule by his officers, who were almost entirely Spaniards and mostly Castilians. Under Charles V the Hapsburg possessions had been governed as a European empire; under Philip they were definitely part of a Spanish empire, and Spanish interest was the main influence on policy. This was to become a major cause of concern to many of his advisers.

Even Spain itself was not a single country—the unification of Aragon and Castile had been in many ways superficial. The power of the nobility, for example, was enormous in Aragon, but in Castile royal power was paramount. Taxation throughout the huge Spanish possessions in Europe was low, because the vast flood of treasure from beyond the Atlantic was able to provide much of the government's needs. But the relatively light economic control that Charles had over his European possessions did not mean that he was willing to allow them to govern themselves. And Philip, on the contrary, believed in the need for firm government. The huge monastery and palace of the Escorial, near Madrid, was the center of Spanish government and it was from the Escorial that Philip tried to control all aspects of life in his empire.

Using a vast inflow of documents from all the provinces and from his ambassadors in foreign countries, Philip, with the help of a small group of advisers, formulated policy, even on minor matters. Yet, despite, or perhaps because of, his attention to detail, Philip often failed to grasp the essential point at issue. Isolated amid his palace of paper—he created a permanent collection of his outdated papers at Simancas in 1567—hundreds, often thousands, of miles from his governors and generals, the King saw reality in a different light than they did. The revolt of the Netherlands was caused as much by Philip's failure to take seriously the complaints of his subjects there as it was by the disputes over religion. Even when the King's analysis of a problem was correct, his orders were often outdated by the time they arrived. Nor did his ministers always carry out his orders; in 1587, when Philip ordered the invasion of England, the Marquis of Santa-Cruz simply refused to carry out the order.

One of Philip's most attractive characteristics was his love of architecture. Buildings such as the Royal Mint at Segovia and the Alcazar and other buildings at Madrid, which became the Spanish capital in 1561, show Philip's taste, but his greatest monument is the huge, if slightly gloomy, Escorial, built in the 1560s.

Even in Spain Philip was often faced with serious problems. In 1591, the populace of Aragon, restive for some years, rose against attacks on their traditional liberties. This was largely due to the King's attempts to impose a unified system of government on the country as a whole. Again, in his determination to impose religious unity, Philip antagonized the *Moriscos*, Moors who had been more or less forcibly converted to Christianity, a group whose loyalty was always doubtful.

Netherlands revolt and overseas expansion

Portugal

But whatever his difficulties in unifying Spain in religion and constitution, Philip was determined to unify it politically. Through chance more than anything else, Portugal had succeeded in escaping the consequences of a whole series of dynastic marriages of members of its royal house with the Hapsburgs. Charles V had married the daughter of a Portuguese prince. One of Charles' sisters had married a daughter of King John III of Portugal, another had married Charles' father-in-law. Philip II, himself half Portuguese, married Maria, the daughter of John III, and Philip's sister had married a Portuguese prince.

The fortress housing the Royal Mint at Segovia.

This web of dynastic marriages failed in its desired effect. After John III's death in 1557, his grandson, Philip II's nephew, Sebastian succeeded to the Portuguese throne. When Sebastian, who was only three years old at the time of his succession, grew up he came to be regarded as a religious fanatic—a considerable achievement in an age of religious fanaticism. He virtually handed over the government of his country to the Jesuits; he refused to marry, despite the succession problem that might ensue after his death; above all, he was determined to conquer North Africa. In 1574, he led a small army there and four years later he returned with a larger force. His religious zeal was not, however, equalled by his military ability. At the battle of Alcazar-el-Kebir in 1578 he was killed along with most of his army.

Sebastian's uncle, Cardinal Henry, who had been regent of Portugal during most of his nephew's minority, as well as Archbishop of Braga, Lisbon and Coimbra, succeeded to the throne. The need for a male heir was now acute, if civil war was to be avoided. Henry hurriedly applied to the pope for a dispensation from his vow of celibacy, so that he could marry his cousin, the daughter of the Duke of Braganza. But whether the sixty-seven-year-old monarch and his thirteen-year-old bride would have produced an heir was to remain an academic question. The wheels of papal justice ground slowly, as Henry VIII of England had found to his fury forty-five years before, and Henry of Portugal died before his dispensation arrived.

Tycho Brahe, the Danish astronomer, in his observatory.

Five claimants for the throne appeared. The dukes of Savoy and Parma were not serious candidates, but two illegitimate members of the royal family, Antonio, Prior of the monastery of Crato and the Duke of Braganza, had serious claims and considerable support within the country. Philip of Spain, however, apart from his strong hereditary claim, had a still more powerful argument. He gathered an army on the border and summoned the Duke of Alva to return from the Netherlands to command it. Portugal was quickly absorbed into Spain, but the unity remained superficial, particularly as the overseas empires were separately administered.

Philip II's empire was very different from that of Charles V. The emphasis had shifted southward to the Mediterranean, and outside Europe to the Spanish and Portuguese colonial empires. This did not prevent Philip from casting his armies into the Netherlands, nor from casting a wishful eye at England which he still regarded as his rightful possession.

Brahe's "new" star

The Danish astronomer Tycho Brahe (1546–1601) was a curious contradiction. The modernity of his instruments and calculations was balanced by the reactionary nature of his intellectual outlook—Brahe regarded astronomy as a "divine" science and rejected the Copernican theory of a heliocentric universe. While studying chemistry at Augsburg, he made a nineteen-foot quadrant and a celestial globe five feet in diameter, and when he returned to Denmark his noble uncle encouraged him to build a laboratory in his castle. From that vantage Brahe observed the "new" star Cassiopeia on November 11, 1572. Brahe's discovery brought him unprecedented royal patronage: Frederick II granted the astronomer the island of Hveen, on which Brahe built his Uraniborg Observatory in 1576. Brahe designed his own instruments and with them achieved new standards of accuracy, but his fame rests primarily on the voluminous observations that he recorded in great detail. Those records form the basis of modern astronomy.

The Gregorian calendar

In 1582, Pope Gregory XIII promulgated a reformed calendar, which was adopted in all Catholic countries in place of the Julian Calendar. Under the Gregorian Calendar, October 4, 1582 was followed by October 15—to compensate for the days over the centuries through the use of the inaccurate Julian Calendar. Most Protestant countries gradually realized the folly of continuing with the Julian system, but Holland held out until 1700, Great Britain until 1752, and Russia until the 1917 Revolution.

If Gregory left his mark on chronology, Sixtus V (1585–90) left his on history. He rid the ecclesiastical estates of bandits and made his rule respected, overhauled the Church's administrative system, limited the College of Cardinals to seventy members and set higher standards for men who hoped to be elevated to the office of cardinal. In his short pontificate he built roads and bridges, laid out the Lateran and attempted to drain the Pontine marshes. His lack of historical sense led him to use the ancient Roman columns of Trajan and Antoninus as pedestals for statues of St. Peter and St. Paul, but he did give Rome a new grandeur. He demanded that the dome of St. Peter's be completed, and employed six hundred men working around-the-clock to finish the work in twenty-two months.

CORONO
EXHILERO
ELIZA, TRIVMPHANS
Guilielmus Rogerus sculp. Aº 1589

The Invincible Armada 1588

There was a time when England and Spain seemed destined for a firm alliance if not an outright political union, but the differences between the Protestant island kingdom and the Catholic monarchy to the south proved irreconcilable. By early 1588, Spain was arming the mightiest naval force ever assembled. The Armada's commander, the Duke of Medina Sidonia, was totally ignorant of naval warfare, and had a distressing tendency to seasickness—yet, pressed by King Philip II, *he led the enterprise northward that summer. A nervous England waited—Queen Elizabeth unhappily contemplating the costs of a large standing army to defend her realm against invasion; the English seadogs eager to have at the Spaniard. The first clashes were inconclusive; then—according to hallowed English legend—"God breathed" and winds dispersed the invading fleet.*

A long peace between England and Spain seemed assured with the marriage, in 1554, of the Catholic Queen Mary and the Hapsburg Prince Philip, soon to be King Philip II of Spain. But within four years Mary died, childless, and was succeeded on the throne of England by her half-sister, the decidedly Protestant Elizabeth. Initially the new Queen remained at peace with Philip II, but two decades later she reversed herself and entered an alliance with the people of the Low Countries, who were trying to throw off the Spanish yoke. In 1585 Elizabeth sent an army led by Robert Dudley, Earl of Leicester, to fight alongside the Dutch rebels against Philip's troops. The fiction of peace with Spain, further jeopardized by the privateering raids of John Hawkins and Francis Drake against Spain's New World possessions, could no longer be maintained.

Philip II confiscated all English ships docked in Spanish ports, and plans for a combined naval and military expedition against England were drawn up by the Marquis of Santa Cruz. When news of the execution of Mary Queen of Scots reached Spain, Philip ordered preparations to go forward speedily. A grand fleet was collected and outfitted, and supplies were gathered for the 8,000 mariners and 22,000 soldiers who were to be transported to Calais, a French seaport across the Channel from Dover, to rendezvous with the Duke of Parma's army. The meeting with Parma required perfect timing, if the expedition were to succeed. Philip anticipated that the combined Spanish forces would be welcomed as liberators by some 25,000 English Catholics. Pro-Spanish sentiment was indeed high in certain regions, and long-range culverins or heavy cannon, made in Sussex and Gloucestershire in 1587, were smuggled to Spain by unpatriotic iron-masters.

England prepared for the anticipated invasion by training county militia and by establishing along the coastal headlands a system of beacons to warn of the enemy's approach. Sir John Hawkins, prudent treasurer and comptroller of the Royal Navy, assured Elizabeth that the fleet was ready for action, but the Queen, who could not afford to keep her "wooden walls" permanently in commission, was obliged to defer mobilization until the last moment. At the time, attack seemed the best method of defense, and in the spring of 1587, Sir Francis Drake boldly led twenty-three vessels into Cadiz harbor, where they destroyed some thirty Spanish ships. On the way home, Drake's fleet captured and burned thousands of empty barrels and other cooper's stores that were being shipped to French ports for use in victualling the Armada. Drake's raid, dubbed the "singeing of the King of Spain's beard," prevented the Spaniards from launching an invasion that year.

European seers had long been predicting that 1588 would be a year of disaster, encompassing the fall of empires and perhaps the Armageddon itself. An early setback for Philip, the death of his admiral Santa Cruz, seemed to confirm those portents. Philip chose the Duke of Medina Sidonia, a thirty-eight-year-old grandee from Castile, as Santa Cruz' successor. Although ignorant of naval warfare and prone to seasickness, Medina Sidonia was a brave and level-headed commander, and he accepted the post against his will. The new commander found the preparations for the invasion inadequate, the vessels poorly equipped and the victualling arrangements deplorable (water casks made of green wood had been substituted for those burned by Drake's raiders, and the water supply was tainted). Medina Sidonia held out for more time, but Philip, usually reluctant to move, insisted on pushing ahead. The fleet now consisted of thirty-two first-line ships: twenty galleons; four Mediterranean galleys (which later found Atlantic conditions so impossible that they turned back); four galleasses, crosses between galleon and galley that used oars when the wind dropped; and four armed merchantmen. These warships, organized in squadrons, were supported by

Lord Howard of Effingham, Earl of Nottingham, Lord High Admiral. His knowledge of naval tactics was as limited as that of the Spanish commander, the Duke of Medina Sidonia.

Opposite A symbolic picture of the triumphant Elizabeth.

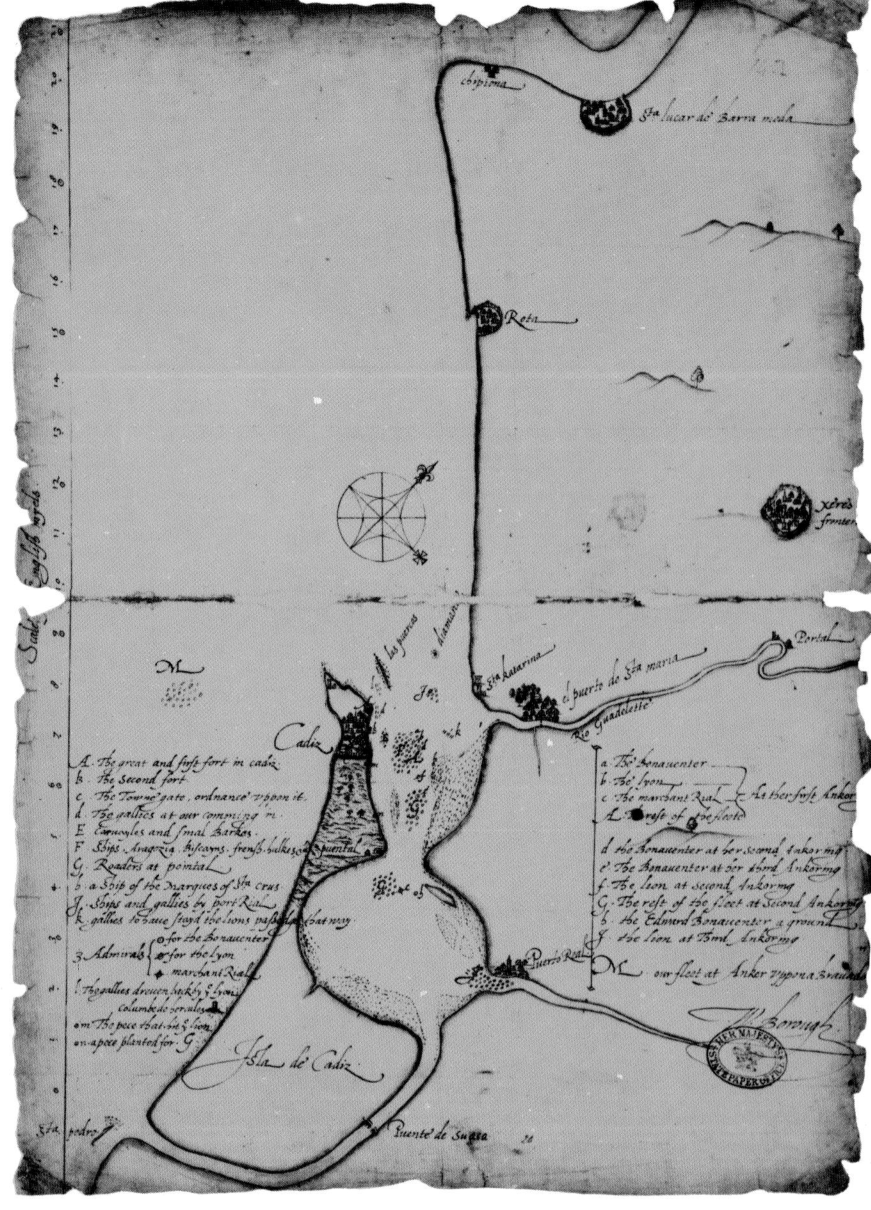

Above Cadiz Harbor with the positioning of the Spanish and English ships at the time of Drake's bold attack in 1587.

Below Part of Drake's letter to Queen Elizabeth, describing his action at Cadiz.

forty merchantmen, twenty-three freighters and two dozen pinnaces, which were used as scout ships.

Pope Sixtus v had blessed the Spanish Enterprise although he had withheld his financial support, and on April 15, 1588, the banners to be carried in the crusade against the heretic Queen were hallowed in Lisbon Cathedral; and every man in the expedition took the Sacrament. By April 30, the fleet was ready to leave, but gales delayed the actual sailing until May 20. Progress up the coast was painfully slow and the weather treacherous, and on June 9 Medina Sidonia anchored at the Spanish seaport of Corunna to wait for stragglers. Finding storm damage extensive and supplies low, he wrote to Philip asking whether he should continue. The King was adamant, and on July 12 the Armada left Corunna. The invaders were in good spirits, but even pro-Spanish Frenchmen were laying 6 to 1 odds that the Armada would never pass Ushant, an island off the Brittany coast.

The English fleet's first line was composed of eighteen large galleons and seven smaller vessels. Elizabeth's ships were more heavily armed than their Spanish counterparts, and their longer and more slender hulls gave them greater maneuverability. Privately owned armed merchantmen and small pinnaces brought the fleet's total to 197 vessels.

In December, 1587, Elizabeth had appointed Lord Howard of Effingham to command her fleet. Like his Spanish opponent, Lord Howard was an aristocrat and—despite his administrative office of Lord High Admiral of England—he had little knowledge of naval tactics. Yet he was able, by force of his strong personality, to impose obedience on the unruly English captains Drake, Hawkins and Frobisher. Initially, Lord Howard's fleet was based at Queenborough, to defend the Thames; Lord Henry Seymour, based at Dover, patrolled the Straits, while Drake's Plymouth-based fleet stood ready to scour the western approaches to the Channel. In May, 1588, Howard moved his main fleet to join Drake's in Plymouth Sound, but the Queen refused to permit the combined force to go marauding—partly because of the cost of stores, and partly because she feared that the Armada might elude Howard and enter the Channel unopposed.

When word reached England in early July that the Spaniards were at Corunna, Howard received fresh authority for loading victuals—and a hint from Elizabeth that he might now seek out the enemy in their own port. An English fleet of ninety ships left Plymouth in haste on July 7 and raced towards Biscay on a strong northeast wind. As Howard's ships neared the northern coast of Spain, the wind suddenly shifted to the south and the fleet was forced to return to Plymouth, reaching port on July 12, the very day Medina Sidonia left Corunna. A week later the captain of an English scouting ship brought news that some Spanish ships were off the coastal Scilly Islands with their sails struck, waiting for stragglers. The English left the Sound by the night tide, and anchored in deep water. The following morning, Saturday, July 20, Howard led fifty-four

The Ark Royal, flagship of Elizabeth's fleet.

ships to leeward of the Eddystone Rocks and sailed straight south—a brilliant move that enabled him to double back on the enemy.

Medina Sidonia formed his fleet into a great crescent, with the strongest galleons at the points and flanks and the weakest in the middle, so that they appeared to Howard as an imposing enemy "with lofty towers, castle-like, in front like a crescent moon." This defensive formation limited the English to an attack on the Armada only where the Spanish were strongest.

The English needed to maneuver into a position in which their cannon could be used effectively, while the Spanish needed to close in with grappling-irons and board the enemy. Grand sea duels between fleets composed of ships-of-the-line were unheard of in warfare, and the tactics were as yet unwritten. The stalemate continued as the fleets moved up the Channel; English attacks on the points of the crescent failed to draw blood, and the only Spanish casualties in the five days of sailing were two ships lost in accidents. The Spanish had wasted 100,000 cannon balls with nothing to show for their fusillades, and the English were also running short of shot.

Though the Cornish beacons had been lit on July 19, not until the Armada was off Portland Bill, four miles south of Weymouth on the southern coast, four days later, did the order go out for the main army to assemble at Tilbury and for the second army, which was to defend the Queen's person, to go to St. James's. On that day, July 23, 1588, Leicester was named Lieutenant-General for the Defense of the Realm, and from all over England the mustered levies began converging on the southeast. Booms were improvised across the Thames to prevent a Spanish raid on London.

Medina Sidonia anchored off Calais on July 27, only to discover that Parma had no flat-bottomed boats available to transport 18,000 men camped between Dunkirk and Nieuport out to the Armada. Howard, too, was in a quandary, for he could not get within gunshot range of the Spanish. He called a council of war, and it was decided to attempt to break up the Spaniards' formation by sending a fleet of large fire ships into the Armada's midst.

Drake volunteered his own ship, the 200-ton *Thomas*, and seven other owners proffered theirs as well. The vessels were filled with anything that would

"Drake's dial," a sixteenth-century navigational instrument used by Drake.

The English attacking the Spanish off Calais. The use of fireships threw the Armada into confusion from which it never recovered.

burn and their guns were double-shotted so that they would explode from the intense heat. The Spanish had feared a secret weapon—and here it was. Soon after midnight the fireships, lashed together, approached the anchorage, cutting through the cordon of pinnaces. In great confusion the Spanish galleons slipped their cables and stood out to sea. None of the Armada's vessels caught fire, but the impregnable crescent had been broken.

At dawn on July 28, Lord Howard divided his squadrons to deal with the scattered enemy. Drake, in the *Revenge*, was to lead the fight and, aided by Frobisher and Hawkins, he pounded the Spanish flagship, whose defenders were reduced to using muskets. Howard had driven the rudderless *San Lorenzo* ashore, and in the four hours of close fighting that ensued the Spanish suffered major casualties. The duel at Gravelines, a French port fifteen miles southwest of Dunkerque, clearly demonstrated the superiority of the English in handling their vessels—but Medina Sidonia still would not give in. Squalls and blinding rain saved the Spanish from certain defeat; when the weather cleared, the English discovered that the Spanish had drifted out of range and reformed the old crescent formation. Two Spanish ships had sunk, however, and most were leaking. His ammunition nearly spent, Howard could not repeat the attack—but he pursued the enemy north along the Netherlands coast.

Early on July 30, when it seemed certain that the Spanish fleet would be driven on the perilous lee shore of the Zeeland sands, the wind suddenly backed to west-southwest, enabling the Spanish to maneuver into the deep waters of the North Sea. At a war council on board the *San Martin*, casualties and damage were reported and it was agreed that if the wind changed again, the Armada would fight its way through the Straits of Dover and attempt to take an English harbor. If the wind held, the fleet would have to sail westward around the British Isles.

The wind did not change, and Medina Sidonia, who had already lost seven of his first-line ships, knew he must at all costs bring the rest of his limping vessels home. The long, hazardous voyage around the Orkney and Shetland islands and west of Ireland would have to be made on meager rations. Seventeen ships broke away from the fleet in a desperate attempt to secure food and water in Ireland, and all but two were wrecked. The remainder battled on. Their fight was now only with the elements, for Howard had given up the chase north of Berwick, on the Scottish border, on August 2, when it became clear that the enemy would not attempt a landing.

The Queen, hedged in by her guards at St. James's,

The Armada Portrait of Queen Elizabeth.

Sir Francis Drake, pirate, explorer and naval captain. Legend obscured history and made Drake the hero of the campaign against the Armada.

felt left out, and decided to visit the coast. Leicester politely forbade the journey, so Elizabeth then decided to visit Tilbury. The Earl did not have the heart to dissuade her, and she went by barge on August 8 to inspect the men. A steel corselet was found for her, and the Queen rode through the ranks "like some Amazonian empress." She stayed nearby and returned to the camp the next day to review the troops and make the speech that, Leicester said, "so inflamed the hearts of her poor subjects as I think the weakest person among them is able to match the proudest Spaniard that dares now land":

> . . . Let tyrants fear. I have always so behaved myself that under God, I have placed my chiefest strength and goodwill in the loyal hearts and goodwill of my subjects; and therefore I come amongst you, as you see, at this time, not for my recreation and disport, but being resolved, in the midst and heat of the battle, to live or die amongst you all; to lay down for God, my kingdom and for my people, my honour and my blood, even in the dust. I know I have but the body of a weak and feeble woman;

One of a pack of playing cards produced to celebrate the victory of 1588; the king of hearts represents the army of the Earl of Leicester, Lieutenant-General for the Defense of the Realm.

but I have the heart and stomach of a king, and a King of England too, and think it foul scorn that Parma or Spain, or any Prince of Europe, should dare to invade the borders of my realm; to which, rather than any dishonour should grow by me, I myself will take up arms . . .

Elizabeth assured her troops that they would be paid for their services and asserted that she did not doubt that they would shortly have a great victory. The cheers were thunderous. During dinner in Leicester's tent that night, news came that Parma was embarking from Dunkirk and would cross on the spring tide. Those eager for action were disappointed, however: Parma's chances had been dashed eleven days before, when the British fireships scattered the Armada.

Lord Howard was later criticized for not having destroyed more ships—although the English had not lost a single ship and no more than one hundred men in the whole engagement. Little was heard about the crews still on shipboard—many of whom died like flies from typhus while their officers quarreled about their pay. The significance of the Armada's defeat soon pierced the haze, and court and capital celebrated. The captured flags were placed in St. Paul's, and the Queen journeyed to London on November 24 to attend a Thanksgiving. John Piers, Bishop of Salisbury, preached on the "Protestant wind"—the same wind that had wrecked Pharaoh's chariots in the Red Sea—and his impassioned oratory earned him promotion to the Archbishopric of York.

To mark the English fleet's victory, Elizabeth took the novel step of issuing various medals, with

The Armada, a contemporary engraving showing the crescent formation of the Spanish fleet.

her bust on the obverse and a suitable engraving of the storm on the reverse; "God breathed and they were scattered," ran one of the inscriptions. She sat for a special portrait that included views of the English galleons proudly returning from Calais and of the Spanish ships foundering, and Sir Thomas Heneage gave her "the Armada jewel," a brooch that incorporated a miniature of herself by Hilliard. The following year, Elizabeth asked Burghley to draw up an honors list including six earldoms, but they both thought better of the idea before the peerages were announced. In 1597 she belatedly advanced Howard to the Earldom of Nottingham; his patent described his brilliant service in 1588.

By the time the Spanish flagship *San Martin* reached Santander on September 13, many on board had died from scurvy or typhus and Medina Sidonia himself was delirious from dysentery. Among the thousands who later died were the Spanish commander's stalwarts, Recalde and Oquendo. The sick Admiral was unable to organize relief for his men; he never returned to sea and never lived down the obloquy of the campaign that was unfairly heaped on him. Philip II took the defeat with dignity, never realizing that the Armada had been set an impossible task, with inadequate provisions and ammunition. No one praised Medina Sidonia for succeeding in bringing home sixty-seven battered ships.

Legends soon obscured history: Drake became the hero of the campaign, and the Queen was credited with the idea of the fireships (which purportedly actually burned some galleons). Above all, the wind was made "God's instrument" in England's victory—when, in truth, the weather had favored the Spanish all along.

The medal struck to celebrate the victory of 1588: the Spanish fleet is scattered and destroyed

The campaign did not cause Philip II to sue for peace with England or lead him to recognize Dutch independence, nor did it end England's fear of invasion. The action was decisive primarily in that it checked the colossus of Spain—which had grown considerably since the Battle of Lepanto and the conquest of Portugal. The fact that the Enterprise had been a holy crusade—and an unsuccessful one—shows that the Counter-Reformation, no less than Spanish prestige, had passed its apogee. French Huguenots no longer felt that the world had ended with St. Bartholomew, or Dutch Calvinists that hope had been buried with William the Silent. The events of 1588 put new heart into the Protestant cause.

NEVILLE WILLIAMS

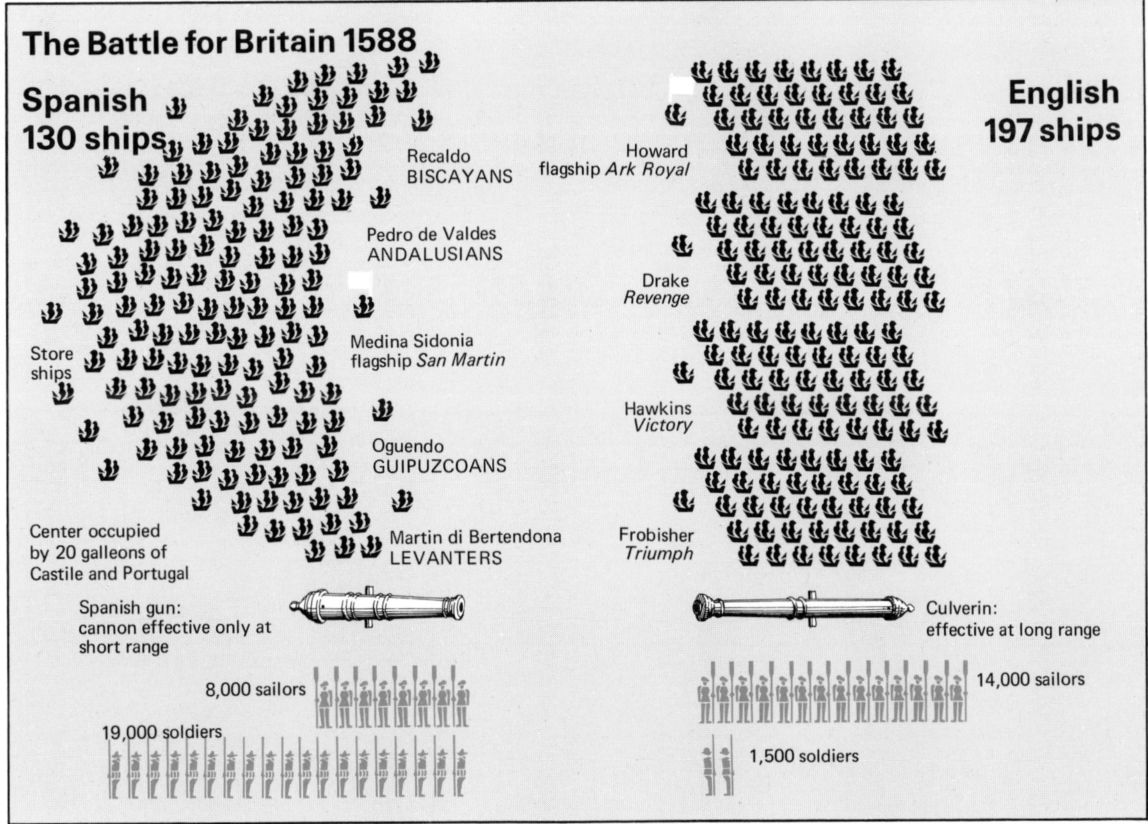

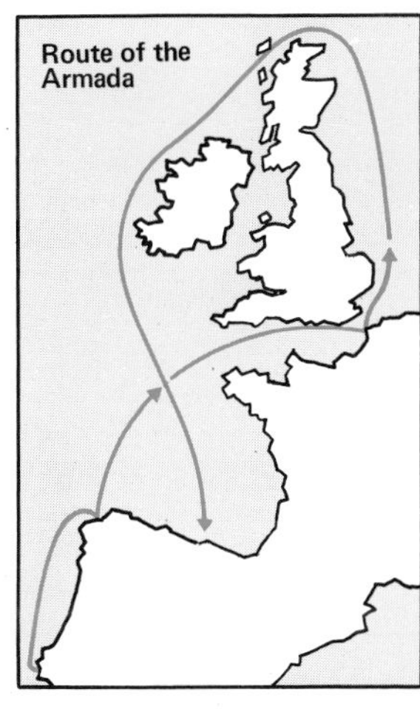

The reign of Ivan IV left Moscow far stronger than it had been before. This strength was apparent both in the Tsar's dealings with his subjects and in his dealings with his neighbors. Ivan's brutal treatment of his enemies—the boyars were not the only sufferers—and his furious temper—he killed one of his sons with a stick—left his subjects cowed, while the Church preached that his authority was absolute. Ivan saw himself as an all-powerful emperor, the Caesar (Tsar) of all the Russians; and his capital, following the fall of the Roman empires in West and East, as the third Rome.

The steady growth of the Muscovite principality at the expense of its neighbors continued. In 1300, the dukes of Moscow had been lords of no more than a few hundred square miles around the capital. By 1467, the principality had expanded nearly tenfold. The reign of Ivan III had brought the huge area to the north and west of Moscow, including the lands disputed with Poland, under control, roughly trebling the land area. Ivan IV, who on his accession was already lord of the largest state in Europe, dwarfing even the huge European empire of Charles V, was no less expansionist in his ambitions than his predecessors had been. Nor was he less successful at achieving his ambitions. He did not, however, waste his resources on relatively futile wars with the Kingdom of Poland. As Poland turned its energies increasingly toward the west, so Moscow looked eastward, largely because the wars between Ivan and Poland were inconclusive. Trade with Western Europe was difficult because there was no outlet to the Baltic as a result of the resurgence of Swedish power, and the cultural differences between Western Christendom and Russia were becoming increasingly pronounced. The port of Archangel on the Arctic Sea provided a valuable link with England, but was closed by ice for most of the year. Ivan gave up his attempts to break through to the Baltic and moved southward instead toward the Black Sea.

He attacked the successor-states to the now defunct Golden Horde, annexing the khanates of Kazan and Astrakhan without difficulty, although the Turks assisted the Crimean Tartars in order to prevent the Russians from breaking through to the Black Sea. Spurred on, like the kingdoms of the West, by hope of vast treasure, Ivan began the eastward expansion of Russia and conquered the largely waste lands of the Khanate of Siberia. During his reign Russia again almost doubled its territory, and these new conquests were gradually settled over the next two centuries.

Ivan's son Feodor (1584–98), who succeeded him, was a man of very different character. Feodor was almost totally absorbed in finding his way to heaven. He patronized the Church and gave the Metropolitan the rank of Patriarch as a reflection of Moscow's position as the third Rome, much to the anger of the Patriarch of Constantinople. In secular matters Feodor showed no such decisiveness.

Boris Godunov

Effective government during Feodor's reign lay in the capable hands of his brother-in-law, Boris Godunov (1552–1605), who acted as the Tsar's guardian. Godunov pursued a largely peaceful foreign policy with the West, although he continued the eastern drive of Ivan IV, pushing deep into Siberia beyond the Obi River. However, the conquest of such large areas of wasteland created a problem of manpower: if the newly conquered lands were to be settled, the old estates of European Russia would be threatened with depopulation. To get over this danger, the nobility demanded the formalization of a state of serfdom for the landless peasantry. In 1587, the peasants were banned from moving from one estate to another. Godunov favored the landlords, but he was determined not to allow the creation of any great feudal estates, and he attempted to crush the leading dynasty, the Romanovs.

Boris Godunov, Russian ruler.

When the childless Feodor died in 1598, Godunov was elected to succeed him. However, despite his ability, Godunov found it almost impossible to rule effectively. The boyars regarded him as no more than one of themselves, and it seemed increasingly likely that the Romanovs would rebel against him. In order to avoid this he banished some of the Romanovs and forced others to become monks, but this did not prevent rebellion. In 1603, a pretender who claimed to be the son of Ivan IV invaded Russia with help from Poland. Godunov marched against him, but died before he had a chance to defeat him. Deprived of any powerful ruler, Russia degenerated into anarchy.

Poland

Poland's problems, which had been growing throughout the first half of the sixteenth century, came to a head in 1572 with the death of the last Jagellionid King, Sigismund II. The problems of Poland were those of an amorphous group of states united solely by obedience to a common ruler. Sigismund called his realm "a commonwealth of states," but neither socially nor geographically was there any real unity. The chief difficulty was the power of the nobility, who were able during the sixteenth century successfully to enserf the peasantry. The kings of Poland, after the extinction of the Jagellionid line, found it hard to resist the demands of the nobility, because the monarchy was elective, and the demands grew from reign to reign. The eastward extension of Poland during the fifteenth century meant that the population tended to move eastward into relatively unpopulated lands, and the nobility reacted by tying the peasantry to their land.

After Sigismund's death the national assembly elected as King Henry of Valois, Duke of Anjou. In order to prevent a new dynasty from succeeding the Jagellionids and to keep the power of electing the king firmly in their own hands, the nobility forced Henry to agree not to marry without the assembly's consent. It also insisted on reduced taxation and attempted to gain control of foreign policy. Henry soon showed that he had no intention of keeping his promises. Worse, he was determined not to subordinate his position in France to his new kingdom. He spent little more than six months in Poland before returning to France to fight the Huguenots. He was determined to succeed his brother as King of France and hoped to unite the two kingdoms. This ambitious plan was rejected by the assembly and Henry was deposed.

The next two elections, in 1575 and 1587, proved how deep rooted Poland's problems were. The assembly was unable to agree on a successor, and because no method of sorting out disputes had been agreed, rivals for the throne disputed the results. The problem was exacerbated by disputes as to whether the king should be a Pole or belong to a foreign dynasty, and if the latter, from which dynasty he should come. Unable to accept one of themselves as king, the Polish nobility were forced to look abroad, and Poland was dragged into the power politics of Europe. The election of the Valois Henry had displeased a substantial minority among the nobles, who wanted to tie the fortunes of Poland more closely to the Empire and to elect a Hapsburg as king. The majority preferred to follow the previous anti-Hapsburg line, and in 1577 Istvan Báthory of Hungary and Transylvania was elected. After Báthory's death ten years later, Sigismund III Vasa, a member of the Swedish royal house, was elected. After the 1575 election the

Istvan Báthory elected King of Poland by the anti-Hapsburg party.

danger of civil war between the pro- and anti-Hapsburg factions was narrowly avoided. In 1586, the Hapsburg Archduke Maximilian invaded the country, but was decisively beaten at Byezyna in 1588, a setback for the Austrian Hapsburgs as serious as was the defeat of the Armada for their Spanish cousins in the same year.

Sigismund attempted to strengthen the authority of the crown, but was unable to push any substantial reforms through the assembly. In addition he was found to be negotiating with the Hapsburgs to hand over Poland in return for Hapsburg support in gaining the crown of Sweden. As a result Sigismund was faced with rebellion in 1607, and although he defeated the rebels, he was unable to use his victory to extract worthwhile political concessions from the assembly. Poland therefore was left with a chaotic constitution and a nobility that was able to ignore the authority of the crown almost entirely.

Hungary

From 1547, Hungary was formally divided into three separate regions: royal Hungary, which was ruled by the Hapsburgs, Turkish Hungary and independent Transylvania. The rule of the Turks was firmly directed from Constantinople, and the Hapsburgs allowed their part of the country little independence, while Transylvania retained its independence largely because of its fear and hatred of both the Turks and the Hapsburgs. The Hapsburg threat seemed more dangerous than the Ottoman, and the Prince of Transylvania, Istvan Báthory, asked for Turkish help when the Hapsburgs invaded his country in 1552 and 1556. Báthory was determined that his principality should remain independent, and all his efforts were devoted to this even after his election as King of Poland.

Sigismund Báthory, Prince of Transylvania.

After Báthory's death in 1586, his great-nephew Sigismund Báthory became Prince of Transylvania. Sigismund cared little for the responsibilities of government and abdicated in favor of the Hapsburg Archduke Matthias. The Hapsburg determination to extirpate Protestantism—the cause of so many of their difficulties throughout Europe—led to rebellion in 1593. Sigismund returned from his retirement to lead the national struggle. It was, however, not he but another Transylvanian noble, Istvan Bocksai, who ultimately, with Turkish help, drove the Hapsburg army out in 1606, and set himself up as Prince.

Mannerism

As the sixteenth century progressed, art and architecture developed into something that had ceased to be Renaissance, but had not yet become Baroque. This intermediate style, which found popularity throughout Europe, has been called Mannerist since the contemporary artist and art historian Giorgio Vasari (1511–74) described it as such. Mannerism was a reaction against the rigid imposition of classical rules, which had become so important during the Renaissance; but the rules remained important simply so that they could be broken. At the same time the exaggeration and distortion of the figures in Mannerism was the basis on which the Baroque was to be built.

The Nymphaeum, courtyard of the Villa Giulia in Rome, by Giorgio Vasari.

The leading practitioner of Mannerist art was Giulio Romano (c. 1500–46), a pupil of Raphael. Guilio's huge *Fall of the Giants* at the Palazzo del Tè at Mantua shows all the characteristics of Mannerism. Other leading Mannerist artists were Jacopo Pontormo (1494–1557), whose *Deposition from the Cross* shows how rapid was the move away from classical perfection, and Francesco Parmigiano (1503–40).

Joseph in Egypt by Jacopo da Pontormo.

Although Mannerism was in origin an Italian style, heavily influenced by the spirituality of the Counter-Reformation and by the Council of Trent, it spread rapidly even in the Protestant north, although more as an architectural than as an artistic style. This speedy development was characteristic of the way in which ideas, styles and thoughts become Europeanized within a few years during the sixteenth and seventeenth centuries, largely as a result of increased contact between the north and south of Europe—particularly at the diplomatic level—and because of printing. Architects such as Vasari, who designed the portico of the Uffizi at Florence, and Pirro Ligorio (1510–83), whose organ fountain at the Villa d'Este is a monument of Mannerist oddity, had an extensive influence on the north as well as the south of Europe. Buildings like Hardwicke Hall in England show how rapidly Mannerism became an international style.

“Paris Is Worth a Mass” 1594

After four years of trying to impose order on his kingdom, the Huguenot Henry IV *embraced Catholicism and put an end to fifty years of civil and religious strife. By recognizing that the French would not permit a Protestant king to rule, and by treating his former followers generously under the Edict of Nantes, Henry ushered in peace and founded France's last royal dynasty—the Bourbons.*

At seven in the morning on March 22, 1594, Henry IV, first of the Bourbon kings of France, entered Paris by the Porte Neuve, the same gate by which his predecessor, Henry III, had fled some six years before. Since the day of that flight, May 12, 1588, Paris had been held by a revolutionary party which, for most of the time, would not even acknowledge that it had a king, much less admit him to the city. The restoration of the monarchy to Paris ended a reign of terror there and opened the final stage of the French wars of religion.

The sixth of those wars, concluded by the Peace of Bergerac in 1577, had resulted from the formation in the previous year of the Holy League, an association of Catholic nobles sworn to destroy Protestantism and restore the sole authority of the Church throughout France. Under the leadership of Henry, Duke of Guise, the League temporarily gained control of the government. Although League leaders professed loyalty to the crown, they had no respect for Henry III and knew he did not share their zeal for the extirpation of the Protestant heresy of the Huguenots.

For his part, the King feared that the destruction of the Huguenots would make him dependent on Guise and his noble partisans and perpetuate the fragmentation of his authority in the kingdom, as they hoped to convert their provincial governorships into hereditary fiefs. A victory for the League would thus have restored religious uniformity at the price of fragmenting France under a new feudal order.

This first Catholic League collapsed after Henry III declared himself, and not Guise, to be its head. Lack of funds, however, prevented him from taking part in the ensuing sixth war of religion (March to August, 1577) and the League's own organization was insufficient to mount a serious military campaign against the Huguenots. The Peace of Bergerac thus ended both this desultory, inconclusive warfare and Henry's obligations to the League. The peace, in fact, prohibited all leagues and secret associations, a ban that applied both to the Holy League and to the Huguenot Confederation. The Huguenots were granted freedom of worship in a limited number of towns. The peace therefore reflected the belief of Henry III and his mother, Catherine de' Medici, that the political unity of the kingdom under royal authority be preferred to its religious unity.

Moderate Catholics had refused to support the League. This central body of opinion, known as *Politiques*, had an assorted membership—nobles, particularly the great House of Montmorency, whose only consistency in policy, apart from private aggrandizement, was hostility to the Guise faction; lawyers and officials, less devoted to their Catholic faith than to their interest in upholding the institutions of lawful government; and merchants and bankers anxious to restore a commerce ruined by fifteen years of civil war. For various motives, therefore, the *Politiques* were prepared to accept the principle of peaceful coexistence with the Huguenots. With their support, Henry III and the Queen Mother were able to preserve the Peace of Bergerac for nearly ten years. (It was renewed after the brief, localized seventh war in 1580.) Economic revival followed this restoration of internal peace, until the calm was shattered by external factors and the question of the royal succession.

In 1584 it became apparent that Henry III was to be the last Valois King of France. With the death on June 15 of his younger brother, the Duke of Anjou (and previously of Alençon), Henry was the only survivor among the four sons of Henry II and, with his preference for male favorites, he now seemed likely, after nine years of marriage, to remain childless. According to the Salic Law barring succession through the female line, Henry III's heir would be the head of the House of Bourbon, which was descended in an unbroken male line from King Louis IX (d. 1270).

Henry IV (of Navarre), King of France. A genial, shrewd man of action he had first to conquer his kingdom. For the sake of French unity he abjured his Calvinist faith, but established a regime of tolerance for the Huguenots.

Opposite Henry IV during the Battle of Ivry at which he defeated the larger forces of the Catholic League under Mayenne. Henry's courage, staying-power and good humor won him the war; his subtlety and patience secured religious peace.

Procession through Paris of the Catholic League. Besieged by Henry IV the Parisians suffered appalling hardship, and processions such as these were meant to rekindle fervor against "the king of heretics."

This was Henry of Bourbon, King of Navarre. Born in 1553, Henry had been brought up as a Huguenot in the mountains of Béarn. Here, on the northern slopes of the Pyrenees, was the tiny remnant of the former Spanish kingdom that gave Henry his first royal title, though he also held other lordships in this largely Protestant part of France. Henry had, of necessity, observed the Catholic faith during his enforced residence at the French royal court after his marriage to Margaret of Valois which had occasioned the Massacre of St. Bartholomew. In 1576 he made his escape, immediately abjured Catholicism, and a year later was recognized as the leader of the Huguenot party. In the sixth and seventh wars of religion, Henry won renown as a fearless, dashing and often successful commander of the Huguenot forces; his readiness to share the hardships of campaigning with his troops, and his warm humanity and easy, cheerful manner, were the basis for his reputation as the most popular of all French kings.

That this heretic should become King of France, however, was a prospect that evoked the most bitter opposition of zealous Catholics, not least the members of the House of Guise who harbored their own aspirations to the crown based on their descent from Charlemagne. Thus in 1584, after Anjou's death, a new Catholic League sprang into being for the purpose of excluding Henry of Navarre from the French throne.

The initiative for forming this national revolutionary party came from a group of clerics and attorneys in Paris. From their pulpits, priests and monks roused the fears and hatred of their congregations against "the king of heretics." A central committee arranged for their recruits to take control of the guilds and organized the Parisian artisans to harry opponents and the unaligned. Other dominantly Catholic towns followed the example of the Parisian League, which built a network of communications with its provincial brethren. Links were also made with the Duke of Guise who, as the League's military leader, replaced royal garrisons of towns with his own officers. The League at this stage was, in fact, a conspiracy against Henry III, who was already prepared to recognize Henry of Navarre as his heir.

By the Treaty of Joinville on January 2, 1585, Guise secured financial support and the promise of military assistance from Philip II of Spain. Philip was, of course, the principal political champion of Catholicism, but his purpose was also to bring about the destruction of France as a European power, in order to prevent further French assistance to his rebellious subjects in the Netherlands. Following the murder of the Dutch leader, William the Silent (1584), and their defeats by the Duke of Parma's Spanish army, the Dutch seemed in such danger that Elizabeth of England sent an expedition to support them against the common foe. This led Philip to conclude that he would have to conquer England in order to crush the Dutch. And as preparations for the Spanish Armada were advanced it was imperative that France be neutralized by internal strife.

Initially, and reluctantly, Henry III came to terms with the League and on July 7, 1585, revoked

Henry IV presented with the keys to Paris, by Gerard. His entry into the city on March 22, 1594, signaled the restoration of the French monarchy.

all his concessions to the Huguenots. The ensuing "War of the Three Henrys" was slow in gathering momentum. After Henry of Navarre defeated a royal army at Coultras (October 20, 1587), Henry III avowed that Henry of Guise was his worst enemy. The King ordered Guise not to enter Paris and directed his Swiss mercenaries to secure the capital. The alarmed Paris leaguers called on Guise to save them from royal repression, and the Duke entered Paris on May 9, 1588.

The preachers in the city had now been able to add to their vituperations against the two royal Henrys the moral to be drawn from the execution of Mary Queen of Scots by Elizabeth of England (February 8, 1587). This event also finally determined Philip II to launch the "Enterprise of England." Through Mendoza, now his ambassador in Paris, he synchronized the sailing of the Armada with the execution of long-laid plans for the city's rebellion against Henry III. The barricades of May 12 so hampered the French King's troops that they were prevented from occupying key points, and the mob was roused to march on the Louvre, shouting for his deposition.

Once flight had won him personal safety, the King resumed negotiations with the League. Powerless, he ceded all its demands, including the summoning of the Estates-General to Blois. Then encouraged perhaps by the failure of the Spanish Armada, he attempted to destroy the League by assassinating its leader. But Henry's murder of the Duke and Cardinal of Guise (December 23 and 24, 1588) only roused the fury of their followers: the Sorbonne declared that Henry's crimes freed his subjects from allegiance; the leaguers of Paris organized the government of the city under a council known as the Sixteen, proclaiming the Cardinal of Bourbon, Henry of Navarre's uncle and prisoner, as "King Charles X." Guise's brother, the Duke of Mayenne, was recognized as the League's new leader and styled Lieutenant-General of the kingdom.

As his rule was now effective only in the Loire valley, Henry III turned to Henry of Navarre for support. In July their combined armies neared Paris. Then another assassination saved the city. On August 2, 1589, Jacques Clément, a fanatical monk, fatally stabbed the King at St. Cloud. On his deathbed Henry III recognized Navarre as his successor.

In this way Henry IV inherited the French crown. His fellow Huguenots accepted him as King with little hesitation. He was also recognized by royalist Catholics and *Politiques* after a declaration confirming Henry III's nominees in their offices; moreover, Henry promised to preserve the Catholic Church and to submit himself to instruction by its doctors. But the League's hostility continued unabated, and, bolstered by Spanish gold and soldiers, it commanded the allegiance of all the great towns, and the whole of northern France from Brittany to Burgundy. Indeed, Henry IV's cause was so uncertain that half his army soon deserted him, its leaders preferring to wait on events and strengthen their own local empires.

Henry III attending a ball. Although more cultured and affable than his brother, the last Valois King of France was eccentric. His murder of the Duke of Guise lost the monarchy what little prestige it retained.

German cartoon of "L'Affaire Brisson," in which the revolutionary Paris Leaguers hanged the President of the Parlement. This act alienated their Lieutenant-General, Mayenne, and hastened the League's disintegration.

Henry therefore abandoned his first attempt on Paris. Instead he turned to the conquest of Normandy, where he twice defeated the larger forces of the League under Mayenne, at Arques (September 21, 1589) and Ivry (March 14, 1590). In May he returned to blockade Paris. As the summer passed, its people were reduced to starvation; some perished by eating bread made from bones from the cemeteries, while fanatics preached that it was better to eat one's children than submit to a heretic king. The siege was raised in September by Parma's Spanish troops from Flanders.

Despite this second failure at Paris, Henry's cause won ground in 1590. The League's army had been annihilated at Ivry. In Provence its noble leaders fell out among themselves. The relief of Paris had shown that Spanish support was essential for the League's survival, but the intervention of France's enemy of a century's standing alienated moderate, loyal opinion. Even Mayenne did not wish to be a subject of Philip II. The Guises and other great princes preferred a king whose authority rested lightly and who would tolerate their virtual autonomy. City corporations had equally selfish motives: the collapse of royal authority favored municipal independence—Marseilles was a republic from 1591 to 1596.

These local ambitions also hampered Henry IV. The exhaustion of France, the ruin of its economy by war and the increasing brigandage of impoverished nobles and starving peasants, deprived Henry of the means to crush the League. Indeed he, too, lived from hand to mouth, a shabby figure with his meager wardrobe, though his invincible good humor and tireless courage kept up the spirits of his troops. He could show, also, that he was ready to forgive former enemies, to confirm the privileges of towns that opened their gates to his army and to retain in their offices and even grant pensions and more powers to nobles who ended their opposition.

Henry's generosity to former enemies dismayed his Huguenot followers. Their long services in arduous campaigns went unrewarded, and their support for him was consequently diminished by desertions and even by hostile intrigues. On the other hand, Henry appeared determined to remain a Huguenot. Although he acknowledged Catholicism to be the state religion of France, he showed no urgency in fulfilling his promise to receive instruction in its doctrine. His Catholic subjects therefore had no more cause to be enthusiastic in their loyalty than were the disillusioned Huguenots.

The military stalemate persisted for three more years. Henry continued the occupation of Normandy and the Île de France, but his siege of Rouen had to be raised in March, 1592, when Parma returned to relieve the League with his Spanish troops. Other Spaniards stiffened the resistance of Henry's enemies in Toulouse and Brittany; in the latter the involvement of English forces made this local war an international affair, though it had little effect on the rest of Europe. Spanish intervention could not be decisive because of Philip's other commitments; as it was, the diversion of his forces to France enabled the Dutch rebels to regain lost ground. The object of the Spanish expeditions was to prevent the defeat of Henry's opponents so that the French civil war should continue.

Henry's survival more than the progress of his campaigns worked toward his ultimate success. The desperate condition of France eventually persuaded all but the most fanatical leaguers that if the country was to be rescued from utter desolation he must be accepted as King. Even in Paris, the heart of the League, continuing privation and distaste for Spain were sapping the will to resist. There the revolutionary junta determined to maintain its hold by a policy of terror. A list of *Politiques* was drawn up, each name having against it a letter meaning "hang," "stab" or "expel." On November 15, 1591, the Sixteen had Barnabé Brisson, President of the Parlement, and two other leading lawyers arrested and hanged. This atrocity actually hastened the League's disintegration. Mayenne reacted by taking the Bastille from the control of the Sixteen; the council was purged and four ringleaders in "L'Affaire Brisson" were hanged. Henceforth the zealots regarded their Lieutenant-General as an enemy.

The League had lost their "King Charles X" with the death of the Cardinal of Bourbon in 1590. There was no agreement about his successor. Philip II pressed the claims of his daughter, the Infanta Isabella, as the granddaughter of Henry II of France. Mayenne and the other Guises preferred their own shadowy claims. Owing to his dependence on Spain, however, Mayenne complied with Philip's demand to hold a meeting of the Estates-General to choose a king. In May, 1593, it listened to the Spanish ambassador's claim for the Infanta and, despite the purge of the Parlement of Paris, its judges upheld the Salic Law and excluded Isabella from the throne.

It was at this point that Henry IV made his historic decision to become a Catholic. His persistence in the Huguenot faith until 1593 indicates the strength of his conviction. By this time he could not be accused of abandoning Protestantism as an

The signing of the Edict of Nantes; a contemporary engraving. The Edict confirmed religious toleration for the Huguenots to be guaranteed by possession of fortified towns and autonomous political and legal institutions.

expedient to rescue himself from a weak political situation, as would have been the case at his accession four years earlier. He was the strongest power in his fragmented kingdom. It was obvious, however, that French reunification waited on his conversion: noble members of the League were declaring themselves ready to submit when Henry was received into their Church. He had to sacrifice his convictions to save his country. He persuaded himself also that as a Catholic king he would be better able to guarantee toleration for the Huguenots.

Thus on July 25, 1593, in the abbey-church of St. Denis, the ancient shrine of the kings of France, Henry made his confession of faith, swore to defend the Catholic Church, and received Mass. There is no proof that he cynically observed that "Paris is worth a Mass," for he was to remain a Catholic for the remainder of his life. Nor did Paris immediately open its gates. Henry made a truce with the League until the end of the year, making it understood that any who did not then submit would be treated as rebels. Many did come to terms with him, among them Lyons, Rouen, Orleans and Bourges. Paris had to be won by intrigue and bribes; the city was not "given" to him, Henry said, but "sold, and for a good price." The League's commanders arranged matters with such secrecy that the royalist troops were able to enter from four sides and gain control of the streets before the Spanish garrison had risen from their beds. Then Henry himself entered, and soon a tumultous mob was crying "Vive le Roi" as he made his way to Notre Dame for a celebratory *Te Deum*.

Henry could now rule as King of France through the legal institutions centered on the capital. The task of reuniting the kingdom went on. When the young Duke of Guise submitted in November, 1594, Henry rewarded him with an appointment as Governor of Provence, which still had to be wrested from its local empire-builders. As Spain continued to assist Henry's French enemies, he declared war in January, 1595, hoping that no cause would be more likely to foster French unity. The exhausted combatants struggled on until 1598 when Philip, on his deathbed, agreed to the Peace of Vervins. The last Guise to submit, the Duke of Mercoeur in Brittany, then made his peace with Henry. Soon afterward, on April 15, Henry issued the Edict of Nantes. confirming toleration for the Huguenots to be secured by their possession of 200 fortified centers and their own political and legal institutions.

The last French civil war of the sixteenth century was its longest, extending from 1585 to 1598. It began in "The War of the Three Henrys," like its predecessors a war of religion, of Catholic against Huguenot. A new factor emerged in 1588 with the rising of the Catholic League against the Valois Henry III, and from this time on it gained the character of a war of succession to prevent the Huguenot Henry of Bourbon gaining the throne. Henry's conversion to Catholicism separated the religious and constitutional aspects of the conflict; it was now a war against Spain and neo-feudalism. For the latter, the private empire-building which had been a constant feature in all the wars of religion, Henry's remedy was, in effect, to buy his recognition as King by tolerating princely pretensions. The Edict of Nantes, creating a Huguenot "state within a state" was therefore only the most conspicuous of these concessions to provincial particularism.

France under Henry IV was a federation. His monarchy was thus far less absolute than that of Louis XI, let alone of Louis XIV. He was indeed the popular founder of France's last royal dynasty; even if his character had been less engaging, the peace of his last twelve years and the restoration of French life after fifty years of civil war would have won his reputation as the father of his people. But the problem of political unity, above all the dangerously privileged position of the large Huguenot minority, remained a source of further strife. Henry's own assassination in 1610, and his succession by a boy of nine, soon revealed the fragility of his achievement.

Henry IV's first Mass as King of France gains significance if one looks at other monarchies of the period. In England and Germany rulers had imposed religious dogmas on their subjects. Unlike the Tudors and the Lutheran princes, Henry had to give way to the determination of the French majority to remain Catholic and have a Catholic king. The will of the majority prevailed because, in contrast with Germany and England, there were among them sufficient men of purpose to organize themselves into an effective opposition. The Catholic League nearly destroyed France and itself eventually fell apart, but its purpose was achieved. This revolutionary party, by its well-knit national organization, its unscrupulous use of propaganda and foreign aid, compelled Henry and moderate French opinion to accept that France could not survive unless the King went to Mass. Henry's conversion was thus the result of a new phenomenon in European politics which is still apparent today—the ability of determined, organized extremists to influence the destiny of nations. ROBIN STOREY

Europe reaps the economic consequences

The Age of Exploration did not end in the 1520s. Throughout the sixteenth century, explorers continued to travel in search of new lands and new treasures, while boatloads of colonists were dispatched to distant shores. Voyages of explorers, such as Hernando de Soto who explored much of Florida in 1539, and Francisco Coronado who penetrated as far as the great prairies west of the Mississippi in 1541, continued, but as the century wore on they became less common, at least for the Spaniards and the Portuguese. The extent of actual settlement, whether in America, Asia or Africa, was small, and in America the arrival of white men,

An engraving showing the horrors of the Spanish conquest of South America; from *Den Vermerderndern Spieghel* (1664).

with their advanced weapons, their carelessness of Indian life and their diseases led to a substantial reduction in population. It has been estimated that the population of central Mexico fell from eleven million in 1519 to two and a half million in 1597. If Europe successfully exported typhoid and smallpox, it suffered in return from the import of Indian diseases, of which syphilis was the most serious.

Unlike the Spaniards, whose chief concern was gold and silver mining, the Portuguese set up colonies along the coasts that might be useful for trading. Portuguese overseas possessions were mainly trading posts, and they were used primarily as the bases of a seagoing nation. Only in Brazil was any large-scale settlement attempted, and by 1600 there were probably around ten thousand Portuguese there.

The new colonial nations

From about 1500, England and France began to show increasing interest in the possibilities of colonialism. In 1555 a group of French Protestants settled in Rio de Janiero, and, although they were driven out by the Portuguese in 1567, just as a similar settlement in Florida had been dislodged two years earlier, the idea of settlement in America as a means of avoiding religious intolerance and persecution in Europe became increasingly attractive during the seventeenth century.

Farther north, both England and France competed with the established colonial powers. The search for the northwest passage continued, and the value of the huge shoals of fish off Newfoundland was quickly recognized. Portugal's nominal ownership was ignored, although Portuguese ships did fish there occasionally. English sailors also searched unsuccessfully for a northeastern passage through the Russian Arctic, which introduced them to the power of the Russian tsar.

During the reign of Queen Mary of England, English ships began to trade with the Spanish colonies in America in an attempt to satisfy the growing needs—particularly for slaves—of the colonists. In theory they were allowed to buy only from Spanish merchants, who charged highly inflated prices. As relations between Philip II and Queen Elizabeth deteriorated, the English quite deliberately tried to break the trade monopoly that Spain had reserved in its colonies. Increasing pressure to end this illegal trade was brought to bear by the Spanish government, and in 1568 the leading English

Illustration of an early form of sextant from a French treatise on navigation.

trader, Sir John Hawkins (1532–95), was attacked by the Spanish fleet, although he managed to escape

After this it was clear to the English that piracy was cheaper and more profitable without being any more dangerous. The French had already realized this. The Spanish ships sailing between America and Seville were both vulnerable and rich. French pirates such as Francis Le Clerc, had a serious effect on Spanish trade. In 1537 nine out of twenty ships sailing to Europe from Spanish America were successfully attacked by pirates, and in 1556 Le Clerc attacked the key port of Havana. To counteract the danger of piracy the Spaniards increased the size of their naval forces in America and Spanish ships were sent across the Atlantic in convoys for protection. Toward the end of the sixteenth century the pirates redoubled their efforts, with the secret assistance of their governments. The new breed of pirates were known as privateers (private men of war).

Late sixteenth-century picture of Portuguese ships and flying fish.

The marauding of Sir Francis Drake, who was Hawkins' nephew, along the Spanish Main opened a new chapter in the history of privateering. In 1573, he brought home 96,000 dollars from raids on Nombre de Dios, and four years later Drake became a national hero when he circumnavigated the globe. His raids on Spanish settlements in the New World and his capture of a hoard of Peruvian silver from the *Cacafuego* netted Drake's investors a return of 1,400 per cent on their initial investments. And when the *Golden Hind* put in to Deptford, after its globe-girdling voyage, Elizabeth knighted "her pirate."

In 1585 Drake sailed to the Caribbean and sacked Santo Domingo and Cartagena. The Queen provided 24,000 dollars and two of her ships for the undertaking. Her action constituted a declaration of war against Spain. Drake's leaving Plymouth on an obvious errand of plunder provoked the confiscation of all English shipping in Spanish ports. That same year, through Sir Walter Raleigh's initiative, an English expedition under Sir Richard Grenville and Ralph Lane planted England's first colony in the New World. They named the ill-fated colony Virginia, in deference to the Queen.

Economic consequences of colonialism

The effect of trade and settlement outside Europe on Europe's trading structure was enormous. The massive scale of the import of previously rare spices, such as pepper, and the introduction of new plants and plant products, such as the potato, cane sugar and tobacco, rapidly transformed the consumer habits of Europe. The western states of Europe—Spain and Portugal, and to a lesser extent England and France—rapidly emerged as Europe's economic leaders.

The economic life of the colonies developed rapidly too. Slaves were the largest import, but there was a need for guns and other manufactured products also. In addition it soon became obvious that in some regions conditions for the breeding of livestock were ideal, and cattle, sheep and horses were all introduced to the American colonies in large numbers as breeding stock. But most of the economic activity was directed to one end, the mining of precious metals.

It became necessary for the Spanish and Portuguese to take an increasingly close interest in the government of their colonies. Philip II's obsessive interest in the details of administration led him to keep a close watch on life in the colonies; the viceroys and governors were almost all Castilian nobles who were allowed to serve for a few years only in order to prevent any of them from becoming too powerful. Trade with the colonies was a Spanish monopoly.

But it was, above all, the importance of mining silver and gold that made royal control vitally important. At first simple methods of extraction—the most primitive washing processes—were used, but in about 1545 the huge mine of Potosi in Bolivia was opened up, and there were other major mines in Mexico and Bolivia. A few of the mines were royal property and were operated under the able administration of Francis of Toledo, Viceroy of Peru from 1569 to 1581, the greatest colonial administrator of Spain's golden century. Most were, however, in private hands. Silver production was taxed in kind, usually at around twenty per cent, and the crown levied taxes on other products and exports too. Although the direct contribution of the American colonies to Spain's royal finances did not exceed about fifteen per cent until after 1560, the King gained indirectly also through increasing taxation levied in Spain itself. Later on in the century, silver, gold and taxation from the New World became an increasingly important and substantial part of Philip II's income. The total annual silver and gold imports to Seville from America, worth about one million *pesos* in 1530, rose to ten million *pesos* in 1550, thirty million *pesos* by 1580, and reached a peak of almost forty million *pesos* in the 1590s. Other trade grew enormously also during the second half of the sixteenth century, and the European economic scene was totally transformed.

The price revolution

The effect of the enormous rise in imports of silver on the value of currencies that were made up largely of silver was only very gradually seen. From the middle of the century, when bullion imports first became really substantial, the economy of Europe was in a dangerous state.

The silver mines of Potosi, Peru, from an atlas of sea charts. The influx of precious metals into Europe led to spiralling inflation.

Paradoxically, the first victim was Spain. Charles V and Philip II were both determined to make Spain's new-found wealth available only to Spaniards, which resulted in attempts to ban the reexport of American silver and gold from Spain. Although Spain enforced its monopoly on exports to the American colonies, it was unable itself to supply the goods required by the colonists. As a result it was obliged to import them from the rest of Europe. This was the main cause of the collapse of the Spanish economy in the middle of the sixteenth century, the first major sign of the difficulties to come. Spain brought the French government into bankruptcy at the same time. The Peace of Cateau-Cambrésis in 1559 allowed the economy of Europe a breathing-space from the Hapsburg–Valois struggle and was the cause of a temporary economic recovery, not only in Spain and France, but in Europe as a whole. But the silver imports continued to rise during the second half of the century and the basic problem of inflation remained.

The reason for the inflation was scarcely anywhere realized. In France Jean Bodin saw that silver imports were a cause of rising prices, but he was almost alone in doing so and never found it possible fully to articulate his views. There were in any case other factors, such as the easy availability of credit, at work. The relatively slight financial control of most governments over the economy of their countries made any regulation almost impossible. The simplest solution appeared to be a devaluation of the ever-increasing money supply against silver, which merely fed inflation.

Woodcut of a sturdy beggar. The sixteenth century saw a drop in the standard of living.

The extent of the inflation has been calculated by economic historians. An index of French prices, for example, expressed as 100 in 1471–72, rose gradually to 262 a century later. But in the years between 1575 and 1598 it climbed steeply to reach 628. The rise of two and a half times in the century from about 1470 to 1570 could largely be absorbed by the rapid growth in the economy and population. But the further growth of two and a half times in the following twenty years could not.

The rise in prices was in part due to a simple devaluation of money, but it went much further than that. Historians have recently begun to try to calculate the change in prices in forms of wage rates—an extremely difficult operation owing to regional and national differences, to changing exchange values and to the problem of tracing price fluctuations accurately—but it is clear that there was a fall in living standards during the late sixteenth century for the vast majority. In real terms wages fell, which affected the income of laborers and workers; agricultural and other rents, which in Western Europe were often fixed for long periods, were static in money terms and fell rapidly in real terms. A small minority prospered but the majority must have found life harder at the end of the century than fifty years before. Spain's economic ills were chronic, and in 1598 the government was again bankrupt, though this was in part due to the revolt in the Netherlands and to an expensive foreign policy.

The Battle of Sekigahara

1600

By diplomacy and force, Tokugawa Ieyasu defeated his rivals at Sekigahara and became the dominant force in Japanese politics. Consolidating his power, again mostly by diplomacy and force, he disposed of all possible rivals and assumed the title of Shogun. His efficient, effective government resulted in a stable state and an unquestioned succession, his line lasting more than two and a half centuries. It was finally overthrown by descendants of those he had originally defeated, who had neither forgotten nor forgiven the humiliation of their ancestors.

On the morning of October 21, 1600, more than 150,000 armed men waited tensely for battle near the village of Sekigahara in a narrow valley east of Lake Biwa in central Japan. North and south of the village were the massed forces of the Eastern Army; facing them, the Western Army in strong defensive positions. These forces symbolized the turmoil of the previous century caused by provincial warlords as the last vestiges of imperial administration disappeared and firearms transformed war and fortification. In recent decades both the dictator, Oda Nobunaga, and subsequently his general, Toyotomi Hideyoshi, had come close to national dominance; both had risen from provincial families and based their power on steel and gunpowder.

In September, 1598, Hideyoshi had died in Fushimi Castle, and left five powerful elders to rule until his young son Hideyori reached maturity. Soon these guardians were divided by disagreements and jealousy and began to gather their armies for civil war. By autumn, 1600, Ishida Mitsunari, a medium-rank vassal of Hideyori, had united his allies into the Western Army to challenge the most powerful elder, Tokugawa Ieyasu. They captured Fushimi Castle and advanced eastward hoping that their enemy would be distracted by northern campaigns. Ieyasu soon rebuffed his northern challengers and despatched two columns from Edo (Tokyo) to confront his rivals at Sekigahara.

Both camps were well armed with light guns and traditional weapons, but the Tokugawa army had important if intangible advantages. Foremost among these were the skills and experience of Ieyasu, whose innate ability combined with long campaigns made him the most brilliant commander in Japan. In his youth he had spent sixteen years as the hostage of rival lords before joining Nobunaga and Hideyoshi as a loyal ally. At age fifty-eight he was muscular, vigorous and subtle and surpassed all his enemies in his mastery of military and political strategy. He had also created a superior military organization and his unified command was far more efficient than the loose confederation of Western leaders.

When the morning mist lifted, Ieyasu's famous war cry rang over the battlefield and his horsemen and infantry charged the enemy positions. At first Ishida's allies successfully resisted the gunfire, spears and arrows of the Tokugawa troops, but Ieyasu's agents had already undermined enemy strategy. According to Ishida's battle plan, Kobayakawa, an ally with troops drawn up on hills to the south, was to charge into the valley and attack the rearguard of the Tokugawa troops. But Kobayakawa had secretly promised to switch sides at the height of the struggle, and instead of bringing triumph to Ishida his forces swept into battle and destroyed over 10,000 Western warriors.

With their military power broken many lords now submitted to Ieyasu hoping to assuage his anger and retain their estates. Their hopes and fears brought sharp debates to Ōsaka Castle where there was disagreement until the final days of October. Some members of the Mōri family from western Honshu favored continued military resistance, but advocates of reconciliation won the day, arguing that this might protect their lands from confiscation.

Ieyasu and his entourage entered Ōsaka Castle on November 1. He was now the military master of Japan, but he avoided insults to Hideyori which might provoke animosity and future wars.

After the campaign it was necessary to seize some enemy lands if only to provide booty for loyal allies. Ieyasu desired a strong political heartland and these considerations led him to redraw the political map and destroy enemy fortifications. Eighty-seven lords had their entire territories confiscated, while four important enemies, including Mōri, lost vast tracts of land to the Tokugawa vassals. In all, land with a productive power of 39,000,000 bushels of rice was redistributed, much to Ieyasu's estates.

A seventeenth-century statue of Tokugawa Ieyasu, the warlord who brought stable government to Japan. Combining tradition, philosophy and military power, he established himself as the head of a rigid social hierarchy, underpinned by a code of morality and merit.

Opposite Painting on a folding screen of the Battle of Sekigahara. By this victory over his rivals Ieyasu became the dominant force in Japanese politics. Leaving the phantom-Emperor undisturbed, he restored the imperial office of Shogun which his dynasty continued to hold for two and a half centuries.

A samurai is brought his mount. Japan's highest class were the military. Their code of ethical and political behavior was laid down by Ieyasu in the Laws of the Military Houses, enacted in 1615.

Both Oda and Hideyoshi had already taken several steps to create more efficient and enduring institutions. They had surveyed lands, standardized taxes and restricted arms-bearing to a small elite. Yet neither had created institutions with sufficient momentum to be able to survive the passing of their founders.

Aware of these dangers Ieyasu sought to combine tradition, philosophy and military power to strengthen the basis of his authority. It was relatively easy to continue the policies of his predecessors, which sought to stabilize society, but other elements were needed if these were to be integrated into permanent administration.

By the seventeenth century the emperors of Japan had long been powerless, but it was always possible for their prestige and symbolic power to be invoked by forces seeking to overthrow a military regime. To eliminate this danger, Ieyasu strengthened Hideyoshi's policy of dominating Kyōtō, the imperial capital, by building Nijō Castle as his personal residence not far from the Emperor's palace. He increased political scrutiny of the imperial court and appointed a corps of officials to keep watch on all activities throughout the city.

Although Ieyasu was outstandingly a man of action, he always recognized the value of history and philosophy as a guide and inspiration for the practical politician. One official chronicler wrote: "he fully appreciated the impossibility of governing the country on horseback ... accordingly, there could be no other way to govern the country than by a constant and deep faith in the sages and the scholars." More specifically he was fascinated by the career of T'ang T'ai Tsung, the founder of the T'ang dynasty. Like a Chinese emperor, Ieyasu collected books, sponsored their publication and conversed with scholars. He studied the classics of Chinese and Japanese politics and strategy and even before Sekigahara had enjoyed discussions with Confucian philosophers, Buddhist abbots and learned courtiers. In all these dialogues he was interested in discovering "the key to government, how to govern oneself, the people and the country," and declared "if we cannot clarify the principles of human relations society and government itself will become unstable and disorders will never cease." After Sekigahara, when he could devote more time to peaceful reconstruction, he turned to more serious studies and appointed the distinguished Confucian thinker Hayashi Razan to be official adviser to his government. Ieyasu partly looked to Confucianism to legitimize his own policies, but it was easy to find much in Hayashi's thought that supported his desire to build an enduring, stable administration. Confucian notions of authority and moral example were of obvious value to a ruler hoping to steer a society from war to peace, and Hayashi's emphasis on hierarchy and deference had much to contribute to the creation of a stable state.

Parallel with his interest in a philosophy of stability Ieyasu was deeply concerned to use Japanese precedents to legitimize and strengthen his regime. In 1192 military realities had compelled the Emperor to delegate sweeping powers to Minamoto Yoritomo who was pronounced Shogun, or Generalissimo. Later shoguns became almost powerless and in 1573 Nobunaga had driven the last Ashikaga shogun from office. For thirty years the position lapsed, but Ieyasu sought the sanctity of imperial approval and in 1603 was declared Shogun, the Emperor's most powerful deputy. Ieyasu's interest in the shogunate was not confined to symbolism and outward show; rather he searched the records of Yoritomo's successors for useful precedents which he used in strengthening his own regime.

Nobunaga and Hideyoshi had failed to establish political dynasties as they left no successors schooled in the arts of government. Ieyasu sought to preserve his own line from a similar fate by retiring from the shogunate in 1605, and handing the office to his third son Hidetada. In the final ten years of his life Ieyasu spent long periods in the town of Shizuoka deciding policy and perfecting the development of the Tokugawa state.

Although Ieyasu sought to turn Japanese minds from war to peace, he was unable to disregard the lords who had sought to destroy him or the circle that gathered round Hideyori. Confiscation of their lands added jealousy to their traditional animosity and they always appeared a threat to Tokugawa power. All the defeated had paid homage to Ieyasu after Sekigahara, but there was no reason to believe that they had finally abandoned notions of revenge. Most former enemies were restricted to lands far from the Tokugawa capital of Edo and they were excluded from important offices in the Shogun's government.

Ieyasu's tact and realism always restrained him from the vain endeavor of turning Japan into a unitary state. He sought to maintain Tokugawa dominance by balance and diplomacy and avoided provocative threats to the autonomy of likely challengers. But he prohibited the construction of new castles and demanded notification when lords planned to repair existing fortifications. Marriages between powerful families could only take place with

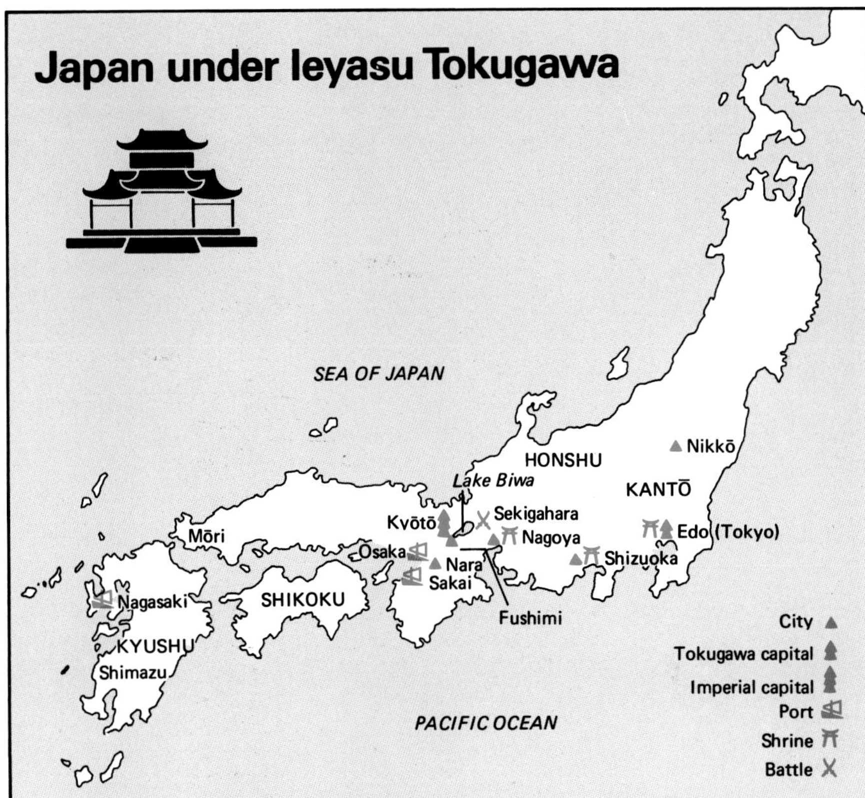

the Shogun's permission, and all these controls were enforced by spying and the supervision of suspected enemies.

Ieyasu never attempted to draw regular revenue from beyond his own domains but he demanded financial help in the construction of major defense works. Lords were asked to contribute to making Edo Castle the strongest fortress in Japan, and thus by strengthening his defenses he depleted the wealth of rival houses.

Underlying these measures were the conceptions of law and politics that were established as a national orthodoxy in the Laws of Military Houses. This code was enacted in 1615 and laid down ethical and political behavior for samurai throughout the land. These rules were heavily laden with references to the Chinese classics and dealt with all the minutiae of daily life as well as matters of high policy. The military class was warned against drinking parties and "wanton revelry," and "sexual indulgence and habitual gambling" were considered "a danger to the state." "The arts of peace and war" were commended and "a frugal and simple life" presented as a model to all samurai. Retainers were forbidden to wear white damask or purple silk and palanquins were reserved for "lords of the various domains, their close relatives and ranking officers, medical men and astrologers, those over sixty years of age, and those ill or infirm." The Tokugawa Code blended ideas of morality and merit to produce a society in which bureaucracy and tradition would prevent the hectic social upheaval of earlier years. Lords were encouraged to "select officials with a capacity for public administration" and the rich were urged not to display their wealth. Austerity and morality were seen as the qualities which would preserve peace under the shoguns.

The Tokugawa peace was based upon a fixed social hierarchy on the model of Confucian China. Japan's highest class were the military, a strange equivalent of China's *literati*. Below them ranked the peasantry who produced the food which sustained society, followed by artisans and craftsmen who manufactured tools, textiles and other essential goods. The lowest official class were the merchants who were thought to make no important contribution to the welfare of the community. Below these was a broad category of outcastes: criminals, executioners and slaughterers who carried out many tasks repugnant to ordinary members of society. These unfortunates were classed as non-human and were so despised that roads through their villages were not measured in official surveys and route maps.

The economic theory that underlies this conception of society was static and agrarian. Commerce was believed to add little to general happiness. And financial operations were regarded as sordid when compared with the military and administrative responsibilities of the samurai.

To reinforce the oath of loyalty which all lords made to Ieyasu, they were encouraged to visit Edo and leave hostages in the city. At first many allies and former enemies visited the Shogun voluntarily, to pay homage and give thanks for favors and marriage agreements. Elements of compulsion were gradually introduced into the practice as the Tokugawa gained in confidence. Some lords were called to the Shogun's capital to help organize the rebuilding of Edo, and in 1609 Hidetada ordered all allies and vassals to spend the New Year's season at his court. By this time the Tokugawa could openly treat all visitors as subjects and the following year all were ordered to leave hostages in the capital. The Laws of Military Houses restricted the size of the retinues that could enter the gates of Edo and by 1615 suspect lords were kept virtual prisoners in the city. After Ieyasu's death the "hostage system" became increasingly formalized. By 1636, all provincial rulers were compelled to keep their wives and families resident near the Shogun's castle, and the practice continued until 1862.

The building of mansions in Edo, like expensive journeys to the city, were further drains on the revenue of provincial nobles. This expenditure stimulated the growth of the city and brought prosperity to innkeepers on the great highways. Merchants benefited from the hostage system but perhaps its most significant outcome was to divert ambitious men from plotting and to secure Tokugawa control of powerful dissidents. With the growing power of the Edo government, barrier gates were established at strategic points to prevent the escape

The fall of Ōsaka Castle, last redoubt of Hideyori's power. At first Ieyasu maintained his dominance by balance and diplomacy. After slow consolidation of his position, however, he sought an opportunity to rid himself of Hideyori, his nominal liege-lord and potential rival.

of hostages or the illegal smuggling of arms into the city.

With the strengthening of this complex of controls Ieyasu felt increasingly secure from military and political challenges. By 1614, with his son firmly in office, he felt ready to destroy Ōsaka Castle, the final redoubt of Hideyori's power. In October, Tokugawa forces marched against Hideyori on the pretext that a bell he had cast was inscribed with the words "in the east the moon in the west the sun," an alleged insult to Ieyasu. Although no lords came to Hideyori's defense, some 90,000 personal vassals and masterless samurai gathered to protect him. After inconclusive skirmishing in November, further Tokugawa forces were committed to the siege and 35,000 casualties were suffered in an unsuccessful winter campaign. In January truce talks were held and fighting ended on January 21, 1615. According to the agreement the outer moats of the castle were to be filled in, but Hidetada broke the spirit of the understanding by also destroying some of the inner defenses of the citadel. By February 16 the outer ring of the fortress had been razed and the Shogun retired to gather new men. In May, with over 150,000 troops at his disposal, he resumed the assault. Bitter fighting continued until the beginning of June when Hideyori's followers assembled for a last stand in front of the castle. On June 3 the final struggle began and by the afternoon Tokugawa men had broken into the inner defenses. The next day Hideyori committed suicide and his mother was killed by a retainer to avoid the humiliation of capture. Shortly thereafter the Shogun ordered the execution of Hideyori's eight-year-old son and organized the massacre of hundreds of enemy supporters. The road between Kyōtō and Fushimi was lined with the heads of Hideyori's loyal soldiers.

Although Ieyasu gave most attention to political reconstruction, he eagerly sought new opportunities to augment his revenue. He confiscated the gold and silver mines of provincial landowners and increased their production. Large quantities of gold and silver currency were minted and on his death he bequeathed a rich treasury to his successors.

By the sixteenth century, Ōsaka, Sakai and Nagasaki had become well-established trading ports with increasing links with China and the Indies. Hideyoshi had encouraged European traders to visit Japan and Ieyasu sought to profit from this commerce.

Ieyasu, like Hideyoshi, feared the subversive influence of Roman Catholicism and in his final years issued decrees prohibiting Christianity and expelling Jesuit missionaries. These measures reflected political fears rather than opposition to trade or xenophobia. Ieyasu took control of key trading ports and employed an Englishman, Will Adams, as his adviser on trade and shipping. His attempts to develop Edo as a foreign trading center

Sekigahara. The seventeenth-century screen painting shows a marked Chinese influence. In many aspects of life the Tokugawa state sought precedents in Confucianism.

failed as ports in Kyushu were far more accessible to Chinese and Western merchants, but his overall attitude to foreign trade was far more positive than that of later shoguns. By 1640 his grandson had confined foreign merchants to the single port of Nagasaki and Japan was almost isolated from the Western world.

When Ieyasu died sixteen years after Sekigahara, the Tokugawa succession was secure. To celebrate the enormous achievements of this remarkable man subsequent shoguns commemorated him in unprecedented style. After a temporary burial at Kunosan near his favorite retreat of Shizuoka, his instructions were carried out and his remains moved to the mountains of Nikkō, north of the Kantō plain. In 1617 the Emperor granted him the title "The East Illumination Incarnation of Bodhisattva" and shrines were built to his memory in Nagoya, Edo and Shizuoka. Seventeen years later the third Shogun, Iyemitsu, determined to build a shrine and mausoleum that would do justice to Ieyasu's brilliant career. Twelve thousand of Japan's best craftsmen were recruited from Kyōtō and Nara and with their assistants they worked for two years to construct spectacular memorial buildings. Almost 2,500,000 sheets of gold leaf were used to emblazon

the gates and sanctuaries, and to this day their ornate walls stand witness to his wealth and power.

The triumph of Sekigahara ended two centuries of civil war. Ieyasu's descendants never equaled his creativity but they preserved his regime until the age of Lincoln, Gladstone and Napoleon III. Throughout the great peace, broken only by peasant rioting, Japan grew into a complex society, far from the abstemious ideals of the first Tokugawa Shogun. Agriculture prospered and commerce grew. Towns expanded and merchants flourished. Swordsmen became scholars; and plays, novels and color prints enriched city life. Schools multiplied and raised literacy to levels higher than in the West. Contact with Europe was limited, but the Dutch at Nagasaki inspired scholars and officials to discover new worlds of science, technology and politics. The Tokugawa failed to shackle trade and innovation, presiding over a flowering of commerce and civilization that was the envy of many visitors.

Despite the evident benefits of the shogunate, Sekigahara was not forgotten. Every year, on the anniversary of the battle, warriors of the defeated Shimazu House buckled on their armor and meditated on the far-off tragedy. Boys in Mōri's territory slept with their feet toward the east to insult the shoguns. They were urged never to forget Sekigahara "even in their dreams." Revenge was no more than a dream until 1854 when Commodore Perry forced the Shogun to open the country's ports to American vessels. More treaties, all unequal and damaging to the Tokugawa House, followed. Many believed that the treaties and warships would destroy Japan's independence, and many samurai turned their thoughts to defending the "divine land."

In 1866 the Mōri and Shimazu signed a treaty to oppose the shogunate. Two years later they defeated the Shogun's army and declared an Imperial Restoration. Tokugawa rule was at an end. Sekigahara had been avenged.

GORDON DANIELS

Above left Himeji Castle near Kyōtō, built in 1609. An example of the splendor of the Shogunate, it has a five-storey tower connected with three-storey keeps by means of covered passages, as well as ornate turrets, walls and gates.

Above An illustration of samurai lawlessness. With the breakdown of imperial government. Japan had gone through a period of civil anarchy, which only conclusively ended when Ieyasu subdued the barons and routed his rival generals.

1500 | 1513 | 1525

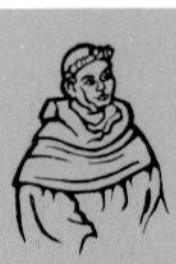

The Ninety-Five Theses 1517
Martin Luther's polemic against the sale of indulgences—intended for debate within the Church—leads instead to the Protestant Reformation

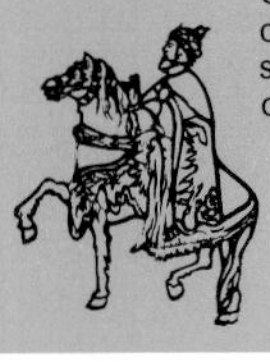

The Election of Charles V 1519
Charles' election as Holy Roman Emperor consolidates Hapsburg power in Europe, but his support of the Catholic Church against Luther dooms Germany to dissension and instability

1521
The Conquest of Mexico
Luck, ingenuity and courage—and the skilful use of horses and firearms—enables Cortes to topple the mighty Aztec Empire

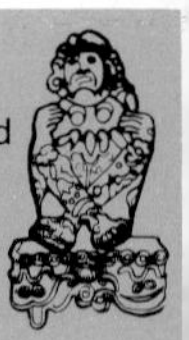

1522
A Bible for the Masses
Martin Luther's secretly published vernacular translation of the New Testament proves the power of the popular press in Europe

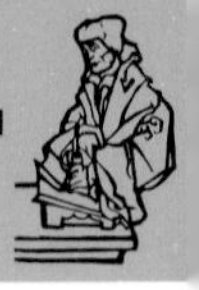

Paul III 1468–1549
Pope

Louis II 1506–25
King of Hungary

Margaret of Parma
Regent of the

Francisco Pizarro *c.* 1470–1541
Spanish conquistador

Francis Xavier (St.) 1506–52
Jesuit missionary, "Apostle of the Indies"

Selim II
Ottoma

Nicholas Copernicus 1473–1543
Polish astronomer

Anne Boleyn 1507–36
Queen of England

Ali Pash
Ottoma

Paul IV 1476–1559
Pope

Humayun 1508–56
Mogul Emperor

Charles
Cardina

Clement VII 1478–1534
Pope

Fernando, Duke of Alva 1508–82
Spanish general, regent of Netherlands

Baber 1483–1530
Founder of Mogul Empire

John Calvin 1509–64
French Protestant leader

Martin Luther 1483–1546
German religious reformer

Gerard Mercator 1512–94
Flemish cartographer

Ulrich Zwingli 1484–1531
Swiss religious reformer

Andreas Vesalius 1514–64
Flemish anatomist

Thomas Cromwell *c.* 1485–1540
English statesman

Tahmasp I 1514–76
Shah of Persia

Henry VIII 1491–1547
King of England

Mary of Guise 1515–60
Wife of James V of Scotland

Ignatius Loyola (St.) 1491–1558
Spanish founder of Jesuits

Francis of Toledo *c.* 1515–84
Spanish viceroy of Peru

Francis I 1494–1547
King of France

Mary I 1516–58
Queen of England

Suleiman I the Magnificent 1494–1566
Ottoman Sultan

Henry II 1519–59
King of France

Atahualpa *c.* 1500–33
Last Inca of Peru

Francis of Lorraine 1519–63
Duke of Guise

Manco *c.* 1500–44
Puppet Inca

Gaspard de Coligny 1519–72
Admiral of France, Huguenot leader

Charles V 1500–58
Holy Roman Emperor and King of Spain

Catherine de' Medici 1519–89
Queen of France

Reginald Pole 1500–58
English cardinal

Pieter Breughel the Elder *c.* 1520–69
Flemish painter

Gregory XIII 1502–85
Pope

Sigismund II 1520–72
King of Poland

Ferdinand I 1503–64
Archduke, then Holy Roman Emperor

Sixtus V 1521–90
Pope

John Knox *c.* 1505–72
Scottish religious reformer

Lamoral, Count
Flemish leader

1513 ● Balboa discovers the Pacific

1519–22 ● Magellan circumnavigates the world

1520 ● Luther excommunicated

1520 ● The Field of Cloth of Gold

● **1521** Diet of Worms: Luther under imperial ban

● **1522** Rhodes falls to the Turks

1524–26 ● Peasants' Revolt in Germany

1525 ● Battle of Pavia: Charles V takes Francis I captive

525 1538 1550

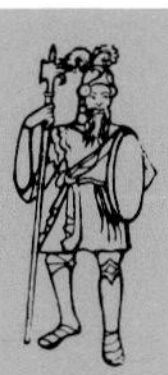

1532
Pizarro Conquers Peru
Conquistador Francisco Pizarro plunders the wealth of the Inca Empire and, snuffing out the native culture, extends Spain's overseas possessions

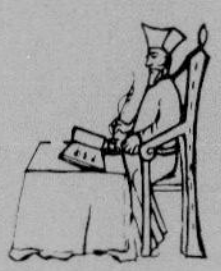

1544
The Council of Trent
Convened by Paul III to reunite Christendom, the Council of Trent confirms the breach, ushering in the Counter-Reformation and authoritatively ruling on questions of faith and doctrine

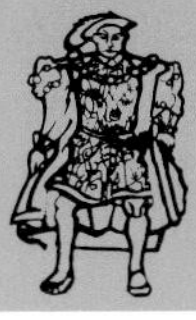

1533
Henry VIII's "Great Matter"
Intent on remarriage for the sake of a male heir, Henry VIII comes into conflict with the Pope, and sets in motion the English Reformation

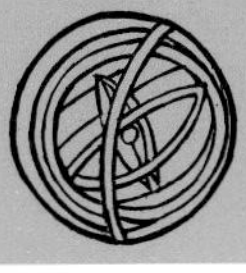

1543
The Earth Dethroned
Copernicus' theory of planetary motion – making the sun and not the earth the center of the universe–inaugurates a scientific revolution

522–86
letherlands

Jane Grey 1537–54 *Proclaimed Queen of England*

ne Sot *c.* 1524–74
ultan

–1571
eneral

f Guise 1524–74
f Lorraine

iiovanni Palestrina *c.* 1525–94
talian composer

Maximilian II 1527–76
Holy Roman Emperor

Philip II 1527–98
King of Spain

Emmanuel Philibert 1528–80
Duke of Savoy

Louis I de Condé 1530–69
Huguenot leader

Ivan IV the Terrible 1530–84
Tsar of Russia

Jean Bodin 1530–96
French political economist and philosopher

Robert Dudley *c.* 1532–88
Earl of Leicester

John Hawkins 1532–95
English privateer and slavetrader

William of Orange-Nassau (the Silent) 1533–84
Leader of Netherlands revolt

Stephen (Istvan) Báthory 1533–92
Prince of Transylvania, King of Poland

Michel de Montaigne 1533–92
French essayist

Elizabeth I 1533–1603
Queen of England

Oda Nobunaga 1534–82
Japanese warlord

Toyotomi Hideyoshi *c.* 1536–98
Japanese warlord

:gmont 1522–68

Edward VI 1537–53
King of England

● **1526**
Mogul Empire established in North India by Baber

● **1529**
Siege of Vienna by Turks

● **1533**
First permanent settlement in Argentina

● **1531**
League of Schmalkalden against Charles V

● **1534**
Act of Supremacy: severance of English Church from Rome

● **1526**
Battle of Mohacs: Turks defeat Hungarians

● **1529–36**
Henry VIII's Reformation Parliament

● **1533**
Pizarro takes Cuzco

● **1521–29**
War between France and Spain

● **1530**
Antwerp: new Bourse financial hub of Europe

● **1534**
Quito falls to three Spanish armies

1527 ●
Sack of Rome by imperial troops

● **1530**
Confession of Augsburg: Lutheran rule of faith

● **1542**
Inquisition established in Rome

1540 ●
Jesuit Order recognized by Paul III

● **1545**
Silver deposits discovered at Potosi, Peru

● **1541**
Calvin establishes theocracy at Geneva

● **1541**
Suleiman invades Hungary

1550 | 1563 | 1575

1564
'He Who Resists Power Resists God"
Tsar Ivan IV adopts a policy of terror against Russia's powerful boyar class in order to impose his concept of autocracy

1572
The Massacre of St. Bartholomew's Eve
Catholics, under the leadership of the Guise family, rise up and attempt to massacre the Huguenots in Paris and the provinces

1573

1566
The Revolt of the Beggars
The Protestant nobility of the Low Countries formally request leniency from Philip II in matters of religion—a request that is to escalate into war for independence

1571
Cutting the Sultan's Beard
Two vast navies—one Christian, one Moslem—engage in a sea duel that destroys the myth of the invincible Turk

Francis Drake *c.* 1540–96
English admiral and privateer

Francis, Duke of Alençon and Anjou *c.* 1554–84
French prince

El Greco *c.* 1541–1614
Cretan painter in Spain

Charles of Lorraine 1554–1611
Duke of Mayenne, leader of Guise party

Mary Stuart 1542–87
Queen of Scots

Abbas I the Great 1557–1629
Shah of Persia

Akbar the Great 1542–1602
Mogul Emperor

Felix Lope de Vega 1562–1635
Spanish dramatic poet

William Byrd 1542–1623
English composer of Church music

Robert Devereux, Earl of Essex 1567–1601
Elizabethan courtier and rebel

Tokugawa Ieyasu 1543–1616
Japanese Shogun

Maurice of Nassau 1567–1625
Dutch national leader

Francis II 1544–60
King of France

Jahangir 1569–1627
Mogul Emperor

Alexander Farnese 1545–92
Duke of Parma and Piacenza

Johannes Kepler 1571–1630
German astronomer

Tycho Brahe 1546–1601
Danish astronomer

Don Juan of Austria *c.* 1547–78
Spanish admiral, Governor General of Netherlands

Don Luis Requesens ?–1576
Spanish soldier and statesman, Governor General of Netherlands

Miguel de Cervantes 1547–1616
Spanish novelist

Charles IX 1550–74
King of France

Henry of Lorraine 1550–88
Duke of Guise

Medina Sidonia 1550–1615
Commander of Armada

Henry III 1551–89
King of France and Poland

Boris Godunov *c.* 1552–1605
Tsar of Russia

Rudolf II 1552–1612
Holy Roman Emperor

Walter Raleigh, Sir *c.* 1552–1618
English courtier

Henry IV (of Navarre) 1553–1610
King of France

1555 ● Peace of Augsburg: Lutheranism tolerated in Germany

● **1557–82** Russian–Livonian war

1562–98 ● French Wars of Religion

1559 ● Treaty of Cateau-Cambrésis: end of Hapsburg-Valois strife

● **1555** Charles V resigns

1565 ● Ivan IV's ultimatum to the Russian nation

● **1565** Siege of Malta: La Valette defeats the Turks

● **1568** Revolt of the Netherlands

● **1571** Battle of Lepanto ends Turkish naval power

● **1572** Sea Beggars gain base at Brill

● **1571** Convocation sanctions Thirty-Nine Articles, basis of Anglicanism

● **1572** Tycho Brahe sights "Cassiopeia"

575 1588 1600

1588
The Invincible Armada
As Spain's mighty naval force approaches, England seems doomed – but "God breathes" and the island kingdom is spared

1600
The Battle of Sekigahara
By defeating his rivals at Sekigahara, warlord Tokugawa Ieyasu becomes the dominant force in Japanese politics and restores the Shogunate

A New Empire for India
By conquering the province of Gujarat, the Mogul Emperor Akbar lays the foundation for a pan-Indian nation

1594
"Paris is Worth a Mass"
The Huguenot Henry IV embraces Catholicism, thus ending fifty years of civil and religious strife in France and establishing the Bourbon dynasty on the throne

Toyotomi Hideyori 1592–1615
Nominal Japanese ruler

1581 ● Act of Abjuration: constitutional start of Dutch Republic

1582 ● Gregorian calendar promulgated

1584 ● Catholic League formed against Henry of Navarre

1585 ● Colony of Virginia founded

1587 ● Execution of Mary Queen of Scots

1587 ● Formalization of serfdom in Russia

1588 ● Henry III flees from Paris

1589 ● Henry III stabbed at St. Cloud

1590 ● Unification of Japan under Hideyoshi

1594 ● Henry IV enters Paris, restoring French monarchy

1598 ● Edict of Nantes grants toleration to Huguenots

1610 ● Assassination of Henry IV

1615 ● Laws of the Military Houses: Samurai code of conduct

Acknowledgments

The authors and publishers wish to thank the following museums and collections by whose kind permission the illustrations are reproduced. Page numbers appear in bold, photographic sources in italics.

14 (1) *Photo Marburg* (2) Staatsbibliothek, Berlin
15 *Mansell Collection*
17 (1) *Archiv Gerstenberg* (2) Staatsbibliothek, Berlin
18 Staatsbibliothek, Berlin
19 Uffizi, Florence: *Scala*
20 (1) Chester Beatty Library, Dublin (2) India Office Library, London
21 (1, 2) *Novosti*
22 *Photo Bulloz*
23 Museo e Gallerie Nazionali di Capodimonte, Naples: *Scala*
24 *Mansell Collection*
25 (1) Museo Civico, Piacenza (2) Staatsbibliothek, Berlin
26 (1) Pinacoteca, Bologna: *Scala* (2) Villa Farnese, Caprarola: *Scala*
27 Herzog Anton Ulrich-Museum, Braunschweig
28 (1) Society of Antiquaries, London (2) National Maritime Museum, Greenwich, London
29 (1) *Mansell Collection* (2) Academia de San Fernando, Madrid: *Foto Mas* (3) Henry Huntingdon Library, California
30 National Anthropological Museum, Mexico City: *Scala*
31 Uffizi: *Scala*
32 (1) Biblioteca Laurenziana, Florence (2) British Museum, London
33 (1) British Museum (2) American Museum of Natural History, New Yorl
34 (1) Biblioteca Laurenziana (2) Biblioteca Nacional, Madrid: *Foto Mas* (3) Bodleian Library, Oxford
35 Bodleian Library
36 (1) *Mansell Collection* (2) Bibliothèque Nationale et Universitaire, Geneva (3) Staatsbibliothek, Berlin
37 *Reportagebild, Stockholm*
39 *Bilderdienst Ullstein*
40 (1, 2) *John Freeman*
41 Victoria and Albert Museum, London
42 British Museum
43 (1) Provincial Museum, Berlin: *Bilderdienst Ullstein* (3) *André Held*
44 (1) *Bilderdienst Ullstein* (2) Provincial Museum, Berlin
45 (1) *Bilderdienst Ullstein* (2) Staatsbibliothek, Munich: *Foto Marburg*
46 (1, 2) *Mansell Collection* (3) Gallerie Capodimonte: *Mansell Collection*
47 (1) The Polish Library, London (2) Topkapi Museum Library, Istanbul
48 Archivo de Indias, Seville: *Foto Mas*
49 *Robert Harding Associates*
50 (1) Thomas Gilcrease Institute of American History and Art (2, 3, 4) British Museum
51 (1, 2, 3) British Museum
52 (1) New York Public Library (2) *Ferdinand Anton*
53 John Judkyn Memorial, Bath: *Orbis Publishing*
54 (1) National Portrait Gallery, London (2) *Mansell Collection* (3) Campion Hall, Oxford
55 (1) National Portrait Gallery (2) *British Tourist Authority*
56 Reproduced by gracious permission of Her Majesty The Queen – copyright reserved
57 National Portrait Gallery
58 (1) Kupferstichkabinett, Staatliche Museen, Berlin (2) Ashmolean Museum, Oxford
59 British Museum
60 *Colour Centre Slides Ltd*
61 (1) *Mansell Collection* (2) National Portrait Gallery
62 (1) Hertford College, Oxford: *Thomas Photos* (2) *Jean Arland* (3) British Museum
63 (1) *Mansell Collection*
64 Royal Society, London: *Derrick Witty*
66 *Hulton Picture Library*
67 (1) Royal Society (2) *Ronan Picture Library*
68 (1) Museum of History of Science, Oxford (2) Science Museum, London
69 Connaissance des Arts: *R. Bonnefoy*
70 (1) Science Museum (2) National Gallery, London
71 (1) British Museum: *Fleming* (2) Prado, Madrid: *Foto Mas*
72 Louvre, Paris: *Scala*
73 Naples Cathedral: *Rocco Pedicini*
74 (1) *Mansell Collection* (2) Palazzo Vecchio: *Alinari*
75 Staatsbibliothek, Berlin
76 (1) Chiesa del Gesù, Rome: *Scala* (2) Museo Civico, Piacenza: *Scala*
78 Ospedale del Ceppo, Pistoia: *Scala*
79 (1, 2) British Museum: *John Freeman* (3) *Hulton Picture Library*
80 (1) Bibliothèque Nationale, Paris (2) National Portrait Gallery
81 (1) Woburn Abbey, Bedfordshire: *Phoebus Picture Library* (2) Bibliothèque Nationale, Paris (3) National Portrait Gallery
82 Nationalmuseet, Denmark
83 *Novosti*
84 *Mansell Collection*
85 *Novosti*
86 Victoria and Albert Museum: *Phoebus Library*
87 British Museum: *John Fleming*
88 (1) Rijksmuseum, Amsterdam (2) *Foto Mas*
89 (1) British Museum: *John Freeman* (2) *Mansell Collection*
91 Mauritzhuis, The Hague
92 (1, 2) British Museum: *John Freeman*
93 (1) *Foto Mas*
94 National Scheepvaartmuseum, Antwerp
95 Monasterio de El Escorial
96 (1) *Mansell Collection* (2) British Museum: *John Freeman*
97 Rijkmuseum
98 (1) Musée Guimet, Paris (2) *Japan Information Centre, London* (3) National Palace Museum, Taipei: School of Oriental and African Studies, London
99 (1) Chester Beatty Library (2) British Museum
100 Escorial, Madrid
101 *Scala*
102 (1) Prado, Madrid (2) *Kerry Dundas*
103 (2) Musée Royale des Beaux Arts, Brussels
104 (1) *Scala* (2) National Maritime Museum
106 (1) *Giraudon* (2) *Hulton Picture Library* (3) Pitti, Florence: *Gabinetto Fotografico Nazionale*
107 (1) Bibliothèque Nationale, Paris: *Giraudon* (2) Versailles: *Photo Bulloz* (3) *Photo Bulloz* (4) *Photo Jean Roubier*
108 Beaux Art, Lausanne: *André Held*
109 Musée Tesse, Le Man: *Giraudon*
110 (1) *Mansell Collection* (2) Bibliothèque du Protestantisme, Paris: *Giraudon*
111 *Snark International*
112 Bibliothèque Nationale, Paris: *Penny Tweedy*
113 *Mansell Collection*
114 Musée Condé, Chantilly: *Giraudon*
115 Musée Condé: *Editions Robert Laffont*
116 (1) National Portrait Gallery (2) By kind permission of Lord De L'Isle: *Phoebus Picture Library* (3) Bodleian Library: *Phoebus Picture Library*
117 (1) British Museum (2) *Hulton Picture Library*
118 Victoria and Albert Museum
119 India Office Library
121 (2) Victoria and Albert Museum
122 (1) Chester Beatty Library (2) Victoria and Albert Museum
123 Victoria and Albert Museum
124 (1, 2) Victoria and Albert Museum
125 (1) India Office Library (2) Royal Society
126 (1) Stedelijk Museum 'Het Prinsenhof,' Delft: *A. Dinjam* (2) British Museum: *John Freeman*
127 (1) *J. Allan Cash* (2) *John Freeman*
129 National Portrait Gallery
130 (1) Public Record Office, London (2) National Maritime Museum: *John Freeman*
131 (1) *Mansell Collection* (2) National Maritime Museum
132 National Maritime Museum
133 (2) National Maritime Museum
134 (1) British Museum: *R. B. Fleming* (2) British Museum
135 National Maritime Museum
136 (1) Moscow Historical Museum: *Novosti* (2) The Polish Library, London
137 (1) *Hulton Picture Library* (2) National Gallery (3) *Mansell Collection*
138 Versailles: *Snark International*
139 *Mansell Collection*
140 (1) Musée Carnavalet: *Photo Bulloz* (2) Versailles: *Photo Bulloz*
141 *Giraudon*
142 *Editions Robert Laffont*
143 Bibliothèque du Protestantisme
144 (1) *Hulton Picture Library* (2) *Giraudon* (3) Bibliothèque Nationale, Paris
145 (1) The Hispanic Society of America (2) *Orbis Publishing*
146 Art Museum, Shiga: *Sekai Bunka Photo*
147 Zojiji Temple, Tokyo: International Society for Educational Information, Tokyo
148 British Museum: *John Freeman*
150/151 Toshogu Shrine, Nikkō: International Society for Educational Information, Tokyo
152 Art Museum, Shiga: *Sekai Bunka Photo*
153 (1) *Japan Information Centre* (2) British Museum: *John Freeman*

Managing Editor: *Jonathan Martin*
Assistant Editors: *Geoffrey Chesler, Francesca Ronan*
Design Consultant: *Tim Higgins*
Art Director: *Anthony Cohen*
Picture Editor: *Judith Aspinall*

Index

References in italics are to illustrations